DISCARD

D1452320

DATE DUE

			PRINTED IN U.S.A.

Voices of Ancient Greece and Rome

Recent Titles in Voices of an Era

Voices of Ancient Greece and Rome

Contemporary Accounts of Daily Life

David Matz

VOICES OF AN ERA

GREENWOOD

AN IMPRINT OF ABC-CLIO, LLC
Santa Barbara, California • Denver, Colorado • Oxford, England

Copyright 2012 by ABC-CLIO, LLC

Library of Congress Cataloging-in-Publication Data

Voices of Ancient Greece and Rome : contemporary accounts of daily life / David Matz, editor.
    p. cm. — (Voices of an era)
Includes bibliographical references and index.
    ISBN 978–0–313–38738–8 (hardcopy : alk. paper) — ISBN 978–0–313–38739–5 (ebook)
1. Civilization, Classical—Sources. 2. Greece—Civilization—To 146 B.C.—Sources. 3. Rome—Civilization—
Sources. I. Matz, David.
DE59.V64   2012
938—dc23   2011043429

ISBN: 978–0–313–38738–8
EISBN: 978–0–313–38739–5

16 15 14 13 12   1 2 3 4 5

This book is also available on the World Wide Web as an eBook.
Visit www.abc-clio.com for details.

Greenwood
An Imprint of ABC-CLIO, LLC

ABC-CLIO, LLC
130 Cremona Drive, P.O. Box 1911
Santa Barbara, California 93116-1911

This book is printed on acid-free paper ∞

Manufactured in the United States of America

CONTENTS

Contents

PREFACE

Voices of Ancient Greece and Rome: Contemporary Accounts of Daily Life contains 45 original documents dealing with various aspects of day-to-day life in the Greco-Roman world. The starting point for the collection is the Trojan War, ca. 1200 BCE; the time span stretches all the way to the reign of the Roman emperor Diocletian, in the early fourth century CE, thus encompassing some 1,500 years of human experience in these two foundational civilizations. This time period continues to attract the interest of modern audiences; witness, for example, the recent box-office success of movies like *Troy*, *Gladiator*, and *300*. Furthermore, the ancient world lives among us and around us virtually everywhere; it is difficult to walk the streets of any downtown American city without seeing the influence of Greek temple architecture in modern buildings: facades displaying pediments, triglyphs, metopes, with Corinthian, Doric, or Ionic columns holding up the roofs. Even our currency has gotten into the act. The architect who designed the famous Lincoln Memorial in Washington, D.C., was greatly influenced by his knowledge of ancient Greek architecture, and anyone who wishes to see a rendering of this monument need only fish around in his/her pocket for a penny, or wallet for a five-dollar bill. Much of our American culture—from architecture to legal codes and systems to sports (think Olympic Games) to government to language to mathematics to philosophy—owes its inspiration, even its existence, to a Greek or Roman predecessor.

PRIMARY DOCUMENTS

If we wish to truly understand history, it is necessary to delve into the writings of people who "lived it," those who participated in the events of their times, or at least witnessed these events. People like the Greek poet Pindar (518–438 BCE), who could arguably be called the western world's first sportswriter, a man who traveled to the great athletic meetings of his time, including the Olympics, and wrote poetry glorifying the victorious athletes. Or people like the Athenian philosopher Socrates (ca. 469–399 BCE), who eloquently served as his own defense lawyer and argued his own case in one of the most famous trials in the annals of western jurisprudence. Or people like Pliny the Younger (62–114 CE), a sophisticated Roman gentleman, who had seen what the rivers of Italy could do when swollen by floodwaters, and wrote about the ways in which flood victims dealt with the unwelcome devastation caused by the onrushing water.

These documents take us behind the scenes of the "grandeur that was Greece" and the "glory that was Rome," and illustrate how people not only coped with the frustrations that came with everyday living, but also reaped the rewards and enjoyed the pleasures of being a part of two of the greatest civilizations in history.

ORGANIZATION OF SECTIONS

The 45 documents are divided among 11 chapter headings, which are representative of many of the major aspects of daily life. The chapter headings, which appear in the volume in alphabetical order, are domestic life, education, employment, food and clothing, health care, housing, intellectual life, politics, religion, safety, and sports. The documents are taken from a wide variety of Greek and Roman authors, in a wide variety of literary genres: plays, poems, letters, biographies, histories, and satires. Some of the documents describe everyday events and situations to which many a modern reader will probably relate: a dispute between father and son over the son's spending habits; the characteristics of a beloved family pet; the best way to do the weekly laundry; how to efficiently organize clothing and furniture in one's home; and controlling appetite and avoiding weight gain. Other documents take on weightier topics: conspiratorial threats against the government, construction of public buildings, and the credibility of oracles.

Each document is preceded by an introduction and a section entitled "Keep in Mind As You Read." As the wording of the rubric suggests, the entries here will offer important background information with which the reader may not be familiar. Then follows the document itself, usually between 350 and 700 words in length, with some words in boldface type. These will be explained in "definition fact boxes" located next to the document. Some (but not all) of the documents will be accompanied by short "sidebars," which contain additional information intended to supplement the content of the document itself. The "Aftermath" section functions as an epilogue to the document: What happened next? What consequences or developments occurred as a result of the events described in the document? Next come two series of questions: in the "Ask Yourself" category, the reader will be invited to think further about the document and reflect upon questions pertaining to its content. The "Topics to Consider" section often offers suggestions for further research, on topics related to the document. In both of the "questions" sections, the reader will often be asked to think of examples from the modern world that might parallel the events or situations presented in the documents. Finally, suggestions for additional reading, including websites, appear under the "Further Information" rubric.

OTHER FEATURES

The volume contains a brief survey of Greek and Roman civilization, followed by an introduction to the nature and use of primary documents, including some information about how to read an ancient text intelligently. The business of putting pen to paper—or fingertips to keyboard—to construct a book, or an essay, or a poem, or a play can often be tricky, and not only in modern times. Ancient authors, too, confronted the challenges of the writing profession, and we will hear from some of them on this matter, including Thucydides, Livy, Plutarch, and others.

Additionally, there is a section featuring brief biographies of the authors of the original documents, as well as a chronological summary.

INTRODUCTION: GREEK AND ROMAN CIVILIZATION

Greeks

The story of ancient Greek civilization probably could be said to have begun with the Minoans and Myceneans, or perhaps even before that, but for our purposes, the Trojan War serves as the starting point. The final days of this terrible conflict (ca. 1200–1190 BCE) between the Greeks and Trojans is chronicled in one of the most famous works of western literature, Homer's *Iliad*. (See Document 42: "The Goddess Was on His Side") We owe much of what we know of the earliest times of Greek culture, language, political organization, military matters, and much more to this famous epic poem.

Historians generally believe that Greece gradually declined into a dark age for several centuries after the Trojan War, reemerging again in the eighth century BCE. Many famous *polises*, or city-states, came to prominence in the years to follow, but none was more important than Athens. Much of what we associate with the "ancient Greeks," or "ancient Greek civilization," was in actuality happening in Athens. Perhaps the first clearly recognizable individual in the city's glorious history was the lawgiver Solon, whose year in the spotlight was 594 BCE. The city was in crisis, on the brink of anarchy, and it was then that an extraordinary decision was made: to concentrate all legislative power in the hands of one person, who would have complete freedom to rewrite, create, or abolish any laws, regulations, or customs that he thought would lead Athens out of its desperate situation. Since Solon had already established a rock-solid reputation for fairness, honesty, and incorruptibility, coupled with a peerless ability as a legislator and a politician, he was the one chosen for the job. After some hesitation, he accepted, and during his one-year term, he single-handedly transformed Athens from a city in chaos to a city on the move. Even today, the word "solon" remains with us, a term applied to a wise and conscientious lawgiver.

Toward the end of Solon's century, another famous, albeit poorly attested, legislator by the name of Cleisthenes took center stage in Athenian politics. Cleisthenes is often credited with originating two of the most noteworthy aspects of the emergent Athenian democracy: *isonomia*, a word meaning "equal rights" and one of the basic requirements of any democracy; and ostracism (see Document 30: "Out with Him! An Athenian Method of Ridding the City of Tiresome Politicians"), a formal procedure whereby an overly ambitious or unscrupulous politician could literally be voted out of Athens, and into a 10-year exile.

The high point of Athenian democracy—and culture, and literature, and art, and drama, and architecture, and philosophy, and economic power, and international leadership—found its fullest expression under the leadership of perhaps the greatest statesman/orator ever to grace its halls of power: Pericles. By virtue of his unprecedented electoral success (he was voted one of the ten *strategoi,* or military generals, 15 consecutive times), Pericles dominated the domestic political scene in Athens in the 440s and 430s BCE; during that time, he spearheaded a tremendous surge in the construction of beautiful and expensive buildings. The most famous of these was undoubtedly the magnificent Parthenon, constructed atop the Acropolis; estimated cost: 5,000 talents, perhaps equivalent to $1.5 billion, more than even the new Yankee Stadium in the Bronx cost. (See Document 11: "Workers Needed for Building the Parthenon.")

But it was not only the building program that marked out Pericles's administration for greatness. Many noted philosophers, playwrights, and poets—some of the most gifted and famous ever—flourished in Periclean Athens. Two of these, the comic playwright Aristophanes and the philosopher Socrates (through Plato), contributed documents to this volume. (For Aristophanes, see Document 2: "A Failure to Launch, in an Athenian Family." For Socrates/Plato, see Document 26: "An Intellectual on Trial")

Unfortunately, this Athenian Golden Age was derailed by the disastrous Peloponnesian War, a terrible conflict between the two superpowers of the time, Athens and its longtime rival *polis* Sparta. The war began in 431 BCE, and dragged on for 27 long years, finally coming to an end in 404. And while it certainly did not destroy Athenian life or civilization—Athens continued to be a cultural, intellectual, and educational center of the ancient world—the Greeks were never again to reach the heights which they attained under the leadership of Pericles.

Historians refer to the next major period as the Hellenistic Age, spanning from 323 to 30 BCE. Between the Golden Age of Athens and the dawn of the Hellenistic Age lived one of history's most compelling figures, Alexander the Great. He traveled widely with his army, perhaps as far as India and Afghanistan, everywhere conquering the opposition and laying the foundations—whether consciously or not—for the continued spreading of Greek culture, one of the defining characteristics of the Hellenistic period that followed.

But by the end of the second century BCE, the power of Rome, too, was spreading, and beyond the Italian peninsula to which it had been largely confined up to this time. In 146 BCE, the Romans conquered Corinth, the last major Greek city not under their control. As a consequence, they annexed Greece as a province, and although the Hellenistic influence continued, it was now clear that the ancient Mediterranean world had a new superpower.

Romans

Ironically, it might be said that Roman civilization began with the Trojan War. Despite the overwhelming Greek victory in that conflict, a few Trojans managed to escape the carnage on the night when the Greek army swarmed into Troy and destroyed the city. One of these few Trojan survivors was Aeneas. He, along with a small band of similarly fortunate stragglers, slipped out of the burning city, commandeered ships, and set sail for points unknown. After numerous hardships and disappointments, they made their way to Italy, where they landed and attempted to establish a permanent home. They met with some resistance to the plan from the indigenous peoples, but after a series of confrontations and battles, they overcame this opposition and settled in Italy, not too far from the future location of Rome. Aeneas was their leader, and later Romans always regarded him as their progenitor, the founder of the Roman race.

But the actual construction of the city of Rome was to come long after Aeneas, over 400 years later, when a young man named Romulus, with a handful of allies, built the walls and foundations for the city. Romulus became its first king; the date was 753 BCE.

Romulus was followed by six more kings. In 509, the last of these, Tarquinius Superbus, was expelled in a coup, and not only he; the monarchy went out with him, replaced by a republican form of government. The Roman Republic lasted for nearly 500 years before it, too, fell by the wayside, superseded by one-man rule, the Roman Empire. The empire survived for another 500 years before finally falling in 476 CE.

In those 1,200 years of Roman history, one of the most serious external threats they faced was posed by the Carthaginian general Hannibal (ca. 247–183 BCE). Rome had had a long and confrontational history with the Carthaginians, and this ongoing mutual hostility exploded into a major war, the Second Punic War, 218–201. The Romans ultimately emerged victorious, but the devastation from the war (much of which was fought on the Italian peninsula) had a major social and economic impact on subsequent Roman history.

Many of the soldiers who fought for Rome in this war were conscripted farmers, and when they returned to their farms after the war—if they survived—they discovered to their dismay that their lands had been amalgamated into large ranches called *latifundia*, owned in many cases by absentee land speculators in Rome. With nowhere else to go, many drifted into the cities, where conditions, unfortunately, were no better. The cycle of poverty, unemployment, and homelessness continued to worsen for decades after the Second Punic War, until Tiberius Sempronius Gracchus appeared on the scene.

In the campaign season of 134 BCE, Gracchus decided to seek the office of tribune; if elected, he would become a tribune for the year 133. During the campaign, he made speech after speech in which he promised to initiate land reform, a proposition that must have seemed dangerously revolutionary to those who occupied and owned the *latifundia*. Much to the undoubted frustration of the landowners, Gracchus was indeed elected, and soon after taking office, he made good on his campaign promise. After some initial opposition, he was successful in transforming his land reform bill into law.

Although the wealthy landowners certainly could not have been pleased by this turn of events, they were able to restrain their angry feelings, knowing that within a year, Gracchus would no longer be a problem: political offices in the Roman Republic were for one-year terms only, with no formal provision for reelection. But when Gracchus made the stunning announcement toward the end of 133 that he intended to run once again for the tribunate, it was more than his opponents could bear.

The campaign was a rough one, with violence and threats of violence rampant. Tiberius Gracchus was a superb public speaker, well versed in the ways of inciting a crowd with his emotion-laden oratory. During one of his campaign rallies, a scuffle broke out; it soon escalated into a full-fledged riot in which several hundred people were injured or killed. One of the casualties was Gracchus himself. The biographer Plutarch writes that this was the first time in Roman history in which Roman blood was shed in a civil dispute, and most modern historians look back at the year 133 as a turning point in the fortunes of the Roman Republic.

The events of that fateful year foreshadowed similar troubles to come, on a far larger scale, in the next century. Demagogues, rogue generals, revolutionaries—all took center stage at one time or another in the first century BCE. Perhaps the outstanding figure of the time was the great Gaius Julius Caesar, who painstakingly worked his way up the political ladder, finally achieving election to the top spot in the Roman Republic, the office of consul, for 59 BCE. But his true goal seemed to have been the acquisition of a large and prestigious province to govern after his year as the consul. Caesar was a man who usually got what he wanted, and the fulfillment of his postconsular ambitions certainly fit with this pattern. He was granted the governorship of the sprawling province of Gaul, modern France, which he ruled for an unprecedented eight years—most governorships lasted a maximum of three years. In that time, he was bent on conquest and acquisition, in Spain, Germany, and England as well as in Gaul. During that extended stay in the province, he had molded a battle-toughened army, one that was fearless, relentless, and most importantly, utterly loyal to Caesar.

Not surprisingly, Caesar's activities in Gaul occasioned no little uneasiness back in Rome, and there were many who feared that he might use his powerful army to attack the city itself and perhaps install Caesar as a king or a dictator. To prevent such a calamity from happening, in 50 BCE, the politicians in Rome demanded that Caesar return home to give an accounting of his Gallic activities and an explanation of his plans for the future. Caesar complied—up to a point. But when he and his army reached the Rubicon River in northern Italy, he had a decision to make. The Rubicon was regarded as the boundary between Italy and the northern provinces, and the expectation was that any general returning from one of those provinces would dismiss his army before crossing the river and proceed to Rome as a private citizen. Caesar knew full well that if he followed the rules and entered Rome without his army, he would be put on trial for provincial mismanagement, and very likely exiled or worse. But crossing the river with his army intact and at his side would almost certainly mean civil war.

With the famous words *alea jacta est*—"the die is cast"—Caesar led his army across the Rubicon. What followed was the bloodiest civil war yet seen in Roman history. For four long years the conflict raged, until finally Caesar prevailed, in 45. With all of his major opposition either dead, scattered, or in hiding, Caesar proceeded to rule Rome single-handedly, and for the next 18 months initiated many reforms and projects. The biographer Suetonius enumerates them: sponsored gladiatorial shows and stage plays; reformed the calendar (from a lunar to a solar calendar, the basics of which we still use in our modern calendar); carried out a census; made various changes in electoral, legal and judicial processes; granted citizenship to physicians and teachers (to entice them to live in Rome); built temples and a theater; opened a public library; constructed highways and canals; and many more.

Unfortunately, Suetonius also points out that many of these projects were curtailed or never completed because of Caesar's untimely death. Remnants of staunch opposition to his rule remained. A conspiracy was formed, eventually consisting of some 60 individuals. They struck on March 15 (the Ides of March), 44.

A bloody, lengthy civil war followed (much as Caesar had predicted, should anything happen to him). The decisive Battle of Actium was fought in 30, pitting the forces of Mark Antony and Cleopatra against those under the command of the young Octavianus, Julius Caesar's great-nephew. The latter side emerged victorious, putting an end to the wars and paving the way for the one-man rule of Octavianus, who, a few years later (in 27), was granted the honorary title "Augustus" by the Roman Senate. All opposition was at an end, and Augustus ruled Rome as an emperor for over 40 years, until his death in 14 CE.

He was followed by a succession of many other emperors, some good, others bad, still others indifferent. The high point was probably the era in which the noted historian Edward Gibbon wrote that "the condition of the human race was most happy and prosperous": 98–180 CE, in which Rome had the good fortune to be ruled by a succession of conscientious and effective leaders—the so-called Five Good Emperors—culminating with Marcus Aurelius, who reigned from 161 to 180.

EVALUATING PRIMARY DOCUMENTS

Historians go about the business of reconstructing the past by studying, interpreting, and assessing primary sources: histories, biographies, plays, poems, letters, and works of philosophy and natural science written by people who lived "back in the day": writers who were observers of the events which they describe, and/or who had access to sources and documents about events they describe but did not personally witness or experience. However, difficulties often arise when historians attempt to evaluate these many and varied documents. Some ancient authors are probably more credible and reliable than others. But how can we know?

The fifth-century BCE Greek historian Herodotus wrote a compendious volume about the history of the Greek world; indeed, Herodotus is often considered the western world's first true historian: an author who attempted to more or less systematically record a continuum of events occurring over the course of many centuries. His work is very detailed, full of information, running over 600 pages in the English translation. As a result of all this, Herodotus is sometimes called "the Father of History." But wait. Since his work also contains many myths, stories, legends, and tall tales, Herodotus is also sometimes saddled with the sobriquet "The Father of Lies." So which is it, history or lies? Modern historians have to make the call.

The Roman biographer Suetonius (ca. 70–140 CE) is occasionally considered second-rate by modern critics, primarily because he includes information—sometimes too much information!—about the private lives of the emperors about whom he wrote. Hence, these modern critics deride Suetonius as a gossipmonger, the Roman equivalent of a modern tabloid journalist. But is that a fair assessment?

The Roman satirist Juvenal (ca. 60–130 CE) is often accused of poetic exaggeration, and therefore the poems he wrote have to be taken with a truckload of salt and are not reliable sources of information about life in the early Roman Empire. True or not?

Making the Call

A historian's first task is probably to determine the genre of the source under consideration. Reading and evaluating a satirical poem by Juvenal as if it were a strictly historical account by the annalist Tacitus would be an error. Interpreting a play by the comic playwright Aristophanes in the same manner as a play by the tragic playwright Euripides would probably be the wrong approach. Assuming that a biographer like Plutarch should have crafted his writings in the same manner as a historian like Thucydides might not yield the most accurate assessment. Proper genre identification is a crucial first step.

Some genres of literature might be more credible than others. A modern historian must handle satire with care, because satire, ancient as well as modern, does rely on exaggeration to convey its message. But that does not necessarily suggest that satirical plays, poems, or stories have no historical value; satire must be based on factual information or events, or the satire will not be effective.

Sometimes, the same cautionary tale must be applied to speeches. For example, Cicero's bitter diatribes against Mark Antony, the *Philippics,* undoubtedly contain elements of exaggeration and emotional overkill, but those excesses, as with satire, were very likely rooted in truth. On the other hand, Cicero's many letters, which he likely did not expect to be published, might provide the modern historian with a more candid view of contemporaneous events than his speeches.

Next, the modern historian might want to take into account the opinions of the ancient critics. Greek and Roman literatures are both rife with comments by writers, about writers. Which ancient writers seem to have earned the respect and esteem of their peers? Which ones did not?

Longevity should also be considered. Simply by virtue of the fact that the surviving works of classical authors have remained extant for such a long period of time—perhaps 2,500 years or more for the most venerable of them—is a powerful argument for their credibility. Second-rate literature, or worse, is not likely to stand the test of time.

Interestingly, ancient authors did not have a sense or perception of plagiarism similar to that which prevails in today's scholarly world. Work-cited pages or bibliographies were unknown to them. The same may be said for footnotes, endnotes, parenthetical citations, and quotation marks. To employ such documentation would have been a foreign concept, or even odd or laughable to them. Many ancient nonfiction authors provide little or nothing in the way of source information. But a few—notably Plutarch—are very forthcoming in the body of their works, with references to authors and works of literature they have consulted.

So a modern historian might rightfully assign a higher degree of credibility to an ancient author who is willing to share this kind of information.

What about financial support? Making a living as a writer in ancient times was very likely impossible, given the lack of a technology for mass-producing books, essays, or poems. Most budding authors could develop their bent for writing only if one (or more) of the following circumstances were in their favor: they hailed from wealthy families or benefited from generous inheritances, or they had patrons who supported them, or they had real-world jobs that paid well enough to enable them to spend their leisure hours in literary pursuits. In the case of patronage, it seems likely that no one would have bankrolled an author whose work was considered substandard. The first-century BCE poets Virgil and Horace both enjoyed the imperial patronage of the emperor Augustus; although their work was and is justifiably highly regarded on its own merits, a modern historian would also be warranted in evaluating their poetry favorably knowing that they had the financial support and approval of the emperor.

On rare occasions, however, an author could make his way in the world strictly through his writing. The best example of this might be the Greek poet Pindar, who wrote poems for athletes who were victorious at the Olympic Games and other prestigious athletic festivals. These athletes, or their families or patrons, paid Pindar handsomely for his odes. Ultimately, however, the marketplace dictated whether Pindar could stay in business as a freelance poet. Clearly, he turned out a quality product, with many satisfied customers, and that kind of success, in turn, would lead a modern historian to make a positive assessment of his work.

On relatively rare occasions, ancient historians and biographers share with the reader some of the frustrations and difficulties they encountered in composing their accounts, and the manner in which they dealt with these obstacles. The Greek historian Thucydides (see below) is the prime example of an author who was thus forthcoming. A modern historian would not wrongly place faith in the reliability of such authors.

Ultimately, however, a modern historian must decide whether (or when) to be skeptical, and whether (or when) to be trusting when it comes to evaluating the works of ancient authors. But extreme skepticism—an attitude asserting that none of our original sources is completely accurate or honest, and therefore none can be trusted fully—has little to recommend it. If we apply such stringent standards across the board, we can bid farewell to a substantive study of history; at some point, we must be willing to trust the sources. While they are not perhaps 100 percent error-free, the general outline of people and events they offer must be considered factual and credible. After all, what other documents do we have to enable us to piece together the past?

Thucydides's Viewpoint

In the introduction to his classic book on the Peloponnesian War, the fifth-century BCE Greek historian Thucydides provides his readers with some unique observations on the difficulties and challenges involved in writing history. Thucydides has a well-deserved reputation as a very thorough researcher, obsessed with accuracy, and so his words should resonate with a modern historian who might be trying to achieve the same goals.

For example, Thucydides points out that so-called common knowledge, "facts" in the public domain as it were, may not be as common or as factual as people assume: "In investigating past history, and in forming the conclusions which I have formed, it must be admitted that one cannot rely on every detail which has come down to us by way of tradition ... The Greeks make many incorrect assumptions not only about the dimly remembered past, but also about contemporary history ... Most people, in fact, will not take trouble in finding out the truth, but are much more inclined to accept the first story they hear." [Thucydides. *Peloponnesian War* 1.20; tr. Warner.]

A modern example? Perhaps the famous story about George Washington cutting down one of his father's prized cherry trees. Many modern historians discount that tale as pure fiction, and yet it has been told and retold so often that the culture accepts it as fact; or, in Thucydides's words, an "incorrect assumption ... about the dimly remembered past."

One of the trickiest literary genres confronting the analytical skills of a modern historian is oratory. Many ancient authors recorded speeches in their historical works, but how do we know whether those versions are accurate? How do we assess them? Do we take them at face value, or do we assume that the author has slanted the content of the speech, perhaps intentionally because of a certain bias, or unintentionally, because of an imprecise memory or other factors? It is not likely that ancient chroniclers had access to transcripts of these speeches (to enable them to report a speech verbatim), so a particularly careful reading of their versions becomes mandatory. Thucydides explains how he dealt with the problem of accurately recording speeches: "In this history, I have made use of set speeches ... I have found it difficult to remember the precise words used in the speeches which I listened to myself, and my various informants have experienced the same difficulty; so my method has been, while keeping as closely as possible to the general sense of the words that were actually used, to make the speakers say what, in my opinion, was called for by each situation."

And what about the matter of eyewitnesses? Can they be trusted? Let us say, for example, that a fender-bender occurs at a busy intersection in the downtown of a large city. When the police arrive, and interview the 10 witnesses who saw the accident, they will likely receive varied accounts; there will certainly be no firm consensus on the exact circumstances or cause of the accident. Thucydides relied heavily on the reports of eye witnesses for information about events at which he was not present, and yet he found it sometimes very frustrating to sort out their stories: "And with regard to my factual reporting of the events of the war, I have made it a principle not to write down the first story that came my way, and not even to be guided by my own general impressions; either I was present myself at the events which I have described, or else I heard of them from eye witnesses whose reports I have checked with as much thoroughness as possible. Not that even so the truth was easy to discover: different eye witnesses give different accounts of the same events."

Clearly, Thucydides is a trustworthy primary source. From the outset, he makes it clear to the reader that his quest for the truth and the facts has been as thorough and as objective as possible. Few ancient authors are as candid as he.

Herodotus's Viewpoint

Herodotus, the "Father of History" (or lies) mentioned above, offers the modern historian only a very short introductory paragraph to his massive *Histories*: "Herodotus of Halicarnassus, his *Researches* are here set down to preserve the memory of the past by putting on record the astonishing achievements both of our own [i.e., Greek] and of other peoples; and more particularly, to show how they came into conflict." [Herodotus. *The Histories* 1.1; tr. de Selincourt.]

Short and succinct, but also basic to the work of any historian: to record "astonishing achievements" and events, and to explain the genesis and unfolding of wars. Interestingly, Herodotus does not confine his attention strictly or primarily to the Greeks, but instead, he intends to look at the bigger picture of Mediterranean culture in general. Should such a broad-based view of history be a criterion by which we evaluate primary documents?

Plutarch's Viewpoint (Part One)

What about the problem of evaluating documents that have as their primary topic events which occurred, or may have occurred, in the very earliest days of Greek and Roman history? These time periods are not documented by contemporary historians; indeed, as mentioned above, the first "real" historian, Herodotus, lived in the fifth century BCE. What about the events and people of earlier centuries, known to us only by way of oral traditions that were later recorded by historians, biographers, and poets?

Plutarch considered this problem when he embarked upon composing a biography of the legendary founder of the city of Athens, Theseus:

> You know, Sosius Senecio [a Roman, one of Plutarch's scholarly friends] how geographers, when they come to deal with those parts of the earth which they know nothing about, crowd them into the margins of their maps with the explanation, "Beyond this lie sandy, waterless deserts full of wild beasts," or "trackless swamps," or "Scythian snows," or "ice-locked sea." Now that in writing my *Parallel Lives* I have reached the end of those periods in which theories can be tested by argument or where history can find a solid foundation in fact, I might very well follow their example and say of those remoter ages, 'All that lies beyond are prodigies and fables, the province of poets and romancers, where nothing is certain or credible . . . [In writing the biography of Theseus, who lived in one of those "remoter ages"] [l]et us hope, then, that I shall succeed in purifying fable, and make her submit to reason and take on the appearance of history. But when she obstinately defies probability and refuses to admit any element of the credible, I shall throw myself on the indulgence of my readers and of those who can listen with forbearance to the tales of antiquity. Plutarch. *Life of Theseus* 1; tr. Scott-Kilvert.

Plutarch's solution to the problem of uncorroborated stories from the "remoter ages" was apparently to recast them and present them to the reader as having taken on "the appearance of history." What are modern historians to make of this approach when evaluating a primary document like Plutarch's *Life of Theseus*? How would we interpret the information and the anecdotes contained in that biography? As factual? As semifactual? Or as nothing more than tall tales taken from "sandy, waterless deserts full of wild beasts"?

Plutarch's Viewpoint (Part Two)

As alluded to earlier, Plutarch is one of the few authors of primary documents who provides his readers with extensive information about his sources. He frequently credits the authors whose works he has consulted, sometimes referencing them, other times quoting them. Quite often, he will include contradictory material from two (or more) sources, leaving the modern historian with a problem: which of these sources is the more/most credible? Plutarch does not assist us; when he reports differing versions of the same event or story, he generally concludes his report with a sentence like: "Let the reader decide which one of these accounts is the true one." Plutarch seldom even offers hints—let alone blunt statements—about his own assessments of his sources, so the modern historian truly must make the call in these cases.

An exception to the foregoing: Plutarch's *Life of Pericles*. Plutarch seems to have been a great admirer of the famous fifth-century BCE Athenian leader; even so, Plutarch is honest enough with his readers that he quotes sources hostile to Pericles, but with a twist: uncharacteristically, he often criticizes these sources and challenges the credibility of their work.

Example: "The [fifth-century BCE] poet Ion . . . says that Pericles had a rather disdainful and arrogant manner of address, and that his pride had in it a good deal of superciliousness and contempt for others . . . But we need not pay much attention to Ion. . ." [Plutarch. *Life of Pericles* 5; tr. Scott-Kilvert.]

Example: "[H]ow are we to believe [the fourth-century BCE biographer] Idomeneus's charge that Pericles arranged the assassination of the democratic leader Ephialtes, who was his friend [and political colleague], out of sheer jealousy of his reputation? This is surely a poisonous accusation, which he has concocted from some unknown source, to hurl at a man. . .who possessed a noble disposition and a spirit. . .dedicated to the pursuit of honor . . ." [10]

Example: "[W]e find that even [the fifth-century BCE biographer] Stesimbrotus of Thasos has dared to give currency to the shocking and completely unfounded charge that Pericles seduced his son's wife. This only goes to show how thickly the truth is hedged around with obstacles and how hard it is to track down by historical research." [13]

Example: "In the ninth month [of the Athenian siege of Samos, an island off the coast of modern Turkey], the Samians surrendered. Pericles demolished their walls, confiscated their fleet, and imposed a heavy fine on them . . . Duris of Samos [a fourth-century BCE historian] magnifies these events into a tragedy and accuses Pericles and the Athenians of great brutality, although there is no word of this in Thucydides, nor Ephorus, nor Aristotle. He certainly does not appear to be telling the truth [when he reports that Pericles countenanced atrocities during the takeover of Samos]. Duris is apt to overstep the limits of the truth . . . and so it seems . . . that in this instance he has drawn a horrifying picture of his country's sufferings simply to blacken the name of Athens." It is most unusual for Plutarch, in effect, to accuse a source not only of incompetent exaggeration, but outright prevarication. [28]

Livy's Viewpoint

Titus Livius ("Livy," 59 BCE–17 CE) wrote a massive, monumental history of Rome, his *Ab Urbe Condita, From the Founding of the City*. He began work on it around 27 BCE; it took him over 40 years to complete. His plan: to cover the entirety of Roman history from its beginnings with Romulus (753 BCE) all the way to his own time.

In the preface to *Ab Urbe Condita*, Livy identifies a problem common to ancient and modern historians alike: the competition. A modern historian who proposes to undertake the writing of an account of nearly any historical period is admonished by editors and colleagues to be certain that his/her putative work claims a niche or displays an approach heretofore unfilled by any other historian. Livy must have felt the same kind of pressure to produce something new, different, unique, original. He writes: "Whether I am likely to accomplish anything worthy of the labor, if I record the achievements of the Roman people from the foundation of the city, I do not really know . . . perceiving as I do that the theme is not only old but hackneyed, through the constant succession of new historians [his competitors!], who believe either that in their facts they can produce more authentic information, or that in their style they will prove better than the rude attempts of the ancients." [Livy. *From the Founding of the City* 1.1-2; tr. Foster.]

Another problem that confronted Livy was the sheer antiquity of the earliest eras that he intended to chronicle. These time periods were poorly attested, shrouded in myth and legend (cf. Plutarch's similar quandary, above). Worse yet, perhaps, Livy fears that his readers would be far more interested in recent or contemporary events, and that accounts of the earliest eras of Roman history would not resonate with them. His words: "[M]y subject involves infinite labor, seeing that it must be traced back [over] seven hundred years . . . and at the same time, I doubt not that to most readers the earliest origins and the period immediately succeeding them will give little pleasure, for they will be in haste to reach these modern times . . ."[1.4]. As for the credibility or historicity of the legends and stories pertaining to Rome's beginnings, Livy promises "neither to affirm nor to refute." Rather, he argues that it is the "privilege of antiquity" to create or promulgate legends that contain a mixture of divine and human actions, "so to add dignity to the beginnings of cities."

Do historians have the prerogative or the credentials to make value judgments concerning the historical periods about which they write? Livy seemed to think so; he took the view that, rather than quibbling over the accuracy of minute details of particular events, students of history ought to focus instead on the bigger picture: "[W]hat life and morals were like; through what men and by what policies, in peace and in war, empire was established and enlarged. Then let [the reader] note how, with the gradual relaxation of discipline, morals first gave way . . . then sank lower and lower, and finally began the downward plunge which has brought us to the present time, when we can endure neither our vices, nor their cure." [1.9]. This view—that previous generations were somehow more moral, more values-driven, and more courageous than the present one—is echoed frequently by those who see a similar "downward plunge" in contemporary American life.

The bottom line: Livy believed that the study of history was a "wholesome and profitable" undertaking, principally because it offers a wide range of examples of human activities and experiences, some praiseworthy, others not. The wise and perceptive student of history can then discern worthy examples to emulate and disreputable examples to avoid.

So how would a modern historian evaluate Livy's *Ab Urbe Condita*? By his own words, Livy certainly seems to have had a fondness for the "good old days" and a corresponding revulsion for more recent Roman history. Do we then conclude that his descriptions of the earliest times are embellished? Overly favorable, to an extent that they distort the truth? And that his accounts of more recent times are unnecessarily pessimistic? There seems to be no need to be skeptical of the accuracy of Livy's history of Rome. The 40-plus years he spent writing it suggest careful research and a diligent quest for the truth. Beyond that, Livy has always enjoyed the respect and esteem not only of his peers—the first-century CE orator Quintilian compared him favorably to the best of the Greek historians, including Thucydides and Herodotus—but also of later generations, up to the present time.

Tacitus's Viewpoint

The Roman historian Cornelius Tacitus (ca. 55–117 CE) has left us with two notable historical works: *Annals,* which spans the years 14 to 68 CE, and *Histories,* covering 69 and 70.

Tacitus provides modern readers with some fairly harsh criticisms of his contemporaries in the history-writing business, nor is their readership spared. In his introduction to the *Histories,* he notes that many historians have written accounts of the previous 822 years of Roman history, from its founding in 753 BCE up to 69 CE. But he makes a distinction between those who covered the Roman Republic (753–31), characterizing their work as displaying "eloquence and freedom," and those who came later, claiming there were no post-31 BCE historians with abilities similar to their forebears. He acerbically writes that "historical truth was impaired in many ways: first, because [historians] were ignorant of politics; . . . later, because of their passionate desire to flatter; or again, because of their hatred of their masters . . . But while [readers] quickly turn from a historian who curries favor, they [readily] listen to calumny and spite . . . [T]hose [historians] who profess inviolable fidelity to truth must write of no [person] with affection or with hatred." [Tr. Clifford H. Moore. *Tacitus: The Histories.* Volume I. LCL, 1937. Page numbers: 3, 5.]

Unfortunately, Tacitus does not mention these ignorant historians by name, so the modern historian is left to speculate which ones are on the receiving end of his critiques. But this raises another dilemma of document evaluation for the modern historian: If we know that an eminent ancient source (like Tacitus) had a low opinion of a particular contemporary historian, or a whole group of them, how much influence should the ancient critic's opinions exert in our assessments of those writers, and their documents, whom he criticizes?

Conclusion

The ancient sources have demonstrated that the writing of history is no simple task. Many pitfalls, snares, obstacles, and wrong turns await the historian, especially in the matter of evaluating primary documents. And yet he or she must do exactly that if a complete record of human achievement—and failure—is to be written with care and accuracy.

Chronology

Ca. 1200–1190	The epic battle between the Greeks and the Trojans—the Trojan War—chronicled later by Homer in the *Iliad*.
776	Founding of the ancient Olympic Games, the quadrennial athletic festival that took place at Olympia, in the southwestern corner of the Peloponnesus.
734	The first Greek colony in Sicily, Naxos, is founded.
621	The Athenian lawgiver Draco is put in charge of codifying and publishing the laws of Athens. He recommends the death penalty for virtually any offense, even the most minor.
594	The Athenian legislator, poet, politician, and businessman Solon (ca. 640–560) single-handedly enacts many legal, economic, and social reforms in Athens. He modifies the harsh penalties prescribed by Draco's law codes.
Ca. 560–510	Pisistratus, and later his sons, Hippias and Hipparchus, rule Athens as tyrants.
Ca. 510	The shadowy Athenian leader Cleisthenes sponsors a number of initiatives that lay the foundation for the flowering of the Athenian democracy in the fifth century.
490	The Persians, led by King Darius I, invade Greece. The Greeks, principally under the leadership of the Athenians, prevail at the decisive Battle of Marathon.
480	The Persians return to Greece, this time under King Xerxes. The Athenian navy, led by Themistocles, defeats the Persians for the second time in 10 years.
Ca. 478	The representatives of several hundred Greek polises assemble on the tiny Cycladic island of Delos to form an anti-Persian alliance generally known as the Delian League.

472	Aeschylus's play *Persians* is staged. It is the only surviving Greek tragic play based on a historical event, the invasion of Greece led by Xerxes. All other extant tragedies draw their themes from myth and legend.
447	Construction begins on the Parthenon, the signature building of the Golden Age of Athens and one of the most famous architectural landmarks in the history of the western world.
444	The famous Athenian leader Pericles (ca. 495–429) is elected *strategos* (military general) for the first time. He would go on to be elected to this annual office an amazing 14 more times in succession.
431–404	The Peloponnesian War, the devastating conflict between Athens and Sparta and their allies, eventually resulting in the occupation and partial destruction of Athens by Sparta.
Ca. 430	Sophocles's tragic play *Oedipus the King*, perhaps the best known and most often revived ancient Greek play, is presented in Athens for the first time.
429	The death of Pericles, who had contracted the highly contagious and nearly always fatal plague that had swept through Athens in this year and in the previous year.
417	The ostracism of Hyperbolus, the last known victim of the Athenian practice that enabled the citizens of Athens to exile, via popular vote, a disliked or unscrupulous politician for 10 years. Ostracism votes were outlawed after this year.
415–413	The disastrous Sicilian Expedition, in which the Athenians inexplicably try to invade the faraway island of Sicily, in the midst of the Peloponnesian War, and are thoroughly defeated.
406	The famous playwrights Euripides and Sophocles both die in this year.
399	The famous Athenian philosopher Socrates is put on trial for impiety and subversion. He is convicted and forced to commit suicide.
384	The philosopher Aristotle and the orator/lawyer Demosthenes are both born in this year. Ironically, they also both died in the same year, 322.
371	Battle of Leuctra, between Thebes and Sparta. The Thebans win and thereby end Spartan dominance over Greece, which the Spartans had established after the Peloponnesian War.
338	Battle of Chaeronea, in which the forces of King Philip of Macedonia defeat the Athenians and Thebans. The nearby town of Chaeronea was the birthplace of Plutarch.
336	The assassination of King Philip of Macedonia. The Athenian orator Demosthenes attacked King Philip and his policies in three of his most famous speeches, the *Philippics* (352; 344; 341).
336–323	The rule of King Philip's son, Alexander the Great.

331	The founding of the city of Alexandria in Egypt by Alexander the Great, who named it after himself.
330	The venerable and famous capital city of the Persians, Persepolis, is captured, vandalized, and set ablaze by Alexander the Great and his soldiers.
Ca. 280	Completion of the Pharos, the huge 300-foot-tall lighthouse at Alexandria, deemed one of the Seven Wonders of the Ancient World.
279	Battle of Asculum, in which the Greek mercenary general Pyrrhus is victorious against the Romans but loses some of his best soldiers in the process. The outcome of that battle occasioned his famous statement that one more success like that would ruin him; hence, the phrase "Pyrrhic victory."
211	Death of the mathematician and physicist Archimedes in Syracuse. He once said that, given a place to stand and a pole long enough, he could move the world.
146	Subjugation of Corinth by the Romans, the last Greek city to hold out against the inevitable. The Romans annex Greece and turn it into a province called Achaea.

CHRONOLOGY OF ROMAN HISTORY FROM THE FOUNDING OF THE CITY TO THE EDICT OF DIOCLETIAN, 753 BCE–301 CE

BCE Events

753	Romulus founds the city of Rome, and becomes its first king.
753–509	Rome is ruled by a succession of seven kings:
	Romulus (753–714)
	Numa Pompilius (714–671)
	Tullus Hostilius (671–642)
	Ancus Martius (642–617)
	Tarquinius Priscus (617–579)
	Servius Tullius (579–535)
	Tarquinius Superbus (535–509)
509	Tarquinius Superbus is removed from power, and with him, the monarchy. The Roman Republic is founded.
509–27	The span of the Roman Republic, when Rome is governed by elected officials and legislative bodies.
458	The Roman farmer-turned-military dictator Lucius Quinctius Cincinnatus is called to duty to extricate a blockaded Roman army. He

answers the call, saves the army, and resigns his dictatorship, all within the space of 16 days.

Ca. 450	The Twelve Tables are promulgated, the first codification of Roman law.
396	The general Marcus Furius Camillus captures the important Italian town of Veii, signaling the fact that Rome is becoming a regional power to be reckoned with.
366	Lucius Sextius is elected consul, the highest political office. He is the first plebeian to hold the office, which had formerly been exclusively reserved for patrician politicians.
366	The passage of the laws of Licinius and Sextius, which specified, among other things, that no individual could hold more than 300 acres of public pasture land.
343–341	The First Samnite War. The Samnites were a warlike people in south-central Italy, against whom the Romans fought this war and two others: the Second Samnite War (328–304) and the Third Samnite War (298–290).
287	The fifth secession (a massive withdrawal from the city) of the plebeians, a tactic they used against the ruling patrician class in order to gain political equality. Four previous secessions are thought to have occurred, in 494, 449, 445, and 342, although the consensus appears to be that only the fifth, in 287, is beyond question a historical fact.
264–241	The First Punic War. The Romans win and impose an extremely harsh peace treaty on their defeated enemy, the Carthaginians.
247	Birth of Hannibal, the intractable Carthaginian leader and implacable enemy of Rome.
218–201	The Second Punic War, between Rome and Carthage. The Carthaginians are led by Hannibal, who almost succeeds in capturing the city and destroying the Roman Republic.
216	The Battle of Cannae, near the Adriatic coast of Italy. The Carthaginians virtually annihilate a 60,000-man Roman army. Future Romans will look back upon this battle as one of their worst military defeats ever.
202	The decisive Battle of Zama, the only time in the Second Punic War that the Romans defeat the Carthaginians in a major battle. Ironically, the battle occurs not in Italy but in North Africa, not far from the city of Carthage. The Second Punic War officially ends in the next year.
184	Marcus Porcius Cato (Cato the Elder), one of the most famous—and cantankerous—politicians in Roman history, holds the office of censor, in which he initiates a number of unpopular reforms, including crackdowns on citizens who stole water from the aqueducts, the imposition of significantly higher taxes on luxury goods, and higher rental rates for public lands.

149–146	The Third (and final) Punic War, in which Rome utterly and totally defeats and destroys Carthage.
135–132	A major slave revolt breaks out in Sicily.
133	King Attalus III of Pergamum dies, having willed his entire kingdom to the Roman people. Pergamum subsequently becomes Rome's first Asian province.
133	Tiberius Sempronius Gracchus takes office as one of the 10 tribunes for the year. He proposes and wins enactment of some highly controversial land reform measures, including the enforcement of the law of Licinius and Sextius (in 366, above).
133	Some 300 people, including Gracchus, are killed in a riot that breaks out during a political rally. Plutarch states that this was reportedly the first time ever in Roman history in which a civil disturbance resulted in the death of Roman citizens.
123	The tribunate of Gaius Sempronius Gracchus, the brother of Tiberius (above). Gaius has a legislative program as ambitious and as controversial as his brother's, and he meets the same fate.
106	The birth of the famous orator/lawyer/statesman Cicero.
100	The birth of Julius Caesar.
90–88	The Italian Social War, a struggle pitting Rome against its Italian allies, who wanted Roman citizenship with its concomitant rights and freedoms.
73	The Thracian slave Spartacus foments a slave rebellion in southern Italy.
70	Cicero successfully argues his first high-profile court case, a prosecution of the corrupt ex-governor of Sicily, Gaius Verres.
63	The year of Cicero's consulship.
63	The disappointed office seeker Lucius Sergius Catilina ("Catiline") organizes an armed conspiracy whose aim is to overthrow the Roman government by force. Cicero discovers the plan and exposes it in a series of four famous speeches, in November and December of this year.
59	The year of Julius Caesar's consulship.
58–50	Julius Caesar's governorship in Gaul, unprecedented in terms of its length; most provincial governorships lasted for one or two years, three at most.
50	Caesar is recalled to Rome by nervous politicians. They want to interrogate him about his actions in Gaul and his plans for the future.
49	In one of the most famous episodes in Roman history, Caesar, uttering his memorable words "The die is cast," crosses the Rubicon River in northern Italy with his army intact. This action precipitates a civil war.

49–45	A period of civil war following Caesar's crossing of the Rubicon River. Caesar's side eventually prevails. The Battle of Munda in Spain, in 45, is the final and decisive battle of the civil war.
44	Caesar receives a lifetime dictatorship, the latest in a whole series of nontraditional offices and powers he obtains in the decade of the 40s, up until the Ides of March (see next entry).
44	The Ides of March conspiracy (March 15) unfolds. The goal of the 60 conspirators: to assassinate Caesar, in hopes of somehow restoring the Roman Republic by his death. Their goal of killing Caesar is fulfilled. Their hope of restoring the Republic is not.
44–31	Another bloody civil war. Shortly before his assassination, Caesar had predicted that should anything happen to him, a second civil war would break out, worse than the one fought from 49 to 45. He was correct.
44–43	Cicero delivers his *Philippics*, the final public speeches of his long and distinguished career. There were 14 of them altogether; most were harsh denunciations of one of Cicero's arch-enemies, Mark Antony.
43	Cicero is hunted down and murdered at the behest of Mark Antony.
31	The Battle of Actium, the last battle of the civil war. The forces of Octavianus (later Augustus) prevail over those commanded by Mark Antony.
29–19	The Roman poet Virgil spends these 10 years writing the *Aeneid*, the renowned epic poem celebrating the founding of the Roman race.
27	Octavianus receives two perquisites from the Roman Senate that ensure the end of the Republic and the beginning of the Roman Empire: (1) He is granted lifetime tribunician powers, meaning, in effect, that he personally can override and nullify the decisions made by any other legislative entity, or the proposals of any individual politician. (2) The honorary title *Augustus*, "the revered one," a word that has divine connotations.
27 BCE–476 CE	The span of the western Roman Empire.

CE Events

14	The death of Augustus. His reign as emperor lasts over 40 years.
14–68	The reigns of the Julio-Claudian successors of Augustus.

        Tiberius (14–37)

        Caligula (37–41)

        Claudius (41–54)

        Nero (54–68)

17	Two notable literati die in this year: the poet Ovid and the historian Livy.
64	A terrible fire sweeps through Rome, during which Nero supposedly "fiddles" as the city goes up in flames. The story of his fiddling is probably apocryphal.
69–96	The reigns of the Flavian emperors:
	Vespasian (69–79)
	Titus (79–81)
	Domitian (81–96)
79	Mount Vesuvius erupts in the summer of 79, burying the cities of Pompeii and Herculaneum, as well as many farms and smaller towns, in volcanic debris.
80	The Flavian Amphitheater, better known as the Coliseum, is dedicated.
96–180	The reigns of the so-called Five Good Emperors:
	Nerva (96–98)
	Trajan (98–117)
	Hadrian (117–138)
	Antoninus Pius (138–161)
	Marcus Aurelius (161–180)
97	Frontinus becomes *curator aquarum*, the official in charge of Rome's magnificent aqueduct system. He later writes a detailed technical manual on the aqueducts, *De Aquis Urbis Romae* ("On the Aqueducts of Rome"), the only book of its kind surviving from antiquity.
122	Work begins on Hadrian's Wall in northern England to obstruct raids from tribes living north of the wall. It eventually extends for about 80 miles and to a height of around 20 feet.
Ca. 212	Construction begins on the Baths of Caracalla. These public baths were huge; the main building measured 750 feet by 380 feet. Built at the order of the emperor Caracalla (reigned 211–217), for whom they were named.
247	Observances are held in Rome to mark 1,000 years of Roman civilization.
271	Construction begins on the Aurelian Wall, extending for 12 miles around Rome and reaching a height of 60 feet.
284–305	The reign of the emperor Diocletian.
293	The emperor Diocletian establishes a tetrarchy, in which four men would jointly rule the empire.
301	Publication of the Edict of Diocletian.

DOMESTIC LIFE

1. GROWING UP IN SPARTA WAS NO PICNIC

INTRODUCTION

Life in ancient Sparta undoubtedly differed quite markedly from life in the other Greek polises, as the biographer and essayist Plutarch informs us.

KEEP IN MIND AS YOU READ

1. Plutarch's essay *The Ancient Customs of the Spartans*, from which the document has been excerpted, is comprised of an annotated list of 42 aspects of Spartan life. Plutarch describes each of the 42 in varying degrees of detail. Some, like the first one, consist of only one sentence: "To each of those who comes in to the public meals, the eldest man says, as he points to the doors, 'Through these no word goes out' " (eerily reminiscent of the code of many modern sports teams: "What is said in the locker room, stays in the locker room."). Others are lengthier, but none is longer than several hundred words.
2. Plutarch also wrote an essay entitled *Sayings of Spartans*, which is considerably longer than his essay on the customs of the Spartans but contains many of the short, pithy statements for which the Spartans were famous. He also authored a (much shorter) work called *Sayings of Spartan Women*.
3. Many of the Spartan customs that Plutarch describes were reportedly initiated or encouraged by the legendary Spartan king Lycurgus, whose dates and even historical authenticity are debated by modern historians. Plutarch wrote a biography of Lycurgus.

Document: Plutarch on Life in Sparta

They learned to read and write for purely practical reasons. But all other forms of education they banned from the country ... All their education was directed toward prompt obedience to authority, stout endurance of hardship, and victory or death in battle.

a beating: Young thieves caught in the act were beaten not because stealing was considered wrong or immoral, but because they were insufficiently stealthy to avoid capture.

give up their seats: Most likely at public events such as religious festivals or athletic competitions.

gymnasium: A large, open-air public building found in most Greek towns, primarily for the use of athletes. However, philosophical discussions and lectures could also take place in gymnasia. The sacred groves near Athens, where Plato famously taught, was called the *Academia* (hence our word "academic"), and a gymnasium was eventually constructed on the site. But even in Plato's day, the area was apparently frequented by athletes in training.

Pylaea: This word has an interesting history. It is related to the word for "gate," and it originally referred to meeting places, near gated areas of a city's walls, for the representatives of various leagues and councils. Not surprisingly, whenever large numbers of people congregated, the informal topics of conversation often drifted into the realm of the mundane and even the gossipy. Hence, the word came to be associated with trivial conversation, which is what it seems to imply in this context: the young man on "the road to Pylaea" apparently referred to his propensity for unfocused conversation, when he should have been concentrating on gymnastic drills and exercises.

without a shirt: Plutarch does not mean they went about unclothed from the waist up, but that they wore no shirt underneath their cloak, the *himation*, here translated as "garment."

They always went **without a shirt**, receiving one garment for the entire year, and with unwashed bodies, refraining almost completely from bathing and rubbing down . . .

It was the custom that the younger men should be questioned by the elder as to where they were going and for what, and also that the elder should rebuke the one who did not answer or tried to contrive plausible reasons. And the elder who did not rebuke a younger who did wrong in his presence was liable to the same reprimand as the wrongdoer. And anyone who showed resentment, if he was reprimanded, [found himself in serious trouble] . . .

Moreover, the young men were required not only to respect their own fathers and to be obedient to them, but to have regard for all the older men, to make room for them on the streets, to **give up their seats** to them, and to keep quiet in their presence. As the result of this custom each man had authority, not as in other states over his own children, slaves, and property, but also over his neighbor's in like manner as over his own, to the end that the people should, as much as possible, have all things in common, and should take thought for them as for their own . . .

The boys steal whatever they can of their food, learning to make their raids adroitly upon people who are asleep or are careless in watching. The penalty for getting caught is **a beating** and no food. For the dinner allowed them is meager, so that, through coping with want by their own initiative, they may be compelled to be daring and unscrupulous . . .

The selling of anything was not permitted, but it was their custom to use the neighbors' servants as their own if they needed them and also their dogs and horses, unless the owners required them for their own use. And in the country, if anyone found himself lacking anything and had need of it, he would open an owner's storehouse and take away enough to meet his need, and then replace the seals and leave it . . .

They used to make the Helots [state-owned slaves] drunk and exhibit them to the young as a deterrent from excessive drinking.

It was their custom not to knock on the outer doors, but to call from outside . . .

They did not attend either comedy or tragedy [i.e., theatrical productions], so that they might not hear anyone speak either in earnest or in jest against the laws.

They reprimanded [a] young man from the **gymnasium** because he knew well about the road to **Pylaea**.

One of the noble and blessed privileges that Lycurgus appears to have secured for his fellow citizens was

---

ARISTOTLE'S COMMENT ON COMMUNITY PROPERTY

One of the many works of the famous fourth-century BCE philosopher Aristotle is entitled *Politics*. In this lengthy treatise, he covers a number of important topics, including the nature of the state; the family; slavery; the origin of money; the various kinds of governments and constitutions, including those of Sparta, Crete, and Carthage; citizenship; revolutions; the best kind of state; and the nature and importance of education. On the matter of property held in common, he writes: "Even now there are some states in which the outlines of such a scheme [of commonly-held property] are so far apparent, as to suggest that it is not impossible; in well-ordered states . . . there are some elements of it already existing . . . In these states, each citizen has his own property, but when it comes to the use of this property, each makes a part of it available to his friends, and each devotes still another part to the common enjoyment of all fellow citizens. In Sparta, for example, men use one another's slaves, and one another's horses and dogs, as if they were their own. And they take provisions on a journey, if they happen to be in need, from the farms in the countryside belonging to other citizens." Aristotle. *Politics* 2.5; tr. Barker.

---

abundance of leisure. In fact it was not permitted them to take up any menial trade at all, and there was no need whatever of making money, which involves a toilsome accumulation, nor of busy activity, because of his having made wealth wholly unenvied and unhonored. The Helots tilled the soil for them, paying a return that was regularly settled in advance. There was a ban against letting for a higher price, so that the Helots might make some profit, and thus be glad to do the work for their masters . . . [Tr. Frank Cole Babbitt. *Plutarch's Moralia* (237–239). Volume III. LCL, 1931. Page numbers: 429, 431, 439, 441, 443, 445.]

AFTERMATH

Plutarch was writing in a time (first/second centuries CE) when the Romans had long since subjugated Greece and most of the rest of the Mediterranean world. In his last chapter in "Ancient Customs of the Spartans," he argues that the Spartans remained strong and independent as long as they followed the precepts and laws of Lycurgus, but once they began to neglect those ordinances, "they became much like the rest [of those under Roman rule], and put from them their former glory and freedom of speech, and were reduced to a state of subjection. And now they, like the rest of the Greeks, have come under Roman sway."

ASK YOURSELF

1. What do you think of the Spartan attitude toward education? Why do you suppose the Spartans "banned from the country" all forms of education except for purely practical forms of reading and writing?
2. What are some of the Spartan customs regarding children and adults, and their interactions and relationships? What are the advantages and disadvantages of these customs?

3. What is your opinion of the custom that "boys steal whatever they can of their food"? What do you think of the stated rationale for this behavior, namely, that it teaches them to be "daring and unscrupulous"?
4. Why do you suppose the Spartans were not allowed to sell anything? How would this prohibition fit in with other Spartan customs mentioned in the document? And what about the idea that "there was no need whatever of making money"? Is this practical?

TOPICS TO CONSIDER

- A good deal of the information that Plutarch incorporates into this document is also recorded in his biography of Lycurgus. Read over that biography, and then compare it to "Ancient Customs of the Spartans." What similarities or differences do you notice?
- Can you think of any contemporary societies or countries that have customs similar to those of the Spartans? Explain the similarities. Some historians argue that Spartan society, and especially its share-the-wealth ethic, is similar to modern socialist societies or countries. Do you think that this is an accurate comparison?
- Plutarch has very little to say in this essay about Spartan girls or women. Why not, do you suppose? Access one of the many websites on the topic for additional information. (Interestingly, Plutarch did write an essay entitled *Bravery of Women*, and another one called *Sayings of Spartan Women*, so he certainly was not averse to including information about women in his writings.)
- What is your opinion of the descriptions in both Plutarch and Aristotle of the Spartan custom of commonly held property? Do you think that this system worked in actual practice? Would such a system be viable today?

Further Information

Cartledge, Paul. *Spartan Reflections*. London, 2001.
Forrest, W. G. *A History of Sparta, 950–192 B.C.* New York, 1968.
Pomeroy, Sarah B. *Spartan Women*. Oxford, 2002.
Pomeroy, Sarah B., Stanley M. Burstein, and Jennifer Tolbert Roberts. *Ancient Greece: A Political, Social, and Cultural History* (Chapter 4: Sparta). New York, 1999.

Bibliography for Document

Babbitt, Frank Cole (tr.). *Plutarch's Moralia*. Volume III. [LCL.] London and New York, 1931.
Barker, Ernest (tr.). *The Politics of Aristotle*. Oxford, 1958.

2. A Failure to Launch, in an Athenian Family

INTRODUCTION

Aristophanes, author of the document that follows, enjoyed a long and successful career as an Athenian comic playwright, in the late fifth and early fourth centuries BCE. His play *Clouds*, one of his earlier efforts, was staged around 423.

KEEP IN MIND AS YOU READ

1. Aristophanes, like all the comic playwrights of his time, injected heavy doses of satire into his plays, so that fact must always be kept in mind when reading or interpreting his works. Nevertheless, even satire must be based on a foundation of truth, so there is clearly historical value in satirical writings.
2. The document is excerpted from the opening scenes of Aristophanes's play, in which an old Athenian man by the name of Strepsiades is lying in bed, tossing and turning and unable to sleep, because his spendthrift son, Phidippides, has wasted large sums of the family's money on chariot racing. The resulting indebtedness is becoming Strepsiades's problem, and he does not see how he will possibly be able to satisfy the family's growing list of creditors. The scene is thus set for a generational confrontation between father and son: the father extols the virtues of thrift and hard work, whereas the son finds nothing wrong with having a good time—an expensively good time—down at the racetrack.
3. As in many Aristophanic comedies, the names of the principal characters are concoctions of the playwright's imagination, and as such, they can often be translated. The name "Strepsiades" is related to the Greek word *strepho*, meaning "twist," or "turn," a word that is aptly descriptive of the old man's nocturnal woes. The son's name, Phidippides, is formed from a combination of the words *pheido*, "thrift," and *hippos*, "horse." The *hippos* suffix also conveys a connotation of wealth, since only well-to-do individuals could afford to own and maintain horses. And the name is only one letter away from the word "Phi*l*ippides," which would mean "lover of horses," also a fitting moniker for the son.
4. The "city life versus country life" theme is raised in one of Strepsiades's early speeches, where he laments having married a city woman who knew nothing of the simple pleasures of country living that Strepsiades had enjoyed before their union.

Amynias: Apparently a kind of a low-life character, who appeared in Aristophanes's play *Wasps*, as well as in plays by other contemporary writers.

bailiff: The Greek word *demarchos*, or demarch, here translated as "bailiff," was literally the chief officer of an Athenian deme, or administrative district. According to K. J. Dover, the demarch "had the custody of the official list of members of the deme . . . he was responsible for exacting the rents on land leased by the deme to individuals . . . and it is a fair inference from this passage that he had the authority to enforce the surrender of securities by a debtor to a private creditor."

Coesyrized: A reference to the mother of Megacles, Coisyra, who was apparently a typically arrogant member of the upper classes of sophisticated Athenian society.

Colias and Genetyllis: According to Jeffrey Henderson, "Colias was the name of an Attic promontory where women held festivals for Aphrodite and the Genetyllides, goddesses of procreation."

hack: *Koppatian*, a kind of horse branded with the Greek letter *koppa*.

the moon in her twenties: More than 20 days into the month, with bills due and payable at the end of the month.

oil: Lamps were fueled by olive oil.

Pasias: Otherwise unknown. This might be one of Aristophanes's invented names. There was a remarkably successful Athenian banker named Pasio (d. 370 BCE), but it seems unlikely that there is any connection between him and the Pasias mentioned in the play.

Document: A Father-Son Heart-to-Heart

(Strepsiades and Phidippides lie sleeping. Strepsiades sits up restlessly.)

STREPSIADES: Oh dear, oh dear! Lord Zeus, what a stretch of nighttime! Interminable. Will it never be day? I did hear a rooster crow quite a while back, but the slaves are snoring. They wouldn't in the old days. Damn you, **War**, for my many worries, when I can't even **punish my slaves**! And this fine young man here won't rouse himself before daybreak either, but farts away wrapped up in five woolen coverlets. All right, then, let's all get under the covers and snore! No use, I can't get to sleep, poor soul. I'm being eaten alive by my bills and stable fees and debts, on account of this son of mine. He wears his hair long and rides horses and races chariots, and he even dreams about horses, while I go to pieces as I watch **the moon in her twenties**, because my interest payment looms just ahead. [Addressing a slave:] Boy! Light a lamp, and bring me my ledger book, so I can count my creditors and reckon the interest. Let's see, what do I owe? Twelve minas to **Pasias**? What were the twelve minas to Pasias for? What did I use it for? When I bought that branded **hack**. Oh me, oh my! I wish I'd had my eye knocked out with a stone . . . But what arrears overtook me after Pasias? Three minas to **Amynias** for a small seat and a pair of wheels . . .

PHIDIPPIDES (*awakening*): Really, father, why do you grouse and toss all night long?

STREPSIADES: There's a **bailiff** in the bedclothes biting me.

PHIDIPPIDES: For heaven's sake, let me catch a little sleep.

STREPSIADES: All right then, sleep! But bear in mind, all these debts will end up on your head. Ah, I wish she'd died a terrible death, that matchmaker who talked me into marrying your mother! Mine was a very pleasant country life, moldy, **unswept**, aimlessly leisured, abounding in honey bees, sheep, and olive cakes. Then I married the niece of Megacles, son of Megacles, I a rustic, she from town, haughty, spoiled, thoroughly **Coesyrized**. When I married her I climbed into bed smelling of new wine, figs, fleeces, and abundance; and she of perfume, saffron, tongue kisses, extravagance, gluttony, **Colias and Genetyllis**. But still, I won't say she was lazy; she used plenty of thread when she wove. I used to show her this cloak of mine as proof and say, "Woman, you go too heavy on the thread!"

SLAVE: We've got no **oil** in the lamp.
STREPSIADES: Damn it, why did you light me the **thirsty lamp**? Come here and take your beating.
SLAVE: Why should I get a beating, then?
STREPSIADES: Because you put in one of the thick wicks! *The slave runs inside.* After that, when this son was born to us, I mean to me and my high-class wife, we started to bicker over his name. She was for adding *hippos* ["horse," connoting elevated social status] to the name, Xanthippus or Chaerrippus or Callippides, while I was for calling him Phidonides after his grandfather. So for a while we argued, until finally we compromised and called him Phidippides. She used to pick up this boy and coo at him, "When you're grown you'll drive a chariot **to the Acropolis**, like Megacles, and don a saffron robe." And I would say, "No, you'll drive the goats from the **Rocky Bottom**, like your father, and wear a leather jacket." But he wouldn't listen to anything I said; instead, he's infected my estate with the galloping trots. So now I've spent the whole night thinking of a way out, and I've found a singular shortcut, devilishly marvelous [i.e., his idea of enrolling Phidippides in Socrates's school]. If I can talk this boy into it, I'll be saved." [Tr. Jeffrey Henderson. *Aristophanes: Clouds; Wasps; Peace.* (Lines 1–24; 30–31; 35–78.) LCL, 1998. Page numbers: 11, 13, 15, 17.]

punish my slaves: He fears that they might flee from him, and possibly wind up in Sparta.

Rocky Bottom: *Phelleus* in Greek; an area around Athens featuring stony ground covered with porous rocks, like lava. According to Plato, it was not always that way, but in bygone days it was a fertile area, rich with arable soil and heavily forested hills and mountains surrounding it.

thirsty lamp: The Greek word *potes*, "thirsty," is sometimes used to describe a person who drinks to excess, a hard drinker. When Strepsiades uses the word in connection with a lamp, it conjures up modern images of cars that get poor mileage: "gas guzzlers." So Strepsiades's lamp is apparently an "oil guzzler."

to the Acropolis: The reference is apparently to the annual Panathenaic festival and the great procession "to the Acropolis"; the procession featured chariots, women carrying sacred relics, young people leading sacrificial animals, and soldiers mounted on horseback. The Acropolis was the citadel of Athens, on which stood the Parthenon and many other famous buildings.

unswept: From the Greek word *akoretos*, which literally means "unsated," but here translated as "unswept." In this context, however, it seems to mean something like "unbothered," a reference to Strepsiades's carefree country lifestyle—before he met his city-bred wife!

War: A reference to the Peloponnesian War (431–404 BCE), principally between the city-states of Athens and Sparta. Aristophanes stingingly satirized this war in his plays *Acharnians, Lysistrata,* and *Peace.*

"MATCHMAKER, MATCHMAKER"

Strepsiades's wish for the matchmaker who saddled him with his wife is not *too* harsh; he only wants her to suffer a "terrible death"! Although the role of matchmakers (*promnestriai*) in arranging marriages was apparently quite well established in Athenian society, matchmakers are surprisingly not well attested in Greek literature. Xenophon's brief discussion of the topic is also one of the most detailed. He puts these words into the mouth of Socrates, in a dialogue in his *Memorabilia* [2.36]: "good matchmakers are successful in making marriages only when the good reports they carry to and fro are true; false reports [are not recommended], for the victims of deception hate one another and the matchmaker too." [Xenophon. *Memorabilia* 2.6; tr. Marchant.]

It seems clear that Strepsiades considered himself a "victim of deception," because he hated both his wife, and the matchmaker who paired them up.

AFTERMATH

Strepsiades has an inspiration, a way to get out of debt and get his son under control at the same time: enroll the boy in Socrates's new school, the "Thinkery," which reportedly teaches its clients how to win arguments by devious reasoning. Strepsiades hopes that his son will learn how to initiate legal actions that will enable him to extricate himself from his mounting debts. Phidippides at first refuses to attend the school—he would rather work on his suntan!—but eventually, he agrees. The lessons backfire, however, when father and son quarrel over whether it is proper for a son to beat his father and mother. Phidippides argues that a son *does* have that right; he has learned sophistic reasoning all too well. Strepsiades thus comes to the conclusion that it would be wrong to cheat one's creditors by using the convoluted reasoning and deceptive argumentation techniques taught in the Thinkery. The play ends with Strepsiades and his slaves setting the Thinkery on fire.

ASK YOURSELF

1. What is it that keeps Strepsiades tossing and turning all night long, and unable to sleep? What does he seem to think would be the best way to solve this problem?

THE *OTHER* PHIDIPPIDES

There was a famous Athenian long distance runner by the name of Phidippides, whose two days of fame came during the first Persian invasion of Greece, in 490 BCE. The Athenians, not wishing to face the full force of the Persian army alone, sent an appeal to Sparta for help. Their desperate message was delivered by Phidippides—on foot! According to the historian Herodotus, he arrived in Sparta the day after he left Athens, thus covering the distance between the two famous polises, 150 miles, in two days. Although the Spartans refused the Athenian request, Athens nonetheless prevailed against the Persians, at the Battle of Marathon. Legend has it that a messenger ran the 26 miles from Marathon to Athens to announce the victory. For reasons which are not entirely clear, Phidippides has been popularly associated with this first "Marathon run," but it was not he; the runner's name is given in Plutarch as Eucles.

2. How would you describe Strepsiades's relationship with his wife? With his son? Do you think that he was a good father and husband?
3. Strepsiades is obviously concerned about his cash flow. What are some of the actions that he thinks could be taken to reduce household expenses?

TOPICS TO CONSIDER

❧ Strepsiades is portrayed as wrestling with some serious debt and family problems. Do you think his situation was typical of that which confronted many fifth-century Athenians of his socioeconomic group?

❧ Strepsiades seems to be making a point about differences in social status when he remarks that his wife had expectations that Phidippides would one day drive a chariot in the prestigious Panathenaic festival, whereas Strepsiades thinks it more likely that the boy would be herding goats in the Rocky Bottom. How do you suppose an Athenian audience would react to the comparison between the Panathenaic festival and Rocky Bottom? Of the two possible futures in store for Phidippides (chariot driving or goat herding), which one do you think would be more likely to occur? Why?

❧ Satire, whether ancient or modern, almost always contains elements of exaggeration. What portrayals (of people or events) in the document seem exaggerated to you? Can you think of any modern satirists to whom Aristophanes might be compared?

Further Information

Dover, Kenneth J. *Aristophanic Comedy*. Berkeley, CA, 1972.
Ehrenberg, Victor. *The People of Aristophanes: A Sociology of Old Attic Comedy*. Oxford, 1943.
Harriott, Rosemary. *Aristophanes, Poet and Dramatist*. Baltimore, 1986.
Murray, Gilbert. *Aristophanes: A Study*. Oxford, 1933.
Strauss, Leo. *Socrates and Aristophanes*. Chicago, 1996.

Websites

The Clouds: An Analysis of the Play by Aristophanes. http://www.theatrehistory.com/ancient/bates025.html
On Satire in Aristophanes's *The Clouds* [especially section "J"]. http://records.viu.ca/~johnstoi/introser/clouds.htm

Bibliography for Document

Dover, Kenneth J. *Aristophanes. Clouds*. Oxford, 1968.
Feder, Lillian. *Apollo Handbook of Classical Literature*. New York, 1964.
Henderson, Jeffrey (tr.). *Aristophanes: Clouds; Wasps; Peace*. [LCL.] Cambridge and London, 1998.
Marchant, E. C. (tr.). *Xenophon: Memorabilia and Oeconomicus*. [LCL.] Cambridge and London, 1923.

3. Even in Ancient Rome, the Dog Was Man's —and Woman's—Best Friend

INTRODUCTION

The Romans enjoyed keeping all manner of creatures as pets, but dogs seemed to be one of their favorite choices for four-footed companionship. The naturalist Pliny the Elder provides an account of these noble animals.

KEEP IN MIND AS YOU READ

1. Pliny, as a scientist, writes in an objective, nonemotional style, but a careful reading of his canine descriptions reveals an author who appreciated and respected the intelligence and loyalty of these animals.
2. In addition to their role as domestic pets, many dogs were put to work, especially on farms, in hunting, and as watchdogs.
3. Pliny the Elder's writings often contain a mixture of scientific data and supporting anecdotal information that illustrates or confirms the data. His discussion of dogs conforms to that pattern.

Document: Pliny Expounds on Canine Appeal

Many . . . domestic animals are worth studying, and before all, the one[s] most faithful to man: the dog, and the horse. We are told of a dog that fought against brigands in defense of his master and although covered with wounds would not leave his corpse, driving away birds and beasts of prey; and of another dog in Epirus [in Greece] that recognized his master's murderer in a gathering and by snapping and barking made him confess the crime. [Here follows an account of heroic dogs in other cultures.]

Among ourselves, the famous **Vulcatius, Cascellius**'s tutor in civil law, when returning on his **cob** from his place near Rome after nightfall was defended by his dog from a highwayman; and so was the senator Caelius, an invalid, when set upon by armed men at Piacenza [a northern Italian town], and he did not receive a wound till the dog had been [done away with]. But above all cases, in

cob: a breed of horse, *asturco*, which, according to Pliny [8.166], does not display "the usual paces in running but a smooth trot, straightening the near and off-side legs alternately, from which the horses are taught by training to adopt an ambling pace." [Pliny the Elder. *Natural History* 8.166; tr. Rackham.]

National Records: This is probably a reference to the *acta diurna populi Romani*, the "daily news of the Roman people," probably the closest that the Romans ever came to putting out a daily newspaper. Julius Caesar initiated the publication of the *acta* during his consulship in 59 BCE. It was probably originally an account only of the official acts of the Roman senate and other government entities, but eventually it also included social news and information about other events. According to the historian Tacitus, the publication was read not only in Rome but throughout the provinces.

Steps of Lamentation: According to the lexicographers Lewis and Short, the Steps of Lamentation were "steps on the Aventine Hill [one of the famous Seven Hills of Rome] leading to the Tiber [River], to which the bodies of executed criminals were dragged by hooks, to be thrown into the Tiber."

Vulcatius, Cascellius: Vulcatius (alt. Vulcacius) Sedigitus was a second-century BCE poet and literary critic who compiled a "top ten" list of the greatest comic poets in the history of Roman literature. The two names on the list most familiar to us today, Plautus and Terence, ranked second and sixth, respectively. Cascellius was a first-century BCE jurist and politician.

our own generation, it is attested by the **National Records** that in the consulship [28 CE] of Appius Julius and Publius Silius when as a result of the case of Germanicus's son Nero, punishment was visited on Titius Sabinus and his slaves, a dog belonging to one of them could not be driven away from him in prison and when he had been flung out on the **Steps of Lamentation** would not leave his body, uttering sorrowful howls to the vast concourse of the Roman public around, and when one of them threw it food, it carried it to the mouth of its dead master. Also, when his corpse had been thrown into the Tiber, it swam to it and tried to keep it afloat, a great crowd streaming out to view the animal's loyalty.

Dogs alone know their master, and also recognize a sudden arrival as a stranger. They alone recognize their own names, and the voice of a member of the household. They remember the way to places however distant, and no creature [except for humans] has a longer memory. Their onset [i.e., an attack] and rage can be mollified by a person sitting down on the ground. Experience daily discovers very many other qualities in these animals, but it is in hunting that their skill and sagacity is most outstanding. A hound traces and follows footprints, dragging by its leash the tracker that accompanies it towards his quarry. And on sighting it how silent and secret but how significant an indication is given first by the tail and then by the muzzle! Consequently, even when they are exhausted with old age and blind and weak, men carry them in their arms, sniffing at the breezes and scents and pointing their muzzles towards cover. [Tr. H. Rackham. *Pliny: Natural History*. (8.144–147). Volume III. LCL, 1940. Page numbers: 101, 103, 105.]

AFTERMATH

Pliny goes on to describe other canine topics, including breeding. He claims that in India, the inhabitants breed dogs with tigers, while Gauls (modern France) cross dogs with wolves. He discusses gestation periods, puppy litters, and methods of determining which newborn puppy will turn out to be the "pick of the litter." He also relates a lengthy anecdote about a huge hound given to Alexander the Great by the king of Albania. This dog was reportedly so ferocious that it could take down a lion or even an elephant. Alexander decided to test the claim, and the dog did not disappoint; it crushed the lion, and brought the elephant to the ground with a thunderous crash.

TRIMALCHIO'S MUTT

In the fancifully lavish dinner party thrown by Trimalchio, the first-century CE buffoonish epicure described by the satirist Petronius in *The Satyricon*, an incident occurs where the host's outsized dog Scylax causes a scene. Trimalchio had noticed that one of the children who frequented his household was trying to force a half loaf of bread down the gullet of an enormously obese puppy; as fast as the child stuffed in the bread, the animal vomited it. Trimalchio, observing the drama, ordered to be brought in his own dog, Scylax, the *praesidium domus familiaque*, "guardian of my home and family." He tossed the mutt a chunk of bread, adding that no one in the entire household was more devoted to him than the dog. That is when the trouble started.

The child, when he saw the attention and affection which Trimalchio lavished on Scylax, put his plump pup down on the floor, and egged it on to a confrontation with the master's dog. Naturally, Scylax took up the challenge, and, with a cacophony of barking, began pursuing his tormenter around the dining room. During the chase, the two canines managed to collide with a glass lampstand; they smashed the glass, and spilled hot oil (such lamps were fueled by burning olive oil) all over some of the guests.

Big-hearted Trimalchio ignored the melee, and the mess, and instead dipped into the exquisite buffet which adorned the dining room, inviting his guests to do likewise.

ASK YOURSELF

1. What are some of the characteristics of dogs that—according to Pliny—set them apart from other animals?

TOPICS TO CONSIDER

- ❧ The Romans did not recognize the wide variety of dog breeds that we do today, but some breeds were distinctive. What were these? Was any one breed prized more highly than the others?
- ❧ Pliny attributes to dogs some characteristics that might be questionable, especially their incisive memory—"no creature [except for humans] has a longer memory"—and their inclination to leave off from attacking a person, if the person sits down on the ground. Are these characteristics accurately assigned to dogs? What about some of the other canine attributes he describes?

Further Information

Beagon, Mary. *Roman Nature: The Thought of Pliny the Elder*. Oxford, 1992.
Healy, John F. *Pliny the Elder on Science and Technology*. Oxford, 1999.
Murphy, Trevor Morgan. *Pliny the Elder's Natural History: The Empire in the Encyclopedia*. Oxford, 2004.

Website

Names for Roman Dogs. http://www.unrv.com/culture/names-for-roman-dogs.php

Bibliography for Document

Lewis, Charlton T. and Charles Short. *A Latin Dictionary*. London, 1879.

Rackham, H. (tr.). *Pliny: Natural History*. Volume III. [LCL.] Cambridge and London, 1940.

Sullivan, J. P. (tr.). *Petronius: The Satyricon and the Fragments*. Baltimore, 1965.

4. A Prearranged Marriage

INTRODUCTION

Roman marriages were sometimes prearranged, especially in the upper socioeconomic groups of citizens. Pliny the Younger wrote a letter to his friend Junius Mauricus, who was seeking a suitable husband for his niece. Pliny had the perfect candidate in mind!

KEEP IN MIND AS YOU READ

1. This was not the only time in which Pliny had helped his friend Mauricus. He also offered to conduct a search for a tutor for the children of Mauricus's brother. Mauricus was exiled from Rome by the emperor Domitian in 93 CE, but was recalled five years later by the subsequent emperor, Nerva. It seems likely that Pliny wrote this letter early in the second century CE.
2. The document, about a marriage arrangement, gives us a window into the world of the wealthier Roman upper classes, and the manner in which they might go about the task of finding suitable spouses for their children. Did people of more modest means attempt to arrange marriages for their children in similar ways? Or at all? These questions are more difficult to answer.

Document: Pliny the Younger as a Matchmaker

You request me to look for a husband for your niece, and it is fitting for you to give me this commission rather than anyone else. For you know how much I esteemed and loved that great man, her father, and with what encouragement he helped me in my youth, and how he caused me to appear to deserve the praises he used to bestow upon me. You could not give me a more important or more pleasant commission, nor could I undertake a more honorable task than to choose a young man worthy of begetting the grandchildren of Rusticus Arulenus [the brother of Mauricus].

application: This is the translation of the Latin word *industria*, which connotes diligent, purposeful activity. So Acilius not only possessed abstract character traits like integrity and wisdom, but he also was focused and productive in his work habits.

Brixia: A city in northern Italy, modern Brescia. Brixia was located not far from Comum, Pliny's hometown.

equestrian order: The prosperous upper middle class in ancient Roman society, called "equestrian" because in the earliest days of Roman history, these were the people wealthy enough to buy and maintain a horse.

Manicius Acilianus: Although this young man is Pliny's candidate for the husband-to-be, there is no information about him elsewhere.

Minicius Macrinus: Six of Pliny's letters to this individual are extant, including one [8.17] that describes a horrific storm and the flooding that resulted, and Pliny's hope that his friend survived with life and property intact.

Padua: Known as Patavium in Roman times, this town was the birthplace of the eminent Roman historian Livy (Titus Livius, 59 BCE–17 CE).

praetorian rank: Apparently because of his distinguished background and accomplishments, he was granted the privileges of an ex-magistrate (a praetor), even though he had never held that office.

rustic simplicity of the olden days: The Latin *rusticitas*, here translated as "rustic simplicity," is a word with an interesting combination of positive, neutral, and negative connotations. It can mean "rustic charm" or "country-born" or "lacking sophistication." Pliny undoubtedly

Such a person would take a long time to find, were not **Manicius Acilianus** ready at hand, almost as if by pre-arrangement. While he loves me very warmly with the affection usual between young men (for he is just a few years younger), he reveres me as he would an old man. For he is as desirous of modeling himself on me and of being instructed by me as I was by you and your brother.

He is a native of **Brixia**, a city of that Italy of ours, the Italy which that still retains and preserves much of the modesty, the frugality, and even the **rustic simplicity of the olden days.** His father is **Minicius Macrinus**, one of the leading men of the **equestrian order**, who desired no higher status; for though elevated to **praetorian rank** by the deified Vespasian [emperor who reigned 69–79 CE], he very steadfastly preferred an honorable repose to this display—or shall I call it rank—of ours. His maternal grandmother is Serrana Procula, of the municipality of **Padua.** You are acquainted with the manners of the place; yet Serrana is even to the Paduans a model of strictness. He is fortunate in having also Publius Acilius as his uncle, a man of almost unequaled gravity, wisdom, and integrity. In short, there is nothing in his entire family which that would not please you as if it were in your own. As for Acilius himself, he has great energy as well as great **application**, joined with a high degree of modesty. He has already passed with the greatest credit through the offices of quaestor, tribune, and praetor [three political offices of the Republic, whose practical significance in Pliny's time had probably diminished], so that he has already spared you the necessity of canvassing for him. He has the look of a gentleman, fresh-colored and blooming, and a natural handsomeness in his whole build, together with a certain senatorial grace. I think that these factors should not be slighted in the least, for this is a kind of reward that should be given to the chastity of maidens.

I don't know whether to add that his father is very rich. For when I consider the kind of person you are, for whose niece I am seeking a husband, I feel it is unnecessary to mention wealth. But when I look at the public morality and even the laws of the state, according to which a person's wealth claims paramount attention, it certainly merits some notice. And indeed, where children—in fact, a goodly number of them—are thought of, this consideration too is to be weighed in arranging matches. You may perhaps think that I have indulged my affection and exaggerated beyond the merits of the case. But I stake my integrity that you will find everything far greater than what I am telling you in advance . . .

Farewell. [Lewis, Naphtali and Meyer Reinhold (eds.). *Roman Civilization: Sourcebook II, The Empire.* Reprinted by Harper Torchbooks, 1966. 1.14, page numbers: 252–253.]

intends to convey here the positive connotation. By "olden days," he probably refers to the bygone times of the Roman Republic, an era to which many Romans nostalgically hearkened back as a sort of golden age of deportment, respect, and hard work.

AFTERMATH

We have no follow-up to this letter, so it is not possible to know whether the proposed marriage ever took place. However, given Pliny's status in society and his sound judgment in such matters, it seems likely that the union occurred.

ASK YOURSELF

1. Why does Pliny claim that it was fitting for Mauricus to give him "this commission [to find a husband for his friend's niece] rather than anyone else"? What qualifications does Pliny have that make him uniquely suited for this undertaking?
2. What personal and family attributes does Minicius Acilianus possess that would make him a suitable match for Junius Mauricus's niece?

TOPICS TO CONSIDER

- How common was it for Roman marriages to be arranged in the manner that Pliny describes in this letter?
- What can you find out about the history, culture, and significance of some of the northern Italian towns that Pliny mentions in the letter? Were there any other famous names in Roman history (in addition to Pliny and Livy) who came from this region?
- Does it seem a bit odd that Pliny devotes the biggest portion of the letter not to the intended groom, Minicius Acilianus, but to Acilianus's family, and especially his uncle and his father? Why do you suppose he placed the emphasis on these two family members?
- Pliny writes that "he [the uncle, Acilius] has already passed . . . through the offices of quaestor, tribune, and praetor, so that he has already spared you the necessity of canvassing for him." The noted commentator John H. Westcott suggests that "there was only one more office to obtain, the consulship, and that was in the [form of a] gift of the emperor." What do you think Pliny was implying by his statement? Is there an implicit expectation that Minicius Acilianus would somehow have assisted his uncle in his political career, but that since the uncle had already held all the important offices, "the necessity of canvassing for him" would not be an issue?

Further Information

Radice, Betty. *The Letters of Pliny the Younger.* London, 1963.
Sherwin-White, A. N. *The Letters of Pliny: A Social and Historical Commentary.* Oxford, 1966.

Websites

Marriage in Ancient Rome. http://victorian.fortunecity.com/lion/373/roman/romarriage
.html

Pliny the Younger (3). http://www.livius.org/pi-pm/pliny/pliny_y3.html

Bibliography for Document

Lewis, Naphtali and Meyer Reinhold (eds.). *Roman Civilization. Sourcebook II: The Empire.*
New York, 1955.

Westcott, John H. (ed.) *Selected Letters of Pliny.* Norman, OK, new edition 1965.

5. AN EXTREMELY DEVOTED WIFE

INTRODUCTION

Certainly one of our best sources of information about the role of a wife in a Roman household comes from a lengthy eulogy, preserved in the form of an inscription. The honoree was a first-century BCE lady by the name of Turia; the document is generally known as the *Laudatio Turiae* (*In Praise of Turia*). The speaker was her husband, Quintus Lucretius Vespillo.

KEEP IN MIND AS YOU READ

1. Turia and her husband lived through some of the most tumultuous years in Roman history: the unsettled times after the assassination of Julius Caesar (44 BCE). Vespillo's name was placed on a proscription list in 43, but he was later exonerated, and even served a term as consul in 19.
2. Although Roman law and custom placed the husband above the wife as the absolute ruler of the household, it seems clear from the document that Turia exercised a good deal of her own judgment and engaged in actions independent of her husband's approval or permission.
3. There is some scholarly skepticism as to whether this lengthy inscription actually does refer to Turia, since the inscription is fragmentary and pieces are missing in places, and the name "Turia" does not appear on the extant sections. However, the document does contain detailed information that is consistent with information about Vespillo from other ancient sources, and so it seems very likely that the wife in question is Turia. The first-century CE Roman historian Valerius Maximus [6.7] writes: "When Quintus Lucretius [Vespillo] was proscribed by the triumvirs [Octavian, Lepidus, Mark Antony] his wife Turia hid him in her bedroom above the rafters. A single maidservant knew the secret. At great risk to herself, she kept him safe from imminent death. So rare was her loyalty that, while the other men who had been proscribed found themselves in foreign, hostile places, barely managing to escape the worst tortures of body and soul, Lucretius was safe in that bedroom in the arms of his wife." [Valerius Maximus. *Memorable Doings and Sayings* 6.7; tr. Bailey.]

Document: Turia's Devotion

Marriages of such long duration, not dissolved by divorce, but terminated by death alone, are indeed rare. For our union was prolonged in unclouded happiness for forty-one years. Would that our long marriage had come to its final end by *my* death, and that I as the older—which was more just—had yielded to fate.

Why recall your natural qualities, your modesty, deference, affability, your amiable disposition, your faithful attendance to household duties, your enlightened religion, your unassuming elegance, the modest simplicity of your attire? Need I speak of your attachment to your kindred, your affection for your family—when you cherished my mother as you did your own parents—you who share countless other virtues with Roman matrons who cherish their fair name? These qualities which I claim for you are your own; few have possessed the like and been able to hold on to and maintain them; the experience of men teaches us how rare they are.

With joint zeal we have preserved all the patrimony which you received from your parents. Entrusting it all to me, you were not troubled with the care of increasing it; thus did we share the task of administering it, that I undertook to protect your fortune, and you to guard mine. On this point I pass by many things in silence, for fear of attributing to myself a portion of your deserts. Suffice it for me to have indicated my sentiments.

You gave proof of your generosity not only towards very many of your kin, but especially in your filial devotion . . . You brought up in our home . . . some worthy young girls of your kinship. And that these might attain to a station in life worthy of your family, you provided them with **dowries.** Gaius Cluvius [Turia's brother-in-law] and myself, by common accord, executed your intention, and approving of your generosity, in order that your patrimony might suffer no diminution, offered our own family possessions instead, and gave up our own estates to provide the dowries settled upon by you. This I have related not to sing my own praises, but to show that we held ourselves in honor bound to execute from our property those obligations incurred by you out of the fullness of your heart . . .

[Vespillo next devotes several lengthy passages to Turia's role in saving his life during the proscriptions which were issued following the assassination of Julius Caesar.]

When all the world was again at peace and **the Republic reestablished,** peaceful and happy days followed for us. We longed for children, which an

divorce: The essayist Aulus Gellius reports (4.3) that for the first 500+ years after the founding of Rome in 753 BCE, divorce was unknown. The first documented divorce occurred in 231, when a distinguished man named Spurius Carvilius Ruga separated from his wife because she failed to bear children. According to Gellius, Carvilius loved his wife very much, but he divorced her because of a legally binding oath he had taken, in which he publicly professed that he had married in order to father children.

dowries: Unfortunately, Vespillo does not specify how many "worthy young girls" received dowries from Turia and/or Vespillo, but it is probable that the total value of these dowries was considerable, since the family seems to have been fairly wealthy.

the Republic reestablished: This is most likely something of an overstatement. Although the future emperor Augustus claimed to have restored the Roman Republic after the civil war following Caesar's assassination, the reality of the situation was that the Republic remained in name only, and that Augustus had become the sole ruler—for life.

envious fate denied us for some time. Had Fortune permitted herself to smile on us in the ordinary fashion, what had been lacking to complete our happiness? But advancing age put an end to our hopes. . . . Despairing of your fertility and disconsolate to see me without children . . . you spoke of **divorce** because of my unhappiness on this account, offering to yield our home to another spouse more fertile, with no other intention than that of yourself searching for and providing for me a spouse worthy of our well-known mutual affection, whose children you assured me you would have treated as though your own . . . Nothing would have changed, only that you would have rendered to me henceforth the services and devotion of a sister or mother-in-law.

I must admit that I was so angry that I was deprived of my mind, and that I was so horrified at your proposal that I scarcely regained control of myself. That you should have spoken of divorce between us before the decree of fate had been given; that you should have conceived of any reason why you, while you were still alive, should cease to be my wife, you who when I was almost an exile from life remained most faithful . . .

Would that our time of life had permitted our union to endure until I, the older, had passed away—which was more just—and that you might perform for me the last rites, and that I might have departed, leaving you behind, with a daughter to replace me in your widowhood.

By fate's decree your course was run before mine. You left me the grief, the longing for you, the sad fate to live alone . . . [Lewis, Naphtali and Meyer Reinhold (eds.). *Roman Civilization: Sourcebook I, The Republic*. Harper Torchbooks, 1951. Page numbers: 485, 487.]

AFTERMATH

Vespillo concludes his eulogy by proclaiming that his wife deserved more in her life, and that he regretted not having the time to repay everything he owed to her. Finally, he prays to the *Manes* (spirits of the dead) to give peace and protection to Turia

ASK YOURSELF

1. What were the ways in which Vespillo said that his wife helped him, or made his life more secure?
2. What was Vespillo's reaction to Turia's suggestion that they divorce? Why did she make such a suggestion in the first place?

TOPICS TO CONSIDER

- How did the Romans view the role of women, especially wives, at this time in their history? Vespillo makes some very complimentary statements about his wife in this eulogy, especially in the second paragraph, where he specifically enumerates her many outstanding "natural qualities." How typical—or nontypical—do you think that Turia was as a wife and a Roman woman?
- In the third paragraph, Vespillo says, "On this point [the matter of the patrimony], I pass by many things in silence . . . " He never specifies what he means by "many things." What might some of those unnamed things be?

> ❧ Note again Vespillo's statement that "the Republic [had been] reestablished." What were the true facts of the situation? In what ways did Augustus cleverly claim to be restoring the Republic, when in actuality he was doing something quite different?
>
> ❧ There are a number of instances recorded in Roman history where husbands divorced their wives because the wives were incapable of bearing children. Research some of these instances. Were the circumstances similar in all cases? If not, what differences do you notice?
>
> ❧ Vespillo mentions that his marriage to Turia lasted 41 years. Can you find other examples of Roman marriages that endured for an exceptionally long time? (A good starting point: Pliny the Younger's letter [8.5] referencing his friend Macrinus, who had lived without quarreling for 39 years with his recently deceased wife Acilia.)

Further Information

Fantham, Elaine et al. *Women in the Classical World.* Oxford, 1994.

Gardner, J. *Women in Roman Law and Society.* Bloomington, IN, 1986.

Lefkowitz, Mary R. and Maureen B. Fant. *Women's Life in Greece & Rome. A Sourcebook in Translation.* Baltimore, 1992.

Treggiari, Susan. *Roman Marriage.* Oxford, 1991.

Website

On the *Laudatio Turiae:* http://www.dl.ket.org/latin2/mores/women/womenful.htm

Bibliography for Document

Lefkowitz, Mary R. and Maureen B. Fant. *Women's Life in Greece & Rome.* Online at: http://www.stoa.org/diotima/anthology/wlgr/wlgr-mensopinions53.shtml [This is the source for the Valerius Maximus quotation in "Keep in Mind as You Read."]

Lewis, Naphtali and Meyer Reinhold (eds.). *Roman Civilization: Sourcebook I, The Republic.* (Adapted from D. C. Munro, *A Source Book of Roman History,* Boston, 1904.) New York, 1951.

Rolfe, John C. (tr.). *The Attic Nights of Aulus Gellius.* [LCL.] Cambridge and London, 1927.

EDUCATION

6. Plutarch's Prescription for a Child's Education

INTRODUCTION

Although Plutarch (d. ca. 120 CE) is best remembered as a biographer, he also wrote a collection of short essays usually entitled *Moralia*, or *Moral Essays*. Nearly 80 of these essays still survive; the variety of topics indicates the breadth of Plutarch's interests. Some of the titles: *How a Young Person Ought to Study Poetry; On Listening to Lectures; How to Distinguish a Flatterer from a Friend; How to Profit from Your Enemies; Instructions for Maintaining Health; The Bravery of Women; Which Is Worse: the Ills of the Mind or the Ills of the Body?; Should Old Men Take Part in Politics?; Are Land or Sea Animals More Clever?; On the Face in the Moon.*

Some scholars claim that Plutarch did not author the essay that appears as the first document, even though it is traditionally grouped with the many other essays that he wrote. Regardless of authorship, however, the essay offers some interesting insights into ancient Greek attitudes about education.

KEEP IN MIND AS YOU READ

1. Plutarch's moral essay entitled *The Education of Children* usually appears first in the ordering of the surviving essays, and under this general rubric, Plutarch addresses many details; examples: the role of good nutrition; the importance of devoted and conscientious parents, and in particular, that parents should not set unattainable goals for their children or impose unreasonable demands on them; parents should not "be utterly harsh and austere in their nature, but they should in many cases concede some shortcomings to the younger person [i.e., their child], and remind themselves that they once were young"; choosing proper nursemaids and servants for a child and choosing competent teachers; teaching children to be truthful at all times; shielding children from inappropriate speech and behavior.

2. As mentioned in the general introduction, there were no formal elementary "schools" in ancient Greece, at least not of the sort that we are familiar with in modern times. So Greek parents would either teach their children themselves—roughly equivalent to the homeschooling movement today—or else hire knowledgeable tutors to do the job. Parents who chose the latter option needed to exercise

great care in selecting tutors, and Plutarch (and other authors) often emphasized to parents the critical importance of making wise choices.

Document: Educating Free-Born Children

according to Plato: The reference to Plato is taken from his *Republic* (Book 7), where he is discussing the proper and effective ways to educate children. Plato, like Plutarch, shuns the idea that physical force, corporal punishment, or harsh discipline have appropriate roles to play in a child's education. Rather, he suggests that a child's lessons should incorporate play and enjoyment if the child is to learn well and thoroughly.

Bion, the philosopher: Bion (ca. 325– ca. 255 BCE) had an interesting life. Because of his father's criminal activity, the entire family was sold into slavery. Fortunately for Bion, however, he wound up serving a rhetorician, and apparently serving him well: his master eventually freed him and left him a fortune in his will. Bion made his way to Athens, and studied with many noted philosophers of the time. Eventually, he became a wandering philosopher, traveling from place to place and earning his living by offering lectures, for a fee.

every branch . . . general education: Here Plutarch seems to be articulating the idea, still current, of the importance of a liberal arts education, wherein students are exposed to all the branches of knowledge and learning.

suitors . . . Penelope: A reference to Homer's *Odyssey*, in which the 100+ young men, all vying for Penelope's hand in marriage,

The free-born child should not be allowed to go without some knowledge, both through hearing and observation, of **every branch** also of what is called **general education;** yet these he should learn only incidentally, just to get a taste of them, as it were (for perfection in everything is impossible), but philosophy he should honor above all else. I can perhaps make my opinion clear by means of a figure: for example, it is a fine thing to voyage about and view many cities, but profitable to dwell only in the best one. And it was a clever saying of **Bion, the philosopher**, that, just as the **suitors**, not being able to approach **Penelope**, consorted with her maid-servants, so also do those who are not able to attain philosophy wear themselves to a shadow over the other kinds of education which have no value. Wherefore it is necessary to make philosophy . . . the head and front of all education. For as regards the care of the body, men have discovered two sciences, the medical and the gymnastic, of which the one implants health, the other sturdiness, in the body; but for illnesses and affections of the mind, philosophy alone is the remedy . . . [I]t is necessary not to be indifferent about acquiring the works of earlier writers, but to make a collection of these, like a set of tools in farming. For the corresponding tool of education is the use of books, and by their means it has come to pass that we are able to study knowledge at its source. It is not proper, either, to overlook the exercise of the body, but we should send the children to the **trainers** and cultivate adequately this side of education with all diligence, not merely for the sake of gracefulness of body but also with an eye for strength; for sturdiness of body in childhood is the foundation of a hale old age. Just as in fair weather, then, one ought to prepare for storm, so also in youth one should store up discipline and self-restraint as a provision for old age. But the amount of bodily exercise should be so limited as not to be a drain on the children and make them too tired to study; for, **according to Plato**, sleep and weariness are the enemies of learning . . . This also I assert, that children ought to be led to honorable practices by means of encouragement and reasoning, and not by blows or ill-treatment, for it surely is agreed that these are fitting rather for slaves than for the free-born. For so they grow numb and shudder at their tasks, partly from the pain of the blows, partly from the degradation. [Tr. Frank Cole Babbitt. *Plutarch's Moralia.* (7 C–D; 8 B, C, D, F.). Volume I. LCL, 1927. Page numbers: 33, 35, 37, 39, 41.]

AFTERMATH

Plutarch's influence on later writers has been profound. Shakespearean plays set in ancient Rome—*Coriolanus, Julius Caesar*, and *Antony and Cleopatra*—borrow heavily on information drawn from Plutarch's works. The French essayist Michel de Montaigne was also greatly influenced by Plutarch; his writings contain over 400 references to Plutarchian works. Ralph Waldo Emerson and other transcendentalists also came under Plutarch's spell.

ASK YOURSELF

1. Plutarch has a very high opinion of the importance of studying philosophy. Does he provide sound arguments for his point of view? Do you agree or disagree with his line of reasoning?
2. For educated Romans, the principle of *mens sana in sano corpore* (sound mind in a sound body, the body-mind connection) was centrally important. Do you get a sense from Plutarch's essay that the Greeks had the same attitude?

TOPICS TO CONSIDER

- Plutarch's recommendations for the education of children are clearly directed at families who have the financial wherewithal to hire tutors and trainers, and to buy books and other materials for their children. But what about children born into less fortunate circumstances? Plutarch does address that issue, in a sort of roundabout way, by acknowledging the reality of it, but then deflecting any blame for it away from himself. He also says that the poor must do the best that they can for their children, and should that be impossible, they must do at least as much as they can. In other words, he does not offer any specific suggestions for funding or supporting the education of the children of needy families. Can you find any information or examples of children in ancient Greek families who rose above impoverished circumstances to have an impact on the course of Greek history?
- Plutarch was a very prolific author, and so it follows that in his many other writings—especially the moral essays—he addressed problems and aspects of education in ancient Greece. Research some of these other writings to discover what else he might have had to say about issues in education.

contented themselves with the "maid-servants" while waiting for Penelope to choose one of them. Since Penelope's husband Odysseus had been away from home for nearly 20 years while fighting in the Trojan War, the assumption was that he had been killed, and would never return.

trainers: Trainers—*paidotribes*, plural *paidotribai*, in Plutarch's Greek—were somewhat like modern physical education teachers. A trainer, as E. Norman Gardiner explains it, "was a private teacher, often with a palaestra [wrestling facility] of his own. His fee for a course in the fourth century [BCE] was a *mina* …Parents took considerable pains in choosing a *paidotribes* for their sons … In Hellenistic times [fourth to first centuries BCE] they [the *paidotribai*] had a number of assistants for special exercises, the *sphairistes* who taught ball play, the *akontistes* and *toxotes* who gave instruction in the use of the javelin and the bow, and the *hoplomachus* who gave lessons in the use of arms."

Further Information

Beck, Frederick A. *Greek Education 450–350 B.C.* London, 1964.

Kenyon, F. G. *Books and Readers in Ancient Greece and Rome.* Oxford, 1932.

Marrou, Henri-Irenee. *A History of Education in Antiquity*, translated by George Lamb. Madison, WI, 1956.

Morgan, Teresa. *Literate Education in the Hellenistic and Roman Worlds.* Cambridge, 1998.

Websites

Ancient Greek Education. http://www.crystalinks.com/greekeducation.html

Education in Ancient Greece. http://www.mlahanas.de/Greeks/EducationAncientGreece.htm

Bibliography for Document

Babbitt, Frank Cole (tr.). *Plutarch's Moralia.* Volume I. [LCL.] London and Cambridge, 1927.

Gardiner, E. Norman. *Athletics of the Ancient World.* Oxford, 1930.

7. SOCRATES AND PROTAGORAS DISCUSS ISSUES IN EDUCATION

INTRODUCTION

The second document comes from the prolific pen of the famous philosopher Plato (427–347 BCE). He is noted for his 25 philosophical dialogues, all of which still survive. Many of these dialogues, including the one excerpted here, *Protagoras*, feature Plato's teacher Socrates in a leading role.

KEEP IN MIND AS YOU READ

1. Protagoras was a leading fifth-century BCE sophist. Like most sophists, he traveled from town to town to present lectures and offer tutorial services, although it is thought that he spent much of his professional career in Athens. He became a close friend of Pericles, and it was through Pericles's influence that Protagoras was assigned the task of drawing up a code of laws for the recently founded (443 BCE) Athenian colony of Thurii, in southern Italy. Protagoras's pedagogical proclivities impressed even the likes of Socrates, who says of him in Plato's *Republic* (10.600) that teachers like Protagoras were so highly respected for their wisdom that their students would be tempted to carry them about on their shoulders. Given his ability to inspire zealous admiration like this—how many teachers down through the ages were so well regarded by their students that the students would be willing to carry them triumphantly on their shoulders?—it is not surprising to learn that Protagoras was the first sophist to command a fee for his instructional services.
2. The second document consists of a conversation between Protagoras and Socrates, and several secondary characters, around 432 BCE, in which they discuss the role and teachings of the sophists and in particular, whether it is possible to teach a person to be virtuous.
3. Although Socrates was undoubtedly one of the most famous individuals in ancient Athens, he never wrote any books or essays (as far as we know) in which he articulated his philosophy, opinions, or beliefs. That task was left to his student Plato, and most of what we know of Socrates's teachings are recorded in the Socratic dialogues and other works of Plato.
4. Socrates never accepted any money for his teachings, never opened a school, never recruited any students or disciples. Instead, he frequented public places and

initiated, or joined, conversations, dialogues, and debates with anyone who happened to be present. These discussions covered a wide range of topics and often lasted for days at a time. (Socrates's apparent indifference to earning an income did not please his wife, Xanthippe, who gained an unenviable reputation as something of an ill-tempered nag.)

Document: Practiced in the Art of Sophistry

[Socrates and Protagoras are conversing about issues in education, and Socrates inquires of Protagoras why he claims that his teaching would be a better choice for a prospective student than the teachings offered by rival sophists.]

[Socrates is speaking]: "My friend Hippocrates finds himself desirous of joining your classes, and therefore, he says he would be glad to know what result he will get from joining them . . .

Then Protagoras answered at once, saying: Young man, you will gain this by coming to my classes, that on the day when you join them you will go home a better man, and on the day after, it will be the same; every day you will constantly improve more and more.

When I heard this, I said: Protagoras, what you say is not at all surprising, but quite likely, since even you, though so old and wise would be made better if someone taught you what you happen not to know. But let me put it another

Greek red-figure vessel of students learning to play the lyre (left); and being instructed in speech, from Cerveteri, fifth century BCE. (Jupiterimages)

way: suppose Hippocrates here should change his desire all at once, and become desirous of this young fellow's lessons who was just recently come to town, **Zeuxippus of Heraclea**, and should approach him, as he now does you, and should hear the very same thing from him as from you, how on each day that he spent with him he would be better, and make constant progress. And suppose he were to question him on this and ask: In what shall I become better as you say, and to what will my progress be? Zeuxippus's reply would be, to painting. Then suppose he came to the lessons of **Orthagoras the Theban**, and heard the same thing from him as from you, and then inquired of him for what he would be better each day through attending his classes, the answer would be, for fluting. In the same way you also must satisfy this youth and me on this point, and tell us for what, Protagoras, and in what connection my friend Hippocrates, on any day of attendance at the classes of Protagoras, will go away a better man, and on each of the succeeding days will make a like advance.

When Protagoras heard my words, You do right, he said, to ask that . . . For Hippocrates, if he comes to me, will not be treated as he would have been if he had joined the classes of an ordinary sophist. The generality of them mistreat the young; for when they have escaped from the arts, they bring them back against their will and force them into arts, teaching them arithmetic and astronomy and geometry and music **(and here he glanced at Hippias)**; whereas, if he applies to me, he will learn precisely and solely that for which he has come. That learning consists of good judgment in his own affairs, showing how best to order his own home; and in the affairs of his city, showing how he may have most influence on public affairs both in speech and in action." [Tr. W. R. M. Lamb. *Plato: Laches, Protagoras, Meno, Euthydemus.* (318 A–E). Volume II. LCL, 1924. Page numbers: 121, 123, 125.]

AFTERMATH

The document is excerpted from the early stages of this fairly lengthy conversation. In the remainder of the dialogue, Protagoras and Socrates continue the debate about whether virtue can be taught and whether other qualities, such as wisdom, justice, and holiness, are categories of virtue or the same thing as virtue. The two philosophers also discuss the distinction between "becoming

Heraclea: A town in south central Italy.

and here he glanced at Hippias: The polymathic Hippias of Elis, one of the attendees at the conversation, was a very smart and successful sophist in his own right, offering instruction in a wide array of topics, including geometry, astronomy, music, painting, sculpture, oratory, and history. (Hippias's ability to teach so many subjects undoubtedly occasioned "the glance" mentioned in the dialogue, where Protagoras is reciting a similar list of topics, as examples of the specialized teachings offered by some sophists.) Hippias reportedly made a fortune during his lifetime and developed a reputation for traveling almost anywhere to dispense knowledge—if the price was right. He also gained a reputation for arrogance about his money-making prowess; in a dialogue entitled *Greater Hippias*, probably but not certainly written by Plato, he boasts to Socrates that (among other things) he once earned more than 150 minas (perhaps equivalent to around $750,000!) in a very short time, in an out-of-the-way little town in southwestern Sicily. It was likely bombastic bragging of this sort that resulted in gaining for sophists their unseemly, if not altogether accurate, image as a crowd of money-grubbing charlatans.

Some sources also credit him with inventing a system of mnemonics; he illustrated its efficiency by demonstrations such as the following: he might listen to someone read off a list of 50 names, and then repeat from memory all 50, and in the order in which he heard them.

Orthagoras the Theban: Orthagoras was well qualified to give instruction in flute playing because he was considered one of the best flutists of his time.

Thebes: A famous and powerful city north of Athens.

Zeuxippus of Heraclea: It seems likely, although not certain, that the name "Zeuxippus" is a variant spelling of the name "Zeuxis." If so, then the famous fifth-century BCE painter Zeuxis—who happens to be from Heraclea—is undoubtedly meant here. He was especially gifted in creating paintings that were both attractive and realistic. In Cicero's textbook on rhetoric, the *De Inventione*, he relates an interesting anecdote about Zeuxis. It appears that the citizens of the southern Italian town of Croton, who had built a magnificent temple in honor of the goddess Juno, wished to have it decorated with top-quality paintings. So they hired Zeuxis, for a handsome stipend, to do the work, since he was considered the best artist of the time. Zeuxis was interested in including in the project a portrait of Helen of Troy, a choice that greatly pleased the Crotoniates, since Zeuxis had the reputation of being particularly skilled in depicting women in his paintings. But before embarking on the portrait, Zeuxis asked his employers to assemble the five most beautiful women in the city, which they did. "He selected five, whose names many poets recorded because they were approved by the judgment of him who must have been the supreme judge of beauty. He chose five because he did not think all the qualities that he sought to

good" and "being good," and whether it is possible for fallible human beings to actually attain "goodness." The dialogue ends pleasantly, with Socrates and Protagoras congratulating each other on the power of their argumentation and agreeing to take up the subject again at some other time.

Interestingly, in Plato's *Meno*, written about 30 years later, Socrates seriously lambasts Protagoras, noting that although Protagoras made more money in his teaching career than even a top-shelf sculptor like Pheidias, he often corrupted his students and made them worse, not better. Socrates sarcastically remarks that a shoemaker who did a shoddy job of cobbling could not stay in business for more than 30 days, whereas Protagoras got away with his pedagogical chicanery for 40 years!

ASK YOURSELF

1. Protagoras was born around 480 BCE and Socrates perhaps 10 years later, so they were roughly the same age. Why, then, do you suppose Socrates refers to Protagoras as "old and wise," and Protagoras calls Socrates a "young man"?

2. We hear much heated debate these days about the propriety of the "liberal arts" philosophy of education, where students are required to take courses on a wide variety of subjects, regardless of whether they have any aptitude for those subjects or even like them. However, the debate about the liberal arts curriculum is not a phenomenon of modern times; it goes back at least as far as the Greeks and Romans. Based on the information in the document, how do you think Protagoras felt about the liberal arts concept? And what do you think Socrates's point of view would have been?

TOPICS TO CONSIDER

☙ Although the sophists often found ready audiences and willing students in Athens, there were other Athenians who were wary and suspicious of their teachings. We might place in the latter category the famous Athenian comic playwright Aristophanes (ca. 445–380 BCE). During his lifetime, he wrote about 40 plays, 11 of which survive. Many of these 11 are highly satirical; Aristophanes was never shy about stating his opinions on a wide range of political, social, and cultural issues. In his play *Clouds*, produced in 423, he attacked Socrates and other sophists for undermining and confusing the youth of Athens by teaching them devious methods of argumentation, in the process making Socrates appear inept at best, dangerous at worst. Some historians believe that this unfavorable portrayal of Socrates was one of the factors that ultimately led to his trial (on a charge of corrupting his young and impressionable students), conviction, and execution, albeit nearly a quarter of a century *after* the play was produced. Your task: find a copy of Aristophanes's play *Clouds*, research the background information, read the play, and decide for yourself if Aristophanes treated Socrates unfairly, or created an inaccurate picture of Socrates's teachings.

❧ As already noted, Socrates did not own buildings or other property that could be used as a meeting place for his friends and others for their discussions. So one of the public places that they sometimes utilized for their intellectual pursuits was a gymnasium, a large, usually rectangular structure generally populated by athletes and soldiers engaged in physical training. (The word ultimately derives from the Greek *gymnos*, "naked," a reference to the practice of athletes practicing and competing unclothed.) Two of the most famous gymnasia of the ancient Greek world were the Academy and the Lyceum. Research these two structures. What two famous philosophers were associated with them?

combine in a portrayal of beauty could be found in one person, because in no single case has Nature made anything perfect and finished in every part." [2.1.1].

According to the first-century CE natural scientist Pliny the Elder, Zeuxis painted a picture of grapes so realistically that birds tried to eat them. Pliny also reports that Zeuxis painted a second picture involving grapes, but this time, he added a child, carrying them. A second time, birds were deceived and attempted to eat the grapes, but on this occasion, Zeuxis was enraged, exclaiming that if he had portrayed the child more accurately, the birds would not have dared to come close to the grapes.

SOPHISTS AND SOPHISTRY

In its modern sense, "sophistry" carries some unpleasant baggage; *Random House Webster's College Dictionary*, for example, defines the word thus: "a subtle, tricky, superficially plausible, but generally fallacious method of reasoning." And so, practitioners of sophistry—sophists—might be viewed in a similarly unfavorable light, as they sometimes were in ancient Greece.

The derivation of the word certainly does not conjure up images of trickiness or deception; it ultimately comes from the Greek adjective *sophos*, "wise," and hence, a sophist is a "wise person." But over the course of years, different nuances of meaning began to be associated with the word sophist, so that by the fifth century BCE, it was generally applied to "wise men" who gave instruction in specific areas of learning, i.e., a professional class of teachers. Just as one could find good and bad workers in any occupation or profession, so it was with the sophists; unfortunately, the unethical sophists saddled the entire profession with an unsavory reputation. Part of the reason for this unfavorable standing had to do with money. As already mentioned, Protagoras was the first paid sophist; others followed suit. In the minds of some Athenians, the accepting of fees seemed somehow inappropriate, as if knowledge and wisdom were commodities that could be bought and sold. Socrates was accused of taking payments for his teaching, a charge he vehemently denied at his famous trial in 399 BCE.

Also contributing to the damage was the nature of the profession itself, one that "tended to produce a certain attitude of mind, which placed emphasis on material success and on the ability to argue for any point of view, irrespective of its truth." [*Oxford Classical Dictionary*.]

COLLECTING TEACHING FEES

Diogenes Laertius (third century CE) wrote accounts of the lives and philosophical teachings of numerous Greek thinkers, including (among very many others) Protagoras. He relates an amusing story about Protagoras's attempt to collect a fee from one of his students, a certain Euathlus. This Euathlus resisted paying up, claiming that since he had not yet won a case, he owed no money to his teacher. Protagoras's reply: "[I]f I win this case against you I must have the fee, for winning it. If you win, I must have it, because *you* win it."

Further Information

Cornford, Francis M. *Before and After Socrates*. Cambridge, 1932.
Field, G. C. *Plato and His Contemporaries*. London, 1930.
Jarrett, James L. *The Educational Theories of the Sophists*. New York, 1969.
Ross, W. D. *Plato's Theory of Ideas*. Oxford, 1951.
Shorey, Paul. *What Plato Said*. Chicago, 1937.

Website

General Bibliography on Plato. http://faculty.tcc.edu/JCarr/PlatoBib.htm

Bibliography for Document

Hubbell, H. M. (tr.). *Cicero: De Inventione; De Optimo Genere Oratorum; Topica*. [LCL.] Cambridge and London, 1949.
Lamb, W. R. M. (tr.). *Plato: Laches; Protagoras; Meno; Euthydemus*. Volume II. [LCL.] Cambridge and London, 1924.

8. FUNDING FOR ROMAN SCHOOLS

INTRODUCTION

Modern American public schools are built, staffed, and funded according to long-established laws and traditions, but in ancient Roman times, the system was much less standardized. Smaller communities, especially those located far from Rome, may have had no organized system of education at all. Such was the case with the town of Comum, tucked far away from Rome, in Italy's northern expanses.

Enter Pliny the Younger (62–114 CE), who happened to be a native of Comum. A generous philanthropist, Pliny offered to donate a substantial sum of money to the town for organizing a school. Pliny had a reputation for such benefactions: He donated 500,000 sesterces for the support and maintenance of the youth of Comum; he gave 300,000 sesterces for the furnishing and maintenance of public baths in Comum; he presented his childhood nurse with a farm worth 100,000 sesterces; at a time when a friend of his did not have enough money to cover the cost of his daughter's wedding, Pliny came to the rescue with a gift of 50,000 sesterces. Many of Pliny's financial gifts were earmarked for children or young people; in this regard, he was perhaps one of the first prominent Romans to participate in an emergent early imperial social custom called the *alimenta*: a philanthropic system in which wealthy benefactors provided financial support for needy children.

KEEP IN MIND AS YOU READ

1. Pliny himself had probably been the beneficiary of the services of a private tutor, and so he is particularly concerned that the residents of Comum hire "teachers of repute" to staff the proposed school.
2. The document is in the form of a letter addressed to his friend Cornelius Tacitus, a highly regarded Roman historian, many of whose works still survive today. Two of Pliny's most famous letters (of the hundreds still extant) describe in detail the eruption of Mount Vesuvius in 79 CE; Pliny was an eyewitness to that horrific event, and Tacitus had requested some information about it so that he could include an account of the eruption in a history of Rome he was writing.
3. It is thought that the document was written around 104 CE.

Document: Pliny the Younger Helps to Fund a School

Comum: Located in northern Italy, Comum was the hometown of Pliny and also of his uncle, the famous natural scientist Pliny the Elder.

If you put your money together: J. H. Westcott (v. *infra*) writes about this passage: "Rhetoricians were first paid by the state under [the emperor] Vespasian [reigned 69–79 CE]. Here is a suggestion that Comum should follow the example of Rome." Quintilian (see the next document) taught rhetoric in Rome in his own school, which opened sometime during Vespasian's reign.

Mediolanum: The modern Milan, a city in northern Italy, kind of a "hub" city, where many roads interconnected. It was about 30 miles from Comum.

teachers: Pliny uses the word *praeceptores*, here translated as "teachers." More specifically, the word may refer to rhetoric professors, at least according to one commentator (J. H. Westcott, editor and annotator of *Selected Letters of Pliny*).

young son: Pliny's word is *praetextatus*, meaning a boy still wearing the *toga praetexta*, and signifying that he had not yet reached the age of manhood, around 17.

I was visiting my native town [**Comum**] a short time ago when the **young son** of a fellow citizen came to pay his respects to me. "Do you go to school?" I asked. "Yes," he replied. "Where?" "In **Mediolanum**." "Why not here?" To this, the boy's father (who had brought him and was standing by) replied: "Because we have no **teachers** here." "Why not? Surely it is a matter of great importance to you fathers (and luckily there were several fathers listening) that your children should study here on the spot. Where can they live more happily than in their native place? Where can they be brought up more strictly than under their parents' eye or with less expense than at home? **If you put your money together**, what would it cost you to engage teachers? And you could add to their salaries what you now spend on lodgings, traveling expenses, and all the things which cost money away from home—and everything is bought abroad these days. Now, as I have not yet any children of my own, I am prepared to contribute a third of whatever sum you decide to collect, as a present for our town such as I might give to a daughter or my mother. I would promise the whole amount were I not afraid that someday my gift might be abused for someone's selfish purposes, as I see happen in many places where teachers' salaries are paid from public funds. There is only one remedy to meet this evil: if the appointment of teachers is left entirely to the parents, and they are conscientious about making a wise choice through their obligation to contribute to the cost. People who may be careless about another person's money are sure to be careful about their own. So you should meet and come to some agreement; be encouraged by my generosity, for I want my own contribution to be as large as possible. You can do nothing better for your children, nothing more welcome for our town. The children born here should be brought up on their native soil, so that from their earliest years they may learn to love it and choose to stay at home. I hope that you will introduce teachers of repute, so that nearby towns will seek education here, and, instead of sending your children elsewhere as you do today, you will soon see other children flocking here to you." [Tr. Betty Radice. *Pliny: Letters and Panegyricus.* (4.13.) Volume I. LCL, 1969. Page numbers: 279, 281.]

TEACHERS AND STUDENTS BACK IN THE DAY

Juvenal's *Satire VII* contains some biting statements about the sad state of education in his time (first/second century CE). He notes, for example, the stories told about the school days of the mighty Greek warrior Achilles, who was instructed by the centaur Chiron. Achilles did not often back down, but he showed reverence and respect to his schoolmaster; *metuens virgae* are Juvenal's words: Achilles was "fearful of the rod" (or, as the old traditional American song put it: "reading and writing and 'rithmetic / taught to the tune of a hickory stick"). But *now*, in Juvenal's time, things have changed! Students make fun of their teachers and sometimes even physically assault them with impunity.

In the same satire, Juvenal also decries the piteously poor salaries paid to teachers and how parents expect teachers always and everywhere to be ready at a moment's notice to spew elaborate and articulate answers to the most arcane questions (name Anchises's nurse; who was Anchemolus's stepmother, and what was her hometown?; how old was Acestes at his death?; when the Trojans set sail from Sicily, how many gallons of wine did Acestes give to them?). And how difficult it can be sometimes for a teacher to maintain order in a classroom—"no easy matter to watch the hands and sparkling eyes of so many youngsters!" [Juvenal. Satires 7.240-241; tr. Ramsay.]

Finally, he notes that a charioteer can earn more money by winning a single race than a teacher receives in an entire year.

AFTERMATH

Unfortunately, we have no information about whether Pliny's initiative, and his financial backing, resulted in a permanently endowed and viable school in Comum. It is probably reasonable to assume that the school remained at least as long as Pliny was still around to help oversee it, but he died less than 10 years after it was founded.

ASK YOURSELF

1. Pliny seems to suggest that schools—or at least the one proposed for Comum— should be funded by voluntary contributions from parents. Do you think that this funding system would work? In the United States, where does the money come from for building and maintaining public schools?
2. What do you suppose Pliny means when he writes that he would have provided the entire amount of money needed to fund the school except that he feared his gift "might be abused for someone's selfish purposes"? Although he does not identify the "someone," nor the "selfish purposes," what kinds of inappropriate behavior might have been worrying him?
3. Are there any components of Pliny's proposal that seem impractical?

TOPICS TO CONSIDER

- Read and research Juvenal's seventh Satire, especially the sections near the end where he describes the low pay, dangers, and humiliations that teachers frequently have to deal with or confront. How close to the truth do you think Juvenal's descriptions are? (Remember: he was a satirist!) Do you think that the same kinds of problems and frustrations are present today for public schoolteachers? The comment at the end, about a charioteer's salary, seems to strike a chord. Would you say that a similar disparity exists today between a teacher's salary and that paid to a professional athlete?

❧ Consider Pliny's overall proposal for the school at Comum. What do you suppose was his motivation for wanting to do this? There is no doubt that Pliny was the epitome of a civic-minded Roman gentleman, but still . . . We do have a long inscription (*CIL* 5.5262), which was posted in a prominent place in Comum and listed many of his benefactions, including the amounts of money he donated for each.

Further Information

Stout, S. E. *Scribe and Critic at Work in Pliny's Letters.* Bloomington, IN, 1954.

Websites

A Select Bibliography to Pliny's Letters. http://classics.uc.edu/~johnson/pliny/plinybib.html
The Younger Pliny. http://encyclopedia.jrank.org/PIG_POL/PLINY_THE_YOUNGER.html

Bibliography for Document

Radice, Betty (tr.). *Pliny: Letters and Panegyricus.* [LCL.] Cambridge and London, 1969.
Ramsay, G.G. (tr.). *Juvenal and Persius.* [LCL.] Cambridge and London, 1918.
Westcott, J. H. *Selected Letters of Pliny.* Norman, OK, new edition 1965.

9. Spare the Rod, and Other Educational Precepts of Quintilian

INTRODUCTION

The ancient Romans (like the Greeks) never developed a formal educational "system," i.e., elementary and secondary public schools, and colleges and universities. Sometimes, children were homeschooled, either by their parents or by an educated slave or other private tutor. But schools also abounded, and three levels of education were established and accepted. (Quintilian, the source of the third document in this chapter, strongly preferred the latter; he felt that large numbers of students are inevitably attracted to the best teachers, whereas one-on-one instruction, or homeschooling, often resulted in an inferior education because of unqualified teachers. He also felt that learning was enhanced by the dynamic resulting from interaction with others, but solitary study bred boredom.)

In the first level of education, young students (around the age of six or seven) were taught the "three R's" (reading, writing, arithmetic) by the equivalent of today's elementary school teacher, called by the Romans a *litterator*. Next up was the *grammaticus*, a teacher who specialized in giving instruction in the analysis and recitation of literary texts. At the age of perhaps 14, the student was ready to progress to the third level, roughly corresponding to higher education today, where rhetoric, logic, argumentation, and public speaking were emphasized.

It is difficult to know how students were evaluated, because there were, to our knowledge, no examinations, no report cards, no diplomas, nor any degrees awarded, at any of the stages of the educational system.

KEEP IN MIND AS YOU READ

1. One of our best sources of information about Roman attitudes toward education was the orator and educational philosopher Quintilian (full Roman name Marcus Fabius Quintilianus, ca. 35 CE–ca. 95). Quintilian wrote a lengthy treatise on the method and content of a course of training for a Roman orator: *The Institutes of Oratory*. Although his book focuses on oratorical training, many of the educational principles he enunciates, particularly in the first two chapters, have a far wider application.

2. Quintilian wrote his book at the request of friends who respected his intelligence, his integrity, his knowledge of the subject, and his experience; he had been

instructing young orators for some 20 years. At first, he was reluctant to undertake the project, partially because there were already many oratorical books available and partially because he felt unequal to the task. But eventually he forged ahead, because he felt obligated to his friends to do so and also because he believed he could approach the topic from a perspective that was a bit different from the one reflected in the other books on oratory and oratorical training.

3. Roman education was generally geared to boys only, although girls also apparently could receive at least some formal training. When referring to a young student, Quintilian invariably uses the Latin word *puer*, usually translated as "boy," although sometimes the word can have a gender-neutral meaning, especially in the plural form: "children."

4. Quintilian was writing in the first century CE, when the Roman educational system had developed some well-established procedures, expectations, and practices after centuries of refinements. Still, there were those who longed for the "good old days," and who criticized modern educational trends and philosophies. One of these critics was Quintilian's contemporary, the historian Cornelius Tacitus (ca. 55–117 CE). In his *Dialogue on Oratory*, he writes: "Everybody is aware that it is not for lack of votaries that eloquence and the other arts as well have fallen from their former high estate, but because of the laziness of our young men, the carelessness of parents, the ignorance of teachers, and the decay of the old-fashioned virtue." (Tacitus, *A Dialogue on Oratory 28*; tr. Peterson). In the same section, Tacitus lashes out at young people who have a "passion for play actors, and the mania for gladiatorial shows and horse racing," and whose unworthy interests are validated and fueled by like-minded teachers, who waste valuable class time discussing such trivialities with their students.

Document: Quintilian's Educational Philosophies

Chrysippus: Chrysippus was a noted third-century BCE Stoic philosopher. Although a prolific writer—he reportedly strove to write 500 lines of text per day—few of his works survive, and his attitude about corporal punishment in schools must be inferred from the words of Quintilian. Chrysippus was not shy about touting his own intellect; one day, he was approached by a man who was looking for a tutor for his son. The man asked Chrysippus whom he would recommend. The

All our students will require some relaxation, not merely because there is nothing in this world that can stand continued strain, and even unthinking and inanimate objects are unable to maintain their strength, unless given intervals of rest, but because study depends on the good will of the student, a quality that cannot be secured by compulsion. Consequently, if restored and refreshed by a holiday, they will bring greater energy to their learning and approach their work with greater spirit of a kind that will not submit to be driven. I approve of play in the young; it is a sign of a lively disposition. Nor will you ever lead me to believe that a child who is gloomy and in a continual state of depression is ever likely to show alertness of mind in his work, lacking as he does the impulse most natural to children of his age . . . **I disapprove of flogging**, although it is the regular custom and meets with the acquiescence of **Chrysippus**, because in the first place it is a disgraceful form of punishment and fit only for slaves, and is in any case an insult, as you will realize if you imagine its infliction at a later age. Secondly, if a child is so insensible to instruction that reproof is useless, he will, like the worst type of slave, merely become hardened to blows. Finally, there will be absolutely no need of such punishment if the master is a thorough disciplinarian. As it is, we try to make amends for the negligence of the boy's **paedagogus**, not by forcing him to do what is right, but by punishing him for not doing what is right. And though you may compel a child with blows, what are you to do with him when he is a young man no longer amenable to such threats, and confronted with tasks of far greater difficulty? Moreover, **when children are beaten**, pain or fear frequently have results of which it is not pleasant to speak, and which are likely subsequently to be a source of shame, a shame which unnerves and depresses the mind and leads the child to shun and loathe **the light** ... I will content myself with saying that children are helpless and easily victimized, and that therefore no one should be given unlimited power over them ... As soon as the boy has learned to read and write without difficulty, it is the turn for the teacher of literature [i.e., the *grammaticus*] ... [T]hose who criticize the art of teaching literature as trivial and lacking in substance put themselves out of court ... The study of literature is a necessity for boys and the delight of old age, the sweet companion of our privacy and the sole branch of study which has more solid substance than display. [Tr. H. E. Butler. *The Institutio Oratoria of Quintilian* (1.3–4.) Volume I. LCL, 1920. Page numbers: 57, 59, 61, 63, 65.]

AFTERMATH

Several works of literature are attributed to Quintilian; however, the only one that can definitely be ascribed to him is the *Institutes of Oratory*, which he wrote sometime in the decade of the '90s CE, and after he retired from his long career as a lawyer and educator. His book had a favorable impact on his students and others, and he is referenced in works by the poets Martial and Juvenal and the epistler Pliny the Younger.

ASK YOURSELF

1. What do you think of the arguments put forward by Quintilian in opposition to the practice of corporal punishment in schools? What might be some counterarguments?

answer: "Me! For if I thought any philosopher excelled me, I would myself become his student."

I disapprove of flogging: Some Roman teachers would not agree with this assertion. Consider, for example, the case of one Lucius Orbilius Pupillus, a *grammaticus* and one of the teachers of the poet Horace. In one of his *Epistles*, Horace uses the epithet *plagosus* ("full of blows") to describe his old teacher Orbilius; apparently, Orbilius did not shrink from resorting to physical punishment if Horace, although only a small boy at the time, faltered in his recitations. Another writer, Domitius Marsus, also apparently a student of Orbilius, recalled that the teacher would not hesitate to employ rods or leather whips in the classroom. In his brief biography of Orbilius, Suetonius has this to say about him: "He ... wrote a book called *Perialogos*, full of complaints of the wrongs which teachers suffered from the indifference or selfishness of parents ... He was sour-tempered, not only towards rival scholars, whom he assailed at every opportunity, but also towards his students ..." [Suetonius. *On Grammarians* 9; tr. Rolfe.].

the light: As in English, the Latin word for light, *lux*, can have both a literal and a metaphorical meaning: literal light, like the brightness of the day or a well-lit room, and symbolic light: knowledge, education, mental clarity. It seems possible that Quintilian is suggesting both meanings in this passage.

paedagogus: A Greek word meaning "child leader." The *paedagogus* was usually a slave in the household of a wealthy family. His primary job was to escort the family's child, or children, to and from school and to make certain that they did not misbehave. Quintilian believed that *paedagogi* should be educated men, or if they were not, that they should not pretend otherwise, and that especially, they should not attempt to instruct their young charges in any academic subject. Sometimes, a particularly fortunate child was also accompanied by a *capsarius*, a slave who carried the child's books and school supplies.

when children are beaten: Compare the opposite approach, as articulated by the poet Horace (*Satire* 1.1): "Wise teachers often give their students sugar cookies, to encourage them to learn their early lessons" (especially the basics of reading).

2. These days, we often hear complaints from taxpayers about the high cost of public education. In response to these complaints, and in order to save money, school districts often reduce or eliminate programs in schools that are considered "frills," such as sports teams. How do you think Quintilian would have reacted to cost-saving measures like that?

3. What do you think Quintilian means by the last words of the document, that the study of literature is "the sole branch of study which has more solid substance than display"?

TOPICS TO CONSIDER

❧ Quintilian expresses great concern about the long-range negative effects on children of corporal punishment. He even seems to go so far as to suggest that corporal punishment in schools equates to child abuse. Can you think of any events in recent American history or culture that might support (or refute) his concerns? What light does modern child psychology shed on this issue?

❧ Consider the three tiers of the Roman educational system (reading and writing, equivalent to American elementary schools; introduction to rhetoric and literature, corresponding to American middle and high schools; and advanced training in oratory, law, rhetoric, logic, and philosophy, similar to American university education). Research these tiers in more depth. How effective do you think they were? If public opinion polls had existed in Roman times, do you think they would have revealed that most educated Romans were satisfied with the education they received or critical of it?

SOUND MIND, SOUND BODY

Quintilian's notion that students need physical exercise and play as much as they need devotion to intellectual pursuits is reflected in the work of several other Roman authors, most notably the satirist Juvenal; his famous phrase (from the tenth *Satire*) *mens sana in corpore sano*, "[One should pray for a] sound mind in a sound body" has worked its way into popular American culture. The idea is also articulated by the first-century BCE poet Horace, in the 31st poem of the first book of his *Odes*, where he prays to the god Apollo for good physical health and a sound mind. In *Satire* 2.2, Horace hints at the same mind-body connection when he writes that a night of imprudent carousing brings mental as well as physical distress the next day, whereas the people who observe moderation in their social and dietary habits will sleep well, and wake up the next morning ready to face the day. The first-century CE philosopher Seneca, in his tenth *Epistle*, suggests much the same: "Ask [from the gods] a good mind, and good health, of mind and also of body."

A ROSTER OF SCHOOLTEACHERS

The biographer Suetonius is probably best known for authoring accounts of the lives of the first 12 Roman emperors (whose reigns covered most of the first century CE), but he also wrote a series of biographies of some noted *grammatici.* Summaries of several of these individuals:

1. Crates of Mallos (second century BCE), who, Suetonius states, was the first *grammaticus* to offer instruction in Rome. On one unfortunate occasion, Crates fell into an open sewer and broke his leg, but continued his teaching duties nonetheless, serving as an excellent example of a dedicated teacher.
2. Saevius Nicanor (dates unspecified) was the first teacher to become widely known in Rome.
3. Marcus Antonius Gnipho (first century BCE) was a kind, good-hearted man, who never made any demands about fees for his services, and ironically was often paid more money than the going rate. He worked for a period of time in Julius Caesar's household and even served as a tutor for the noted orator/lawyer Cicero.
4. On the other hand, Marcus Pompilius Andronicus, a contemporary of Gnipho, had the reputation of being a rather lazy and underqualified teacher, so he turned to writing books to make a living; he sold one of his volumes for 16,000 sesterces, a handsome sum by the standards of the time.
5. Lucius Ateius Philologus (whose last name means "lover of words") was known, according to Suetonius, as "a rhetorician among grammarians, and a grammarian among rhetoricians." He wrote numerous learned commentaries on history, literature, and rhetoric, and furnished the historians Sallust and Asinius Pollio with information they incorporated into their writing projects.

  ❧ Well-to-do Roman parents, especially fathers, sometimes sought out tutors for their children, but the task of finding a suitable tutor could be a daunting one. Pliny the Younger, a noted civil servant, scholar and epistler, and contemporary of Quintilian, once received a request for help from a friend of his who was searching for a tutor for his nephews. Read Pliny's response, addressed to Junius Mauricus—it appears in Book 2, number 18, in Pliny's collected *Letters*—to get a sense of Pliny's reaction to this request. Pliny also addresses the issue of tutor-hiring in another letter, to a friend of his by the name of Corellia Hispulla (3.3). What sorts of characteristics and qualifications do you think that a Roman parent would desire in a tutor?

Further Information

Balsdon, J. P. V. D. *Life and Leisure in Ancient Rome,* (especially Chapter Five, "Family Life," s.v "Schooling"). New York, 1969.

Bonner, Stanley F. *Education in Ancient Rome: From the Elder Cato to the Younger Pliny.* Berkeley, CA1977.

Wheelock, Frederic M. *Quintilian as Educator: Selections from the Institutio Oratoria of Marcus Fabius Quintilianus.* New York, 1974.

Websites

Schools in Ancient Rome: Roman Teachers and Levels of Education. http://roman-history .suite101.com/article.cfm/schools_in_ancient_rome

Ancient Roman Education. http://www.mariamilani.com/ancient_rome/ancient_roman _education.htm

Bibliography for Document

Butler, H. E. (tr.). *The Institutio Oratoria of Quintilian*. Volume I. [LCL.] Cambridge and London, 1920.

Peterson, Sir William (tr.). *Tacitus: Dialogus; Agricola; Germania*. [LCL]. Cambridge and London, 1914.

Rolfe, J. C. (tr.). *Suetonius*. Volume II. [LCL.] Cambridge and London, 1914.

EMPLOYMENT

10. Pay It Back! Apollodorus and His Day in Court

INTRODUCTION

Just as is the case for people today, making a living was a major concern for most Greeks and Romans. And while a majority of the workers in both civilizations toiled in the agricultural field, there were many other career choices available: government and public service, construction, banking, architecture, oratory and legal work, food and clothing production, and small business enterprises. Older citizens of Athens often depended on work as paid jurors in court cases to help make ends meet. There were even specialty career opportunities; for example, in ancient Athens, some artisans made their living solely by fabricating the elaborate masks worn by actors in dramatic productions. And, perhaps not surprisingly, there was always a need for soldiers and sailors.

KEEP IN MIND AS YOU READ

1. Pasio was one of the most successful—and richest—ancient Athenian bankers that we know of. Pasio's background was anything but affluent; in fact, as a young man, he was a slave, in the possession of two bankers by the names of Antisthenes and Archestratus. He went to work for them in the banking business, and through diligence, perseverance, and loyal service to his masters, he eventually gained his freedom and became the owner of his own bank. In addition to the bank, he also owned a shield-making factory. Both businesses were very successful, netting an estimated annual profit of two talents (perhaps equivalent to $600,000 or more). When Pasio died, around 370 BCE, his fortune amounted to about 40 talents.

2. Perhaps one of the most distressing financial controversies involving Pasio and his bank came about when the Athenian naval commander Timotheus (d. 354 BCE) applied for a loan. In those days, Athenian military leaders often had to engage in fund-raising activities to pay for soldiers and equipment; the Athenian government generally did not supply adequate funds for these purposes. So Timotheus borrowed a large sum of money from Pasio—4,438 drachmas, perhaps equivalent to $225,000 or more—but the money had never been repaid. So the bank initiated a suit to recover the money. The document consists of an excerpt from a speech made in court by Pasio's son, Apollodorus, on behalf of the bank.

3. Athenian banks, just like modern banks, sometimes made unwise loans, which created financial crises when debtors defaulted on their loans. This was the case with the events described in the document.

4. Timotheus apparently believed that he could get away without repaying the money in part because Pasio had recently died at the time that his son, Apollodorus, brought the suit forward.

Document: Apollodorus Speaks

grievous danger of losing his life: The delays caused by the necessity of raising money meant that the campaign of 374 did not go well. Timotheus was recalled to Athens to stand trial for mismanagement, and might well have been condemned to death if not for the intervention of two of his wealthy and influential friends.

king: After his trial, and eventual acquittal, Timotheus, hoping to restore his reputation and improve his personal financial status, offered his services to the king of Persia.

men of the jury: Athenian juries were huge, not limited to the "12 good men—or women—and true" of today's typical jury. Athenian juries frequently numbered in the hundreds; the jury that condemned Socrates had 501 members; the odd number guaranteed that there would be no tie votes. (Three hundred and sixty voted to convict Socrates.) Juries were always composed of men only, often elderly ones; the smallish stipend paid to jurors were particularly coveted by older men who needed the money to make ends meet.

most generous: According to A. T. Murray, editor/translator of the document, the loan could be itemized thus: 1,351 drachmas and two

[Apollodorus is speaking; he is referring to Pasio with the words "my father."] "Let no one of you think, **men of the jury**, that it is a thing beyond belief that Timotheus should have owed money to my father. On the contrary, when I have called to your minds the occasion on which the loan was contracted and the events in which the defendant [Timotheus] was at that time involved and the **straits to which he was reduced**, you will then hold that my father was **most generous** to Timotheus, and that the defendant is not only ungrateful, but is the most dishonest of humankind; for he got from my father all that he asked, and received from the bank money at a time when he was in great need and when he was in **grievous danger of losing his life**; yet he has not only made no return, but even seeks to rob me of the money which was granted him. And yet, if matters had gone badly with Timotheus, my father's money, too, was lost, for he lent it without security [i.e., without collateral; an unsecured loan] and without witnesses. But, if the defendant got off safe, it rested with him to choose when, having the funds available, he should pay us back. But for all that . . . my father did not count the holding of large sums of money as important a matter as to supply Timotheus with what he needed in the time of his distress. No, my father thought . . . that, if Timotheus then got safely out of those dangers and returned home from the service of the **king**, when the defendant was in better circumstances than at the time, he would not only recover his money, but would be in a position to obtain whatever else he might wish from Timotheus. But as matters have not turned out as my father expected, since the money which Timotheus asked of my father and gratefully received from the bank, he is determined, now that my father is dead, to pay back only if forced to do so by hostile legal procedure, and by convincing proof of his indebtedness, and, if he can convince you by deceitful arguments that he is not liable, to rob us of the money—I count it necessary to inform you fully of everything from the beginning: the several loans, the purpose for which he expended each sum, and the dates at which the obligations were contracted. And let no one of you wonder that I have accurate knowledge of these matters; for bankers are accustomed to write out memoranda of the sums which they lend, the purposes for which funds are desired, and the payments which a borrower makes, in order that his receipts and his payments may be known to them for their accounts." [Tr. A. T. Murray. *Demosthenes V: Private Orations* (including *Against Timotheus* 1–6.). Volume V. LCL, 1939. Page numbers: 377, 379.]

---

obols for the fleet in 374 BCE; 10 minas to repay a previous loan; 1 mina, 257 drachmas for a second previous loan; 1,750 drachmas for shipping charges for lumber given to Timotheus by a Macedonian king.

straits to which he was reduced: In 375 BCE, Timotheus had successfully engaged a Spartan fleet, but in the following year, more hostilities commenced, and it was for this purpose that he needed a fresh infusion of money.

AFTERMATH

According to the biographer Plutarch, the famous orator Demosthenes "ghost-wrote" the speech that Apollodorus used against Timotheus; Plutarch also reports that Apollodorus won the case, which is generally thought to have been litigated in 362 BCE. (Some contemporary historians, however, dispute the contention that Demosthenes was the author.) Timotheus had always had an uneven career in Athenian public life, but his ultimate downfall occurred a few years after the celebrated trial, when, as a military commander, he was blamed for a naval defeat. Once more finding himself in legal hot water, he was tried, convicted, and fined the astronomical sum of 100 talents (perhaps equivalent to $30 million). Not surprisingly, he was unable to pay. He went into exile instead and died shortly after.

Apollodorus continued his forays into the legal system as an advocate, apparently sometimes using speeches that Demosthenes wrote for him, sometimes writing his own. Despite the controversies that enveloped him and the enmity that he sometimes brought on himself

APOLLODORUS: LOYAL SON OR SNAKE IN THE GRASS?

Pasio had two sons, Apollodorus and Pasicles; 14 years separated Apollodorus from his younger brother. The ancient evidence, gleaned primarily from lawyer/orators like Demosthenes and Isocrates, implies that Apollodorus was a loyal son, working diligently to protect both the bank and his father's good name, especially in controversies like the ones described elsewhere in this part of the chapter.

But there was also a dark side to his nature. Pasio had a trusted business manager, Phormio, who, upon Pasio's death, married Pasio's widow and became Pasicles's legal guardian. Some 20 years after Pasio's death, Apollodorus sued Phormio, demanding from him a payment of the astounding sum of 20 talents (perhaps equivalent to $6 million!); Apollodorus alleged that Phormio had embezzled this amount from the estate. Demosthenes, who defended Phormio in the case, fired off a few salvos of his own against Apollodorus, accusing him of rapacious behavior, plundering money from the estate that should have been shared with Pasicles.

Apollodorus should have let it alone. Not only did he lose his case, but he failed to gain even one-fifth of the votes of the jurors. The Athenian system provided for a special penalty for any plaintiff who got swamped in the jury voting to that degree: the *epobelia*, or "one obol on the drachma." He would have to pay the defendant one-sixth of the damages claimed (since an obol was worth one-sixth of a drachma). In this case, that would presumably have amounted to about 3.3 talents!

But Apollodorus had at least one more arrow in his legal quiver. He subsequently prosecuted one of the witnesses, a certain Stephanus, who spoke on behalf of Phormio, charging him with perjury.

A SUCCESSFUL FUND-RAISING GENERAL

The general Timotheus, as we have seen, created some trouble for himself by failing to repay a bank loan for money he borrowed to finance his military activities. But Aristotle, in his treatise *Athenian Constitution* [22.3], records the method whereby Themistocles successfully raised 100 talents for building warships. In 483 BCE, a rich vein of silver was discovered in a state-owned mine near Athens; the yield was a 100-talent profit for the Athenian government. Some leaders thought the windfall should be distributed among all the people, but Themistocles argued that the money should be lent to the 100 wealthiest citizens, one talent per man. His opinion carried the day, the 100 talents were accordingly lent, and then Themistocles prevailed upon the 100 "lucky winners" to use their newfound money to oversee the construction of warships. Each recipient did so, and none too soon; the Athenians needed those 100 new ships to defeat the mighty Persian navy in the Battle of Salamis in 480.

as a result, he lived a comfortable life, made possible by the money he inherited from his father. He died around 340 BCE.

ASK YOURSELF

1. The portion of the document that has been quoted is taken from the very beginning of Apollodorus's speech to the jury. Do you think he is off to a good start? Do his arguments make sense? If you were the opposing lawyer, what counterarguments might you make?

2. Timotheus is obviously being made to look like a crook and a villain. Do you think that this would be a fair characterization of him? After all, he was put into a position where he had to do a job (providing funds for the fleet) that probably should have been done by the authorities in Athens. What, if anything, could he have done differently?

TOPICS TO CONSIDER

• These days, we hear many news accounts of "frivolous lawsuits." Perhaps the best example of this kind of case was the suit brought against a noted fast-food chain by a customer who was irate because she burned herself when she spilled some of the hot coffee served to her in the restaurant's drive-through. The incident occurred in 1992, but the case was not resolved until 1994, when the parties settled out of court for an undisclosed sum of money, but apparently the amount was well into the six figures. The Athenian legal system, too, was plagued by what might well be termed frivolous lawsuits. (The comic playwright Aristophanes [ca. 445–380 BCE] ridiculed and satirized the litigious inclinations of his fellow Athenians in a play entitled *Wasps*, which features, among other amusing incidents, a dog put on trial for stealing a piece of cheese!) We have numerous transcripts of court speeches and cases argued by skilled orator/lawyers like Demosthenes, Isocrates, Aeschines, Isaeus, and Dinarchus, all of whom lived in the fifth and fourth centuries BCE. Could you find among these cases examples of petty or frivolous legal actions, akin to suing a fast-food chain for the temperatures at which it serves coffee or putting on trial a cheese-thieving dog?

❧ Aristophanes, in his aforementioned play *Wasps*, does more than simply create a ridiculous situation like a court case against a dog. Research this play, and find out what else about the court and jury system the playwright found objectionable.

Further Information

Bolkestein, Hendrik. *Economic Life in Greece's Golden Age*. Leiden, 1958.
Calhoun, George Miller. *The Business Life of Ancient Athens*. Chicago, 1926.
Frost, Frank J. *Greek Society* (especially Chapter Four: "The Economies of the Greek World"). Lexington, MA, 1987.

Website

Demosthenes Biography. http://biography.jrank.org/pages/5026/Demosthenes.html

Bibliography for Document

Murray, A. T. (tr.). *Demosthenes V: Private Orations*. Volume V. [LCL.] Cambridge and London, 1939.

11. WORKERS NEEDED FOR BUILDING THE PARTHENON

INTRODUCTION

The fifth-century BCE politician, statesman, and orator Pericles was to a very great extent the face of Athens during its Golden Age, at the midpoint of the century. He came from a wealthy and distinguished Athenian family, and as a handsome, intelligent, and well-spoken man, he might seem to be a "natural" for the world of politics. After some initial hesitation, he took the plunge, eventually gaining election to the office of *strategos*, a post to which he was elected 15 consecutive times, from 444 to 429. (Ten *strategoi* were chosen annually, and although technically military leaders—the word *strategos* means "general"—they often exerted wide influence in politics and public policy debates and decisions. Usually, one of these 10 emerged as the most influential, and this was clearly Pericles's defining characteristic and the source of his political power in Athens.)

The key to Pericles's electoral and political success was undoubtedly his oratorical ability, a skill that remains critical to this day for aspiring politicians. He was widely regarded as the best public speaker of his time. In 430 BCE, at the conclusion of the first year of the Peloponnesian War, Pericles was chosen to make a speech in honor of Athenian casualties. He used the occasion to deliver a stirring address about the glory of Athens and its democracy. Among other things, he proclaimed that for a person in poverty, the real shame was not in the poverty, but in the individual's failure to take measures to escape it.

Pericles was the guiding and driving force behind the explosion of creative activity in art, architecture, literature, economics, and geopolitics that occurred in Athens during his string of electoral victories: a brief but important era called the Athenian Golden Age. Not only did the efforts expended during this time result in the creation of lasting achievements, but they had an equally strong impact on the employment picture in Athens, for virtually any Athenian who wanted a good-paying job could obtain one. The building projects, in particular, generated all sorts of employment opportunities. And while Pericles's oratorical skills may have been central to his success as a politician, the job-creation component of his policy initiatives must certainly also have endeared him to the electorate.

KEEP IN MIND AS YOU READ

1. A construction project of this magnitude would require massive injections of cash. Most of the money came not from taxpayer funds, or contributions from wealthy

donors, but rather from the Delian League's treasury. The Delian League was a sort of mutual defense organization of Greek poleis, formed around 478 BCE, shortly after the Xerxes-led Persian invasion of Greece. The league's purpose was to deter future Persian invasions by showing a united, pan-Hellenic front. Although the League was theoretically composed of equals, it did not take much time for Athens to assert leadership and then dominance. League members contributed money, in the form of annual tributes, while Athens provided ships, sailors, and soldiers. Over the next three decades, far more money was flowing into league coffers than was necessary to build and maintain ships, and to recruit and train military personnel. So Athens began treating this surplus as its own; Pericles dipped into these monies to fund the construction projects.

This funding method brought howls of protest from league members, and even some Athenians found it to be disreputable. But Pericles defended the practice by saying merely that the Athenians were under no obligation to justify their actions to anyone, as long as they continued to furnish the military manpower and equipment necessary to keep the Persians at bay.

2. Part of the reason the buildings were so expensive is that Pericles did not stint on materials. "Ivory, gold, ebony, and cypress-wood" were not cheap. And the project was highly labor intensive, with the best architects, craftsmen, and artists employed, and all commanding excellent wages. Untold numbers of unskilled workers also participated, and these individuals were undoubtedly paid well.

3. The amount of time required to complete these building projects was mind-bogglingly fast to an ancient Athenian but might seem overly lengthy to us. For example, the great temple on the Acropolis, the Parthenon, took about 15 years of construction time. By modern standards, that would appear to be a long time, but the world of the ancient Athenians obviously lacked modern aids such as mechanized construction equipment or computer-assisted building plans.

Document: Construction Zone: Authorized Personnel Only! Plutarch Describes the Building of the Parthenon

Acropolis: The Acropolis (the name derives from two Greek words meaning "top of the city") was a prominent elevation in Athens, its dimensions about 1,000 feet wide and 460 feet long. Several important buildings, in addition to the Propylaea and the Parthenon, were located there, including the Erechtheum, a much-admired Ionic temple in honor of the deities Athena, Poseidon, and Erechtheus;

[Pericles] was . . . anxious that the unskilled masses, who had no military training, should not be debarred from benefiting from the national income, and yet should not be paid for sitting about and doing nothing. So he boldly laid before the people proposals for immense public works and plans for buildings, which would involve many different arts and industries and require long periods to complete, his object being that those who stayed at home, no less than those serving in the fleet or the army or on garrison duty, should be enabled to enjoy a share of the national wealth. The materials to be used were stone, bronze, ivory, gold, ebony, and cypress-wood, while the arts or trades which wrought or fashioned them were those of carpenter, modeler, coppersmith, stone-mason, dyer, worker in gold and ivory, painter, embroiderer, and engraver, and besides these the carriers and suppliers of the materials, such as merchants, sailors, and pilots for the sea-borne traffic, and wagon-makers, trainers of draught animals, and drivers for everything that came by land. There were also rope-makers, weavers, leatherworkers, road builders, and miners. Each individual craft, like a general with an army . . . had its own corps of unskilled laborers at its disposal, and these worked in a subordinate capacity . . . and so through these various demands the city's prosperity was extended far and wide and shared among every age and condition in Athens.

So the buildings arose, as imposing in their sheer size as they were inimitable in the grace of their outlines, since the artists **strove to excel themselves** in the beauty of their workmanship. And yet the most wonderful thing about them was the speed with which they were completed. Each of them, [it was thought], would take many generations to build, but in fact the entire project was carried through in the high summer of one man's [i.e., Pericles's] administration . . . The director and supervisor of the whole enterprise was **Pheidias**, although there were various great architects and artists employed on the individual buildings. For example, **Callicrates and Ictinus** were the architects of the Parthenon [see sidebar] . . .

The **Propylaea**, or portals of the **Acropolis**, of which **Mnesicles** was the architect, were finished within the space of five years. While they were being built, a miraculous incident took place, which suggested that the goddess **Athena** herself, so far from standing aloof, was taking a hand and helping to complete the work. One of the workmen, the most active and energetic among them, slipped and fell from a great height. He lay for some time severely injured, and the **doctors** could hold out no hope that he would recover. Pericles was greatly distressed at this, but the goddess appeared to him in a dream and ordered a course of treatment, which he applied, with the result that the man was easily and quickly healed. It was to commemorate this that Pericles set up the bronze statue of Athena the Healer near the altar dedicated to that goddess . . .

[Tr. Ian Scott-Kilvert. *Plutarch: The Rise and Fall of Athens, Nine Greek Lives.* (*Pericles* 12, 13.) Penguin Classics, New York, 1960. Page numbers: 178, 179, 180, 181.]

a small temple also in honor of Athena; numerous statues, altars, and other temples. Some of the early kings of Athens were said to have homes on the Acropolis, although the Acropolis was not primarily a residential area. On the south slope, there were two magnificent outdoor theaters, and a long portico. Adjacent to the larger of the two theaters was a recital hall for musical contests, the Odeon.

Also located on the Acropolis was a large rectangular building called the *chalkotheke*. Only traces of this structure remain today, and its purpose is uncertain, but it apparently served as a repository for objects made of bronze—its name is etymologically connected to the Greek word for bronze—and it may also have been used as a treasury building.

Athena: The patron goddess of Athens and a deity whose name and image were well represented by the statues and temples constructed on the Acropolis.

Callicrates and Ictinus: As Plutarch states, these two individuals were the architects of the Parthenon. Callicrates flourished during the Athenian Golden Age, although little is known of his life or of his other architectural projects, with one exception: the third Long Wall. There were originally two Long Walls, built ca. 461–456 BCE, running parallel from Athens to its port cities, meant to provide the Athenians safe access to the sea in the event of an attack. A third Long Wall, between the first two, was built under the supervision of Callicrates, around 455. Ictinus was most famous for his work on the Parthenon, but he was also noted as the primary architect of the Temple of Apollo at Bassae, in Arcadia, in the central Peloponnesus. The travel writer Pausanias notes that this building was considered one the most beautiful temples in all of the Peloponnesus, second only to the Temple of Athena at Tegea, designed by another noted sculptor, Scopas, who flourished in the fourth century BCE.

Interestingly, the names of Pheidias and Ictinus (although not Callicrates), along with many others, are carved into the frieze surrounding the perimeter of the Art Institute in Chicago.

doctors: Plutarch does not provide the names of the physicians, but it is interesting to speculate that physicians were apparently on site, or at least on call, to treat injuries suffered by the workers. And accidents like the one described in the document probably happened with some regularity; construction zones are inherently risky places even now, but in the fifth century, without regulations or policies specifically protecting the workforce, they must have been even more dangerous.

Mnesicles: A fifth-century BCE architect about whom nothing is known except what Plutarch conveys to us in the document: that he was the designer of the Propylaea.

Pheidias: The famous sculptor-architect is thought to have been born ca. 490 BCE and to have died in 432. He was, and is, generally considered the best artisan of his time, high praise indeed when one considers the great number of artists flourishing during that era. His reputation primarily rests on

AFTERMATH

Unfortunately, the Athenian Golden Age was brought to a crashing halt by two chief factors from which the Athenians never really recovered. The first of these was the death of Pericles from the highly contagious, and usually fatal, plague that swept through Athens around 430 and the following years. Pericles died around 429. Although a popular leader for many years, he had his share of enemies, too, and they were never shy about leveling angry criticisms at him, for almost all of his policy decisions.

The second factor was the Peloponnesian War (431–404 BCE), the long and bitter conflict between the city-states of Athens and Sparta, an event that permanently derailed further intellectual and creative achievements in Athens. It is certainly true that Athens did not cease to exist after the war, and noted Athenian philosophers, scientists, writers, and orators flourished in the centuries to come. But it also seems safe to say that Athens never recaptured the heights to which it had risen in its fifth-century Golden Age.

ASK YOURSELF

1. As mentioned earlier (in "Keep in Mind as You Read"), Pericles siphoned off large sums of money from the Delian League treasury to pay for the labor and materials required to construct the expensive buildings. Was he justified in doing so? Were his critics right to complain about what he did?

2. Large, impressive, expensive buildings are often built as displays of power, as landmarks that enable a city to flaunt its wealth, and as sources of civic pride. Would the Parthenon have been an example of Athenian power, wealth, and pride? Would there have been other advantages for Athens in having a building of this magnitude in the city? After all, it was no accident that this huge temple was constructed at the very top of one of the highest elevations in all of Athens!

TOPICS TO CONSIDER

> ❧ Consider Pericles's beautification-of-Athens plans. One of his motives in devising and promoting his ambitious building plan was apparently to provide jobs for people who were unemployed or underemployed. Politicians today often try to do the same thing. Can you find other examples in ancient history, or in western history generally, in which these kinds of full-employment programs

were tried? How successful were they? What criteria could we use to determine whether Pericles succeeded?

❧ Consider the anecdote about the worker who was injured on the job: What kinds of conclusions or inferences can we draw from it? For example: How dangerous was it to "work construction" in the ancient world? How skilled or proficient was the medical profession in treating work-related injuries?

❧ With regard to that injured worker, Plutarch states that "the goddess [Athena] appeared to him [Pericles] in a dream and ordered a course of treatment, which he applied, with the result that the man was easily and quickly healed." Today, this explanation for the healing might seem a little, or a lot, far-fetched. Is it possible, however, that the ancient Athenians believed it? If Pericles merely made up the story about Athena appearing to him in a dream, why do you suppose he would have done that? What advantages would it bring, or what would he gain from it? Can you think of modern examples in which political or religious leaders claim to have visions or messages from God about a particular course of action?

Further Information

Kagan, Donald. *Pericles of Athens and the Birth of Democracy*. New York, 1991.
Ober, Josiah. *The Athenian Revolution*. Princeton, NJ, 1996.

Website

438 B.C. Pericles Triumphant. http://www.pbs.org/empires/thegreeks/characters/pericles_p8.html

Bibliography for Document

Scott-Kilvert, Ian (tr.). *Plutarch: The Rise and Fall of Athens; Nine Greek Lives*. Penguin Classics. New York, 1960.

three of his greatest sculptures: the Athena Promachus, the statue of Athena in the Parthenon, and the statue of Zeus at Olympia. The Athena Promachus—like the Parthenon—was erected on the Acropolis. Pheidias created a polished spear and shining helmet for the bronze, colossal statue. It was said that the glint of the sunlight on the spear point and the helmet crest could be seen from miles away. Pheidias's Olympian Zeus was considered not only his best work but the best ever created by any ancient Greek sculptor. It was a chryselephantine statue (like the Athena in the Parthenon), massively made—over 60 feet tall—and seated on a heavily decorated throne. The statue was so impressive that it was regarded as one of the Seven Wonders of the Ancient World.

Propylaea: The Athenian Propylaea, built in the 430s, was an elaborately designed and constructed entryway to the Acropolis. It contained five doors: one for processions and their necessary components, such as wagons pulled by animals, and four other doors reserved for the general public. The Propylaea was also outfitted with auxiliary buildings, one on each end. One of these was used as a kind of picture gallery.

strove to excel themselves: Ancient Greek artists—like most typical ancient Greeks—loved to compete with one another to determine which of them could produce the best works of art.

A HOME FIT FOR A GODDESS

The Parthenon is perhaps the most recognizable landmark in all of ancient Athens. Photos of it have probably appeared in more travel brochures, more feature newspaper articles, more history books, and on more Internet sites than any other ancient building. And why not? It came to symbolize the power and the wealth of the Golden Age of Athens under Pericles's inspired leadership.

The word derives from the Greek *parthenos*, meaning "young girl," one of the chief epithets of the goddess Athena, in whose honor the Parthenon was built. Located at the top of the Acropolis (see glossary, above), it was a massive rectangular structure, so large that it could reportedly be seen by sailors on ships in the Mediterranean Sea, from 20 miles or more away. Its exterior featured 34-foot-tall Doric columns, 17 of them on the two long sides of the building, 8 on the short sides. (By contrast, typical rectangular temples generally featured 13 columns on the long sides and 6 on the two ends.) The columns were ingeniously designed in such a way that they bulged very slightly in the middle and tilted very slightly toward one another. The Greek architects were trying to create an optical illusion with this bulging and tilting; they knew that from a great distance, a curved line looks straight, and a straight line looks curved. They wanted the columns to appear to be perfectly straight when viewed by those sailors on the sea and by others who might be seeing the building from a distance.

Perhaps the most stunning feature of the temple was the magnificent statue of Athena, placed on the inside of the building. Standing some 40 feet tall, created by the super-talented sculptor-architect Pheidias, it was a chryselephantine (gold and ivory) colossus. The gold alone that it contained has been estimated to have been worth 44 talents, equivalent to approximately $13 million (see the following sidebar). Some archaeologists believe the statue's great height required a sort of skylight to be carved into the roof of the Parthenon to accommodate it; otherwise, it would not have fit inside the building.

ANCIENT GREEK MONEY

Greek money in Pericles's day was divided into four basic denominations: obols, drachmas, minas, and talents; the latter two were never minted. The drachma seems to have been the basis of the monetary system, much like the dollar in modern American currency. So the question arises: how much, in American dollars, was the drachma worth?

First, some equivalencies: six obols = one drachma

100 drachmas = one mina

6,000 drachmas = one talent

It is difficult, perhaps impossible, to determine the exact dollar amount for one drachma. But educated guesses are possible. For example, it appears that one drachma was about the average daily income for a middle-class, employed Athenian in the fifth century BCE. If we assume an approximate contemporary minimum wage of $6.00/hour, and an eight-hour workday, then we might suggest a value of $50 (rounded up from $48) for one Athenian drachma. (If this calculation is even roughly accurate, it then becomes apparent why the Athenians never minted one-talent coins. A one-talent coin would have been worth $300,000. Where, and on what, would such a coin be spent? What merchant could make change for it?)

Hence, 44 talents for the gold in the statue of Athena would be equivalent to $13,200,000. The overall cost of the Parthenon has been estimated at a stupendous 5,000 talents, or about one and a half *billion* dollars, a staggering sum even by today's standards, surpassing the price tag even of a modern sports palace like Yankee Stadium. A couple of factors that drove the cost so high: the expense of the building materials (only top-quality marble was used) and the labor costs. The document has revealed how many people were employed generally in the Athenian Golden Age, and certainly a good many of these workers were assigned to Parthenon construction. And of course, they all had to be paid.

12. Cicero Advises His Son on a Right and Proper Career

INTRODUCTION

The orator/statesman/lawyer Marcus Tullius Cicero (106–43 BCE) produced a tremendous output of written works during his lifetime, including many philosophical treatises. Among these is his *De Officiis*, or *On Duties*.

Cicero's public life had taken a very gradual decline after his consulship in 63 BCE, and in the 50s and 40s, he turned increasingly to thinking about, studying, and writing philosophy. *De Officiis*, penned about 45 BCE, is the last, and possibly best, of his 15 philosophical tracts. The piece is addressed to his 21-year-old son (also named Marcus Tullius Cicero), who was at the time in Athens studying with the noted philosopher Cratippus. (The elder Cicero was apparently acquainted with Cratippus and even used his influence to help him gain Roman citizenship.) Cicero wrote *De Officiis* with his son in mind.

Sadly, at the very end of the book, Cicero expressed his hope that he and his son could discuss in person the issues raised in it, but he never saw his son again. The famed orator was killed in the proscriptions of late 43 BCE.

KEEP IN MIND AS YOU READ

1. Cicero, as an educated and sophisticated Roman gentleman, had a sort of benign contempt for people he considered beneath his social status, especially manual laborers such as "fishmongers, butchers, cooks, poulterers, and fishermen." Interestingly, however, he professes a high regard for those engaged in agriculture (although he probably refers in the document to the owners and managers of the farms, not the field workers).

2. Cicero, and many Romans of his rank in society, looked down upon professions, and their practitioners, that today are held in (mostly) high esteem: actors, physicians, architects, and athletes, for example. This disconnect is especially striking in the case of charioteers and gladiators. Romans of all social classes flocked to the amphitheaters and the racetracks in huge numbers; the great chariot-racing venue in Rome, the Circus Maximus, is estimated to have had a seating capacity in excess of 250,000. But these same rabid spectators would have considered individual gladiators and charioteers a contemptible lot.

Document: Cicero's Advice to His Son

corps de ballet: Cicero again enumerates a list of disreputable occupations, culminating with the *corps de ballet*, or in Latin, *ludus talarius*, a kind of melodramatic vaudeville show, often with bad acting, bad singing, and bad dancing. Cicero here is denigrating the actors who participate in such displays.

fishmongers, butchers, cooks, poulterers, fishermen: It is not exactly clear why Cicero, or Terence for that matter, would consider these sorts of occupations the "least respectable," or why workers engaged in these occupations would be founts of lies and misrepresentations. It could be that the marketplaces where these goods were sold sometimes harbored unsavory characters—thieves, pickpockets, muggers—and so the reputations of even the honest tradesmen were thereby besmirched.

liberal: This word is not to be understood with the modern political connotations. As used in the document, its etymological connection to the Latin word *liber*, "free," helps to define it: occupations that are worthy of a free Roman citizen or those "becoming to a gentleman."

Terence: (Full Roman name: Publius Terentius Afer.) The Roman playwright Terence wrote six plays; all survive. *Eunuch* (161 BCE) recounts the story of a love triangle involving an Athenian youth, a courtesan, and a soldier.

vulgar: The Latin word, which has been translated as "vulgar," is *sordidus*, a word of many and varied

Now in regard to trades and other means of livelihood, which ones are to be considered becoming to a gentleman and which ones are **vulgar**, we have been taught, in general, as follows. First, those means of livelihood are rejected as undesirable which incur people's ill-will, as those of tax-gatherers and usurers. Unbecoming to a gentleman, too, and vulgar are the means of livelihood of all hired workmen whom we pay for mere manual labor, not for artistic skill; for in their case, the very wage they receive is a pledge of their slavery. Vulgar we must consider those also who buy from wholesale merchants to retail immediately, for they would get no profits without a great deal of outright lying. And verily, there is no action that is meaner than misrepresentation. And all mechanics are engaged in vulgar trades, for no workshop can have anything **liberal** about it. Least respectable of all are those trades which cater for sensual pleasures: "**Fishmongers, butchers, cooks,** and **poulterers,** and **fishermen.**" [A quotation from the play *Eunuch*, by the Roman playwright **Terence,** ca. 195–159 BCE.] Add to these, if you please, the perfumers, dancers, and the whole ***corps de ballet***.

But the professions in which either a higher degree of intelligence is required or from which no small benefit to society is derived—medicine and architecture, for example, and teaching—these are proper for those whose social position they become. Trade, if it is on a small scale, is to be considered vulgar. But if wholesale and on a large scale, importing large quantities from all parts of the world, and distributing to many without misrepresentation, it is not to be greatly disparaged. It even seems to deserve the highest respect, if those who are engaged in it, satiated, or rather, I should say, satisfied with the fortunes they have made, make their way from the port to a country estate, as they have often made it from the sea into port. But of all the occupations by which gain is secured, none is better than agriculture, none more profitable, none more delightful, none more becoming to a free man. [Tr. Walter Miller. *Cicero: De Officiis* (1.150.) LCL, 1913. Page numbers: 153, 155.]

AFTERMATH

As noted earlier, Cicero is thought to have written this philosophical tract around 45 BCE, near the end of his long and distinguished career in Roman public and intellectual life. *De Officiis* was his penultimate published work; only the *Philippics*, a series of 14 speeches directed mostly at his hated rival Mark Antony, appeared later. Crossing Mark Antony was not a wise thing to do; his influence was on the rise in the 40s as Cicero's declined. For the last 18 months of his life, Cicero was reduced to not much more than a fugitive, wandering across Italy. (Fortunately, he owned several properties at various places, so presumably he was able to find accommodations.) When he was eventually tracked down and murdered, in December of 43, his severed head and hands were put on public display, apparently at the behest of Mark Antony.

meanings. In this context, its sense is one of impropriety; these occupations are not worthy of an honorable person. Note the contrast to occupations "becoming to a gentleman."

ASK YOURSELF

1. Why do you suppose Cicero believed that fishermen, butchers, cooks, and chicken farmers engaged in professions that "cater[ed to] sensual pleasures"? Why would he have considered basic foods such as fish, meat, and poultry to be somehow linked to sensual pleasures?

2. Cicero does not explicitly urge his son not to earn his livelihood in any of the occupations that he scorns in the document. Do you think, however, that this is the implicit message?

TOPICS TO CONSIDER

~ How would you feel if a parent or other close relative sent you a book-length letter (the *De Officiis* is several hundred pages long) filled with admonitions, career counseling, injunctions, and other advice that might seem a bit inappropriate? We do not know how the young Cicero felt about his father's many words of advice, but could you speculate about his reaction?

TWO ACTORS WHO ROSE ABOVE IT

Cicero (as we have seen) and other respectable Roman gentlemen and ladies were cynically contemptuous of those who took up the acting profession. But the orator/educator Quintilian (ca. 35–95 CE) relates the stories of two actors who seemed to be universally appreciated for their talents, Demetrius and Stratocles: "[T]he one [Demetrius] was at his best in the roles of gods, young men, good fathers and slaves, matrons and respectable old women [male actors played both male and female roles], while the other [Stratocles] excelled in the portrayal of sharp-tempered old men, cunning slaves, parasites, pimps, and all the more lively characters of comedy." [Quintilian. *Institutes of Oratory* 11.3; tr. Butler.] Quintilian states that both actors had strong voices, but each one also had his own unique talents. Demetrius possessed a pair of extremely expressive hands, a manner or power of speech that charmed his audiences, and an ability to make his costumes "seem to puff out with wind as he walked." It helped that he was a tall and handsome man, advantages that successful modern actors also enjoy!

Stratocles had the ability to move quickly and with great agility, and an infectious laughter that he sometimes employed at unexpected or inappropriate places in the play, just to get the audience to laugh along with him. He also was able to manipulate his head and neck in such a way that it seemed as if the former were sinking into the latter.

Quintilian notes that if either man had tried to incorporate the other one's idiosyncrasies into his own verbal and physical repertoire, he would have failed as an actor.

TRIMALCHIO'S COOK AND OTHER PROFESSIONS

In his satirical book *Satyricon*, the Roman novelist Petronius (d. ca. 65 CE) described an outlandish dinner party given by the obnoxious and filthy-rich Trimalchio. Trimalchio had a (usually misguided) opinion on every subject imaginable, including the art of cooking. In a memorable scene from the book, a waiter carried into the dining room a huge roast pig and placed it before the dinner guests. Trimalchio was pleased at first, but then he began to look more closely at the pig and discovered that it had not been gutted. Furious, he demanded that the cook come out of the kitchen and answer for this unforgivable act of forgetfulness. When the cook appeared, all nervous and contrite, Trimalchio was about to order that he be horsewhipped. But the diners interceded on his behalf and begged Trimalchio to rescind the punishment; accidents happen! Trimalchio smiled and relented, and instructed the cook to gut the pig right then and there, in full view of all. As the cook complied, and went to work with his carving knife, sausages and blood-puddings tumbled out of the pig's belly. Everyone cheered, and the cook—who only moments before had faced the unhappy prospect of a beating—was rewarded with a drink, a silver coin, and an expensive goblet.

Elsewhere in the story, Trimalchio ranks some of the professions according to the degree of difficulty. He considers the writing of literature the most challenging. After that come medicine and banking.

Cicero evaluated various professions not only in the document, but elsewhere in his writings. Consider these comments, from his philosophical essay *On Divination* [1.24]: Doctors, for example, practice the art of medicine, but make many mistakes. Captains of sailing vessels are also capable of errors in judgment; for example, when the Greek fleet finally sailed away from Troy after 10 long years of warfare, their euphoria over leaving got in the way of their good sense. They gazed at the scenery, daydreamed, unmindful of a coming storm. Military generals, too, make bad and costly decisions. Politicians are not exempt from fallibility; Cicero gallantly notes that even he had made a mistake or two over the previous 40 years! All these examples were adduced in order to demonstrate that soothsayers should not be overly criticized because of an occasional incorrect prophecy, because most of the time, their proclamations are reliable.

    The Christian author Tertullian (ca. 160–225 CE) wrote a treatise entitled *De Spectaculis* (*Concerning Spectacles*) in which he sharply criticized the attitude of the Roman populace toward charioteers and gladiators, and in particular, their love of the games and shows, but their contempt for the individual athletes. Why do you suppose this double standard existed? Can you think of any examples in modern sports—or in any other occupation or profession—in which there is a similar double standard?

Further information

Cowell, F. R. *Cicero and the Roman Republic*. London, 1948.
Stockton, David. *Cicero: A Political Biography*. Oxford, 1971.

Websites

Cicero: On Duties. http://bostonleadershipbuilders.com/cicero/duties/epitome.htm
Cicero: On Duties. http://www.iep.utm.edu/cicero/#SH7s

Bibliography for Document

Glover, T. R. (tr.). *Tertullian: Apology; De Spectaculis*. [LCL.] Cambridge and London, 1931.
Miller, Walter (tr.). *Cicero: De Officiis*. [LCL.] London and New York, 1913.

13. The Sky Is No Longer the Limit: Diocletian's Cap on Wages and Prices

INTRODUCTION

At the close of the third century CE, the Roman Empire was facing some serious economic challenges, including runaway inflation. The emperor Diocletian (reigned 284–306 CE) attempted to address the problem by issuing an unprecedented decree limiting the prices for commodities and services, and also capping wages. This decree, the *Edictum de maximis pretiis*, or *Edict Concerning Maximum Prices*, was issued in 301. Penalties for violating the edict were severe: death or exile.

The document is remarkable for the detailed information it provides about the relative prices of consumer goods at the time, as well as the wage scale in effect for a large number of occupations and professions.

KEEP IN MIND AS YOU READ

1. This detailed document forms the longest continuous text pertaining to economic issues still surviving from the ancient world, either Greek or Roman.
2. In the years of Diocletian's reign prior to the issuance of the edict, he and his armies had been engaged in seemingly endless wars and in putting down revolts in various parts of the empire. The tremendous expense associated with these campaigns may well have been a major factor in the economic crisis that precipitated the need for a cap on wages and prices.
3. Military adventurism may not have been the only problem. The contemporary Christian writer Lactantius implies that Diocletian's ambitious building programs also played a part in bringing about the empire's economic woes: "he had a certain endless passion for building, and no small exactions from the provinces for maintaining laborers and artisans and for supplying wagons and whatever else was necessary for the construction of public works. Here basilicas, there a circus, here a mint, there a shop for making weapons, here a house for his wife, there one for his daughter." [Lactantius. *On the Deaths of the Persecutors* vii; tr. Lewis and Reinhold.]
4. Most of the specified maximum salaries are per day or per month, but some are calculated according to the number of clients served, (or animals, in the case of veterinarians).

65

Document: An Ancient Roman Wage/Price Freeze

[Excerpts from the preamble:]

If the excesses perpetrated by persons of unlimited and frenzied avarice could be checked by some self-restraint—this avarice which rushes for gain and profit with no thought for mankind . . . or if the general welfare could endure without harm this riotous license by which . . . it is being very seriously injured every day, the situation could perhaps be faced with dissembling and silence, with the hope that human forbearance might alleviate the cruel and pitiable situation. But the only desire of these uncontrolled madmen is to have no thought for the common need. Among the unscrupulous, the immoderate, and the avaricious it is considered almost a creed . . . to desist from plundering the wealth of all only when necessity compels them . . .

It is our pleasure, therefore, that the prices listed in the subjoined schedule [i.e., the text of the edict] be held in observance in the whole of our Empire . . . Therefore, it is our pleasure that anyone who resists the measures of this statute shall be subject to a capital penalty for daring to do so. And let no one consider the statute harsh, since there is at hand a ready protection from danger in the observance of moderation.

[The initial clauses in the document specify maximum prices for all sorts of food and drink: wheat, barley, beans, rye, peas, rice, wines, beer, olive oil, salt, pork, beef, pheasant, chickens, sparrows, venison, butter, fish, oysters etc. The last clauses set the maximum prices for various commodities, including boots, shoes (men's and women's), fir and pine timber, silk, wool, gold, freight and transportation charges. The middle clauses set the maximum wages for a number of occupational titles, including the following:]

Occupational title	Maximum wage (daily, unless otherwise noted)
Farm laborer	25 denarii
Carpenter	50 denarii
Wall painter	5 denarii
Picture painter	150 denarii
Baker	50 denarii
Shipwright working on a seagoing ship	60 denarii
Shipwright working on a river boat	50 denarii
Camel driver	25 denarii
Shepherd	20 denarii
Muleteer	25 denarii
Veterinarian, for clipping and preparing hoofs	6 denarii per animal
Veterinarian, for bleeding and cleaning the head	20 denarii per animal
Barber	2 denarii per man
Sewer cleaner, working a full day	25 denarii
Scribe, for the best writing	25 denarii for 100 lines
Scribe, for second-quality writing	20 denarii for 100 lines
Notary, for writing a petition or legal document	10 denarii for 100 lines

Tailor, for cutting and finishing a hooded cloak of first quality	60 denarii
Tailor, for breeches	20 denarii
Tailor, for leggings	4 denarii
Elementary teacher, per boy	50 denarii per month
Teacher of arithmetic, per boy	75 denarii per month
Teacher of shorthand, per boy	75 denarii per month
Teacher of Greek or Latin language and literature, and teacher of geometry, per student.	200 denarii per month
Teacher of rhetoric or public speaking, per student.	250 denarii per month
Advocate or jurist, fee for a complaint	250 denarii
Advocate or jurist, fee for pleading	1,000 denarii
Teacher of architecture, per student	100 denarii
Check room attendant, per bather	2 denarii

[Tr. Lewis, Naphtali and Meyer Reinhold. *Roman Civilization: Sourcebook II, The Empire.* (Excerpts from Volume III of the *Corpus Inscriptionum Latinarum*, or *CIL*). Harper Torchbooks, New York, first edition published in 1966 (book was originally published by Columbia University Press, in 1955). Page numbers: 464, 465, 468, 469, 470.]

> **denarii:** A denarius was a commonly circulated silver coin, equivalent to four *sestertii*. For a discussion of the value of a *sestertius*, refer to the chapter on sports and games, p. 240.

AFTERMATH

Unfortunately, Diocletian's bold effort at controlling inflation with a wage/price freeze was unsuccessful, and the edict was revoked a few years after it was promulgated. Lactantius claims that violence erupted when attempts were made to enforce the law, that commerce was suppressed, and that prices actually increased. In any event, it was apparent that the edict was not producing the desired effect. Diocletian abdicated his imperial office around 306 and lived the last decade of his life in relatively obscure retirement.

ASK YOURSELF

1. Some of the wage specifications seem to make sense. An artist creating a mural painting for a wall probably deserved to be paid a better wage than a worker who merely whitewashed the wall. But others seem a little odd. For example, why do you suppose a differentiation was made between a shipwright who worked on a sea-going vessel and one who did the same kind of work but on a riverboat? Or why would a wall painter qualify for a higher maximum than a carpenter?

2. Probably one of the most important occupations in the ancient world—both Greek and Roman—was agriculture. Some experts estimate that as many as 80 percent or more of the work forces of both civilizations were involved in some way with farming work. So if this kind of work was such an important part of the economy, why do you suppose that two of the lowest pay ceilings listed in the document were for farm laborers (25 denarii maximum per day) and shepherds (20 maximum)?

3. The maximum salaries for teachers vary greatly, depending on the subject(s) taught. Do these maximums tell us anything about the importance the ancient Romans attached to the various subjects?

TOPICS TO CONSIDER

- Some version of a wage/price freeze has been recommended, or even tried, at various points in western history, in order to control inflation. Can you find other examples (in addition to Diocletian's edict)? How successful, or not, have these efforts been? If they succeeded, why did they succeed? If not, why not?
- It has already been mentioned that Diocletian's edict was not successful. The contemporary Christian author Lactantius provided several reasons for this. Can you think of additional reasons?
- The document has always been known as the Edict of Diocletian, but how likely is it that Diocletian himself was personally responsible for incorporating the various maximums and other details contained in it? It seems reasonable to assume that his economic advisers put together the nitty-gritty details. But is there any way to know for certain?

Further Information

Barnes, Timothy. *The New Empire of Diocletian and Constantine*. Cambridge, MA, 1982.

Corcoran, Simon. *The Empire of the Tetrarchs: Imperial Pronouncements and Government*. Oxford, 2000.

Jones, A. H. M. *The Later Roman Empire, 284–602: A Social, Economic, and Administrative Survey*. Oxford, 1964.

Websites

Edict of Diocletian. http://www.1911encyclopedia.org/Edict_of_Diocletian

What Things Cost in Ancient Rome. http://www.constantinethegreatcoins.com/edict

Bibliography for Document

Lewis, Naphtali and Meyer Reinhold. *Roman Civilization: Sourcebook II; The Empire*. New York, 1955.

FOOD AND CLOTHING

14. PLUTARCH AND FRIENDS TALK DIRTY (LAUNDRY)

INTRODUCTION

Plutarch's *Moralia* (*Moral Essays*), the source for the document, encompass a wide variety of subjects, including the kinds of issues that might be discussed at a dinner party.

KEEP IN MIND AS YOU READ

1. The scene: a dinner party in which three of the guests—Plutarch, Theon, and Themistocles—discuss the merits using freshwater instead of seawater for washing clothes.
2. Although the conversation ostensibly concerns laundry issues, notice that Plutarch also manages to incorporate into it a good deal of information about other topics.
3. Artistotle and Homer are generally considered the ultimate authorities on almost any topic, even something as mundane as the weekly washing, so it is not surprising to find that both of them are referenced in the document.

Document: Laundry Day in Ancient Greece

When we were being entertained at the house of **Mestrius Florus**, Theon the critic raised the question with Themistocles the Stoic why **Chrysippus** never gave an explanation for any of the strange and extraordinary things he frequently mentions: for example, "salted fish are fresher if wetted with brine"; "fleeces of wool yield less easily if one tears them apart violently than if one parts them gently"; and "people who have fasted eat more deliberately than those who have taken food beforehand." Themistocles answered that Chrysippus mentioned such things incidentally, by way of example, because we are easily and irrationally trapped by what appears likely, and contrariwise disbelieve what appears unlikely, and turning to Theon, he continued: "But what business have you, sir, to raise a question about these matters? For if you have become inquisitive and speculative in the matter of explanations . . . tell us for what reason Homer has made Nausicaa [see sidebar] do her washing in the river instead of the sea,

Women doing their laundry. Greek, red-figured *pelike* (two-handled, free-standing jar), fifth century BCE. (Erich Lessing/Art Resource, NY)

though the latter was nearby and quite likely was warmer, clearer, and more cleansing."

"But," said Theon, "this problem you propose to us Aristotle long ago solved by considering the earthy matter in sea water. Much coarse, earthy matter is scattered in the sea; being mixed with the water, this matter is responsible for the saltness, and because of it, sea water also supports swimmers better and floats heavy objects, while fresh water lets them sink, since it is light and unsubstantial. For the latter is unmixed and pure, and so because of its light consistency, it soaks into cloth and, as it passes through, dissolves out stains more readily than sea water. Don't you think what Aristotle says is plausible?"

"Plausible," I said, "but not true. For I observe that people frequently thicken their water with ash, or soda, or, if these are not at hand, with a powdery solid. The earthy matter, it would seem, is more easily able by its roughness to wash out dirt, while the water alone because of its lightness and weakness does not do this [equally effectively]. It is not, therefore, the coarseness of sea water that prevents this action, nor is sea water a less efficient cleanser because of its acridness, for this quality cleans out and opens up the mesh of the cloth and sweeps away the dirt. But since everything oily is hard to wash and makes a stain, and the sea is oily, this would surely be the reason for its not cleaning efficiently.

That the sea is oily Aristotle himself has said. For salt water contains fat, so making lamps burn better. And sea water itself, when it is sprinkled into flames, flashes up with them . . .

What is more, the phenomenon can also be explained in another manner. Since cleansing is the aim of washing, and what dries quickest appears cleanest, the washing liquid must depart with the dirt . . . The sun easily evaporates fresh water because of its lightness, but salt water dries up with difficulty since its coarseness holds it in the mesh of the cloth. [Tr. Paul A. Clement. *Plutarch's Moralia* (626E–627D). Volume VIII. LCL, 1969. Page numbers: 87, 89, 91, 93.]

Chrysippus: Chrysippus was a third-century BCE Stoic philosopher. He was a very prolific author of books and treatises on Stoicism; his works were so widely circulated and read that, in philosophical circles, he became more well-known than virtually any of his Stoic predecessors.

Mestrius Florus: According to the translator of the document, Paul A. Clement, Florus was a "prominent Roman, consul under Vespasian [Roman emperor, reigned 69–79 CE] . . . close friend of Plutarch . . . participant in no less than ten of the Dinner Conversations . . ."

AFTERMATH

Plutarch was born in the little town of Chaeronea, in Greece, not far from Athens. It is known that he visited Rome at some point in his life, but eventually returned to his hometown, where he wrote most of his famous works, including *Moral Essays*. Toward the end of his life, he became involved in the civic life of Chaeronea, where he held various offices.

ASK YOURSELF

1. What are the main arguments for washing clothes in river water, not seawater? Are these arguments persuasive?
2. Aristotle's opinion was that freshwater, because of its "light consistency," soaks into clothing more effectively than saltwater and therefore dissolves stains better. Theon seems to agree, and he asks his friends whether they think Aristotle's view is plausible. What do you think?
3. Why does Plutarch believe that Aristotle's view is "plausible but not true"?

LAUNDRY DAY IN PHAEACIA

In Book 6 of the *Odyssey*, Homer describes a pleasant scene in which Nausicaa, daughter of the king of the Phaeacians, Alcinous, hauls a load of laundry—via mule cart—down to a river, to do the weekly washing. An odd task for a princess, perhaps, but she is accompanied by several servants who will assist her. Homer's description:

When now they came to the fair river's current, where the pools were always full—for in abundance clear water bubbles from beneath to cleanse the foulest stains—they turned the mules loose from the wagon . . . Then from the wagon, they took the clothing in their arms, carried it into the dark water, and stamped it in the pits . . . And after they had washed and cleansed it of all stains, they spread it carefully along the shore, just where the waves washed up the pebbles on the beach. Then bathing and anointing with oil, they presently took dinner on the river bank and waited for the clothes to dry in the sunshine. [Homer. *The Odyssey* 6; tr. Palmer.]

GET THAT STAIN OUT!

In another one of his dinner conversation dialogues, Plutarch notes that olive oil stains are among the most stubbornly difficult to remove from clothing. He attributes this phenomenon to the high degree of liquidity present in olive oil.

TOPICS TO CONSIDER

- ❧ Plutarch states that Chrysippus the philosopher brought up the topics of "salted fish," "fleeces of wool," and "people who have fasted," but that he never explained why he mentioned those topics, other than to state that they were examples of how people often irrationally believe what appears likely or disbelieve that which does not. How would these examples prove his point?
- ❧ Can you tell if anywhere in the document, Plutarch recommends any kind of additive—that is, laundry detergent—for use in washing clothes? Or is the consistency and composition of freshwater alone sufficient to launder clothes?
- ❧ Why do you suppose Plutarch—and Aristotle—claim that seawater is "oily"? What do you think they mean by this description?
- ❧ Do you agree with Plutarch's notion that saltwater is inferior to freshwater for washing clothes, because "salt water dries up with difficulty since its coarseness holds it in the mesh of the cloth"?

Further Information

Barrow, Reginald Haynes. *Plutarch: His Life, His Lives, and His Morals.* Bloomington, IN, 1967.

Gianakaris, C. J. *Plutarch.* New York, 1970.

Pelling, Christopher. *Plutarch and History: Eighteen Studies.* London, 2002.

Russell, D. A. *Plutarch.* London, 2010.

Website

Plutarch: *Moralia.* http://www.attalus.org/info/moralia.html

Bibliography for Document

Clement, Paul A. (tr.). *Plutarch's Moralia.* Volume VIII. [LCL.] London and Cambridge. 1969.

Palmer, George Herbert (tr.). *The Odyssey: Homer.* New York, 1962.

15. After a Long Day of Marching or Fighting, What Did the Homeric Heroes Eat?

INTRODUCTION

Athenaeus's lengthy book on dinner conversations offers an account about the menu options for the Greek epic heroes who fought in the Trojan War, and also some of the foods mentioned in the *Odyssey*.

KEEP IN MIND AS YOU READ

1. Athenaeus's (fl. ca. 200 CE) *Deipnosophistae* (*Sophists at Dinner*) is a vast compendium of all kinds of information that one might reasonably expect to be discussed over the dinner table by knowledgeable and clever dinner guests. The work is divided into 15 books, all organized as dialogues; 14 guests are present, with the host, Athenaeus, bringing the total number of diners to 15. The translator of the document, Charles Gulick, aptly notes: "Greek conviviality was not incompatible with more or less sober discussions, and to make a banquet the scene and setting of philosophical discourse seemed natural. Plato's *Symposium*, Xenophon's *Symposium*, [and] Lucian's *Symposium* . . . testify to the popularity in ancient times . . . of this literary form" [p. x].
2. The document is excerpted from Book 1 of *Deipnosophistae*.
3. Athenaeus frequently quotes short passages from both the *Iliad* and the *Odyssey*, indicating the primacy of those works and also the high degree of familiarity with them that Greek (and Roman) authors possessed.
4. The Phaeacians (first sidebar) lived on an island not far from Athens. Odysseus was shipwrecked there, on his voyage home from Troy, after the Trojan War. The Phaeacians received him hospitably, and, after a sumptuous banquet, he told them of his many adventures during the voyage. Books Nine through Twelve of Homer's *Odyssey* are comprised of this recitation.

Document: Menu Options Described in Homer's Iliad *and* Odyssey

fig on fig: See the sidebar, below.

Tantalus: The famous mythological figure who, because of a trick that he played on the gods, was condemned to stand eternally in a pool of water, with the branches of a fruit tree nearby. Each time he bent over to take a drink, the water receded just beyond his mouth, and each time he reached to grab a piece of fruit, a gentle breeze arose, and blew the branch just out of his reach.

etc.: The rest of the passage reads thus: "ten apple [trees], forty figs. And here you marked off fifty rows of vines to give, each one in bearing order." [tr. Palmer.]

The heroes had vegetables . . . served to them at meals. That they are acquainted with the growing of vegetables is clear from the words "beside the farthest line of trimly planted garden beds" [*Odyssey* 7.127]. Moreover, they ate onions, too, though they are full of unhealthy juices: "thereto an onion, as relish to the drink" [*Iliad* 11.630]. Homer also portrays them as devoted to the culture of fruit trees: "For pear on pear waxes old, **fig on fig**" [*Odyssey* 7.114.]. Hence he bestows the epithet "beautiful" on fruit-bearing trees: "Beautiful trees grow there— pears, pomegranates, and apples." [*Odyssey* 7.120] . . . The use of these fruit trees was older even than the Trojan war. **Tantalus**, for example, is not released from his hunger for them even after he is dead, seeing that the god who metes out punishment to him dangles fruit of this kind before him . . . yet prevents him from enjoying them at the moment when he comes near to realizing his hopes. Odysseus, too, reminds [his father] Laertes of what he had given him in his boyhood, "Pear trees thou gavest to me, thirteen," **etc**. [*Odyssey* 24.340].

That they also ate fish is disclosed by Sarpedon [a leader of the Trojan army], when he compares captivity to the catch of a great [fishing net]. And Eubulus [an early comic playwright], with comic wit, says jokingly: "Where has Homer ever spoken of any Achaean [i.e., Greek] eating fish?" And flesh, too, they only roasted, for he represents nobody as boiling it . . . Nor did the heroes allow the air to be free to the birds, for they set [traps] and nets to catch thrushes and doves. They also trained for bird-shooting . . . But the poet is silent about the eating of vegetables, fish, and birds because that is a mark of greed, and also because it would be unseemly for the heroes to spend time in preparing them for the table, since he judges it beneath the level of heroic and godlike deeds. But that they did use boiled flesh he makes clear when he says: "Even as a cauldron boileth . . . melting the lard of some fatted hog." [*Iliad* 21.362]. Then, too, the ox foot which was hurled at Odysseus [*Odyssey* 20.299] is a proof of the boiling, for nobody ever roasts the foot of an ox. Again, the line [*Odyssey* 1.141] "he [a servant] took and placed besides them [the suitors who had invaded Odysseus's palace in his absence] platters of all sorts of meat" shows not merely the variety of meats, such as fowl, pork, kid, and beef, but also that their preparation was varied, not uniform, but attended with ingenious skill. [Tr. Charles Burton Gulick. *Athenaeus: The Deipnosophists* (1.24–25). Volume I. LCL, 1927. Page numbers: 109, 111.]

AFTERMATH

Following the descriptions and anecdotes that appear in the first book of the *Deipnosophistae*, Athenaeus goes on to expound upon many other dining and food-related topics, including

---

PHAEACIAN BOUNTY

On his long journey home after the end of the Trojan War, Odysseus was shipwrecked for a time on the island of the Phaeacians (not far from the Greek mainland); the Phaeacians received him hospitably. Homer describes in great detail the wide variety of foods cultivated by the Phaeacians, on four acres of ground:

> Here grow tall thrifty trees—pears, pomegranates, apples with shining fruit, sweet figs, and thrifty olives. On them fruit never fails; it is not gone in winter or summer, but lasts throughout the year . . . Pear ripens upon pear, apple on apple, cluster on cluster, fig on fig. Here too the teeming vineyard has been planted . . . heating in the sun; elsewhere, men gather grapes, and elsewhere still, they tread them . . . Nearby, two fountains rise, one scattering its streams throughout the garden, one bounding by another course beneath the court-yard gate toward the high house. From this the townsfolk draw their water. [Homer. *The Odyssey* 7; tr. Palmer.]

---

characteristics of various kinds of seafood; the merits of lentils and lentil soup; the use of silver utensils at dinner parties; the best kinds of fish for eating; the themes and scenes embossed onto drinking cups.

ASK YOURSELF

1. What kinds of foods does Athenaeus report that the Greeks ate during the time of the Trojan War and shortly after? For the most part, does this seem like a healthy range of foods?
2. In the second sidebar, the humorous story is told of the man who gargled with hot water to acclimatize his throat to hot liquids, so that he could eat up all the hot food at a party, before anyone else had a chance to partake of it. What do you think of this story? Would it really be possible to "toughen" one's throat in this way?

TOPICS TO CONSIDER

- Why do you suppose Homer apparently characterized the eating of vegetables, fish, and birds as a "mark of greed"?
- In the "Keep in Mind as You Read" section, it was noted that the translator of the document, Charles Gulick, suggested that Athenaeus's elaborate story of a dinner party followed in the tradition of similar accounts by Plato, Xenophon, and Lucian. Find out the kinds of stories and topics that

---

SOME LIKE IT *VERY* HOT!

One of the diners at the banquet described by Athenaeus relates the following amusing anecdote: "I remember a certain gourmand, who was so far lost to all feelings of shame before his companions . . . that in the public baths, he accustomed his hand to heat by plunging it into hot water, and gargled his throat with hot water that he might not shrink from hot food. For they used to say that he had actually won the cooks over to serving the dishes very hot, his object being to eat up everything alone, since nobody was able to follow his example." [Athenaeus. *The Deipnosophists* 1.5; tr. Gulick.]

---

those authors included in their accounts. What similarities and/or differences do you notice between what they wrote and what Athenaeus wrote?

Further Information

Braund, David and John Wilkins. *Athenaeus and His World: Reading Greek Culture in the Roman Empire.* Exeter, UK, 2000.

Dalby, A. *Siren Feasts: A History of Food and Gastronomy in Greece.* London, 1996.

Wilkins, John, D. Harvey, and M. Dobson. *Food in Antiquity.* Exeter, UK, 1995.

Website

The Deipnosophists, or, Banquet of the Learned, of Athenaeus. http://digicoll.library.wisc .edu/Literature/subcollections/DeipnoSubAbout.html

Bibliography for Document

Gulick, Charles Burton (tr.). *Athenaeus: The Deipnosophists.* Volume I. [LCL.] London and New York, 1927.

Palmer, George Herbert (tr.). *The Odyssey. Homer.* New York, 1962.

16. SPINNING THREAD AND MAKING CLOTHING

INTRODUCTION

The natural scientist Pliny the Elder (23–79 CE) provides us with information about wool making and a brief history of fabric making and clothing.

KEEP IN MIND AS YOU READ

1. The Romans used silk and cotton as materials for making clothes, but wool was apparently the most commonly used fabric.
2. Marcus Terentius Varro (116–27 BCE), from whom Pliny derives a good deal of his information on these topics, wrote a noted—and still-surviving—treatise on agriculture, and hence he is regarded as an authority on sheep and other livestock.
3. Pliny the Elder's massive treatise on natural history was a gigantic undertaking: he consulted some 2,000 works, produced by 473 different authors, from whom he derived over 20,000 facts. Every conceivable subject, from astronomy to topography, to botany, to gems and metals, to plants, birds, and animals—and many more topics—found its way into his writing. So it is perhaps not surprising that he included information on cloth making and clothing production.

Document: Pliny the Elder's Account of Making Clothing

Marcus Varro informs us . . . that the wool on the **distaff and spindle** of **Tanaquil** . . . was still preserved in the temple of **Sancus**; and also in the shrine of Fortune a pleated royal robe made by her, which had been worn by Servius Tullius [her son-in-law]. Hence arose the practice that maidens at their marriage were accompanied by a decorated distaff and a spindle with thread. Tanaquil first wove a straight tunic of the kind that **novices** wear with the plain white toga, and newly married brides. The pleated robe was the first among those most in favor; consequently the **spotted robe** went out of fashion. **Fenestella** writes that togas

Attalus: The name of a dynasty of Asian kings—it is unclear which Attalus is referenced by Pliny—who were known for their great wealth; hence, *Attalicus* became a byword in Latin for opulence.

distaff and spindle: The two chief tools used in the production of woolen thread were the *colus* (spindle) and *fusus* (distaff). The newly shorn wool was wound around the distaff, a stick about 12 inches long. The mass of woolen strands were then drawn from the distaff and twisted into thread on the spindle, a wooden rod that tapered at each end; the strands were simultaneously wound around the spindle, thus producing a neat coil of thread, ready to be spun into clothing.

Etruscans: The Etruscans were a dynamic and cultured people who lived in central Italy and were dominant in that region prior to the rise of Roman civilization.

Fenestella: A Roman historian who lived during the Augustan era, late first century BCE and early first century CE.

novices: *Tirones*, in Latin. The word generally refers to beginners in various occupations, and especially to soldiers, gladiators, orators, and business people. Pliny does not specify which of these occupations he has in mind, so the word probably could be associated with any of them.

Phryxian: Trojan; apparently a top-quality kind of wool. The first-century CE philosopher Seneca, in his essay *On Benefits*, [1.3.7], mentions that the three Graces (attendants of Aphrodite) were attired in plush robes of Phryxian wool.

poppy-cloth: *Papaveratus* in Latin, which, according to the *Oxford Latin Dictionary*, means "treated

of smooth cloth and of **Phryxian** wool began in the latest times of the [divine emperor] Augustus. Togas of closely woven **poppy-cloth** have an older source, being noticed as far back as the [second-century BCE] poet Lucilius . . . Bordered robes found their origin with the **Etruscans**. I find it recorded that striped robes were worn by kings, and they had embroidered robes as far back as Homer, these being the origin of those worn in triumphs. Embroidering with the needle was discovered by the Phrygians [that is, the Trojans], and consequently, embroidered robes are called Phrygian. Gold embroidery was also invented in Asia, by King **Attalus**, from whom Attalic robes got their name. Weaving different colors into a pattern was chiefly brought into vogue by Babylon, which gave its name to this process. But the fabric called damask [a multicolored cloth that could be made from various fabrics], woven with a number of threads, was introduced by Alexandria, and check patterns by Gaul. Metellus Scipio [first-century BCE politician] counts it among the charges against Capito that Babylonian coverlets were already then sold for 800,000 sesterces, which lately cost the emperor Nero 4,000,000. The state robes of Servius Tullius, with which the statue of Fortune dedicated by him was draped, lasted till the death of Sejanus [31 CE], and it was remarkable that they had not rotted away or suffered damage from moths in 560 years. [Tr. W. H. S. Jones. *Pliny: Natural History* (8. 194–197.) Volume VIII. LCL, 1963. Page numbers: 137, 139.]

AFTERMATH

Clothing styles changed after the time of Pliny the Elder, most noticeably in the manner of enhanced decorative touches, such as embroidered plant, animal, or human designs. Preferences for clothing made of silk gradually displaced the traditional reliance on sturdy materials like wool, a trend that had begun to take shape even in Pliny's time and one that he decried: "Nor have even men been ashamed to make use of [silken clothing], because of [its] lightness in summer. So far have our habits departed from wearing a leather cuirass that even a robe is considered a burden!" [Pliny the Elder. *Natural History* 11.78; tr. Rackham.]

ASK YOURSELF

1. Who was Tanaquil? What were her contributions to the history of Roman clothing?

2. What were the different varieties of robes and other clothing used by the Romans? What accounts for such a wide range of colors and materials?

TOPICS TO CONSIDER

- Pliny does not explain why it was considered improvident for women to "twirl their spindles" (see the sidebar) while they were walking along country roads. Can you think of any reason for this superstition?

- Pliny mentions "the poet Lucilius," but he does not provide any context for mentioning him. Why do you suppose Pliny refers to him here? What kinds of poetry did Lucilius write?

- What magnanimous gift did King Attalus III (reigned 138–133 BCE) bestow upon the Romans? Is it likely, then, that he was the Attalus to whom Pliny refers in the document?

- Pliny states that coverlets costing 800,000 sesterces in the first century BCE had risen in price to 4,000,000 by the time of the emperor Nero, in the mid-first century CE. What factors do you suppose could account for the astronomical increase in price?

with poppy, that is, with an extract that acts as a whitening or bleaching agent."

Sancus: Sancus was the Roman god of trust, oaths, commerce, and contracts.

spotted robe: An interesting turn of phrase with an uncertain meaning. The Latin word, in this context, for "spotted," *sororiculata*, is seldom seen and not clearly understood.

Tanaquil: Tanaquil was the wife of Rome's fifth king, Tarquinius Priscus (reigned 617–579 BCE), and the mother-in-law of the sixth king, Servius Tullius (reigned 579–535 BCE). Among other things, she was greatly respected for her skill in weaving, as Pliny indicates.

Further Information

Forbes, Robert J. *Studies in Ancient Technology.* Amsterdam, 1964.

Johnston, Harold Whetstone. *The Private Life of the Romans.* Chicago, 1903.

Sebesta, Judith Lynn and Larissa Bonfante (eds.). *The World of Roman Costume.* Madison, WI, 1994.

Website

Clothing in Ancient Rome. http://en.wikipedia.org/wiki/Clothing_in_ancient _Rome#References

Bibliography for Document

Jones, W. H.S. (tr.). *Pliny: Natural History.* Volume VIII. [LCL.] London and Cambridge, 1963.

DO NOT WALK AND SPIN THREAD AT THE SAME TIME!

According to the Elder Pliny, it was forbidden that farm women should "twirl their spindles while walking along the road, or even to carry them uncovered, on the ground that such action blights the hopes of everything, especially the hope of a good harvest." [Pliny the Elder. *Natural History* 28.26; tr. Jones.]

DYE IT PURPLE

The color purple as a sign of royalty dates back to the earliest days of Roman history. Pliny writes that the first Roman king, Romulus (reigned 753–714 BCE), owned purple cloaks, but by the time of the third king, Tullus Hostilius (reigned 671–642 BCE), kings were wearing purple-bordered robes; perhaps the contrast of the purple border with lighter colors elsewhere emphasized the king's majesty. The historian Cornelius Nepos (d. first century CE) states that when he was a young man, purple dye was considered the peak of fashion, but later, reddish-purple dyes became popular. He also reports that "double-dyed" clothing gained favor.

The first-century BCE politician and orator Cicero wrote a letter to his friend Caelius in the year 49 in which he described some of the political maneuvering of the time: "I expect that you have been told that Oppius is having a *toga praetexta* [an embroidered robe worn by Roman magistrates] woven for him; for our friend Curtius has set his heart on a double-dyed robe [i.e., a kind of robe called a *trabea*, one of purple and saffron, worn by augurs, priests who interpreted signs and omens from the gods]. But he finds his dyer's 'job' takes time." [Cicero. *Letters to His Friends* 2.16; tr. Williams.] W. Glynn Williams, the translator of the passage, notes that the literal translation of the final sentence is "his dyer [i.e., Julius Caesar] keeps him waiting," and that the operative verb has the double meaning of "waiting" and "corrupting." The implication: that Curtius has accepted a bribe to support Caesar's political aspirations, but that Caesar has been slow to pay up.

Rackham, H. (tr.). *Pliny: Natural History*. Volume III. [LCL.] London and Cambridge, 1940.

Williams, W. Glynn (tr.). *Cicero: The Letters to His Friends*. Volume I. [LCL.] Cambridge and London, 1927.

17. Controlling Appetite and Curbing Weight Gain

INTRODUCTION

The essayist Aulus Gellius was nothing if not a diversified writer. The document below, one of his essays, touches upon two topics that seem very contemporary: artificial stomach contraction as a dieting and weight control method, and bulimia.

KEEP IN MIND AS YOU READ

1. Erasistratus, whom Aulus Gellius quotes at length in the document, was a third-century BCE Greek physician. His writings no longer exist except in fragmentary form, but his influence on subsequent physicians was considerable.
2. Neither the Greeks nor the Romans, of course, had developed bariatric surgery as a way to control appetite and weight gain, but Aulus Gellius seems to be describing a similar method, whereby the stomach is artificially contracted to make difficult the passage of food into it.

Document: Aulus Gellius and Erasistratus on Dietary Issues

I often spent whole days in Rome with **Favorinus**. His delightful conversation held my mind enthralled, and I attended him wherever he went, as if actually taken prisoner by his eloquence; to such a degree did he constantly delight me with his most agreeable discourse. Once when he had gone to visit a sick man, and I had entered with him, having conversed for some time in Greek about the man's illness with the physicians who chanced to be there at the time, he said: "This ought not to seem surprising either, that although previously he was always eager for food, now after an enforced fast of three days all his former appetite is lost. For what Erasistratus has written is pretty nearly true," said he, "that the **empty and open fibers** of the intestines, the hollowness of the belly within

empty and open fibers etc.: Erasistratus was known more as a medical researcher than as a practicing physician, and this section of Aulus Gellius's essay reveals that Erasistratus had a solid knowledge of human anatomy.

Favorinus: Favorinus, a native of Gaul, lived in Rome during the second century CE; charming and sophisticated, he was a friend of both Aulus Gellius and Plutarch. He was reputedly born a eunuch, and yet at one point was accused of adultery, which gave rise to a famous boast of his: that even though he was a eunuch, he was capable of adultery; even though a Gaul, he could speak and write Greek; and even though he sometimes offended the emperor, he lived to tell about it.

ox-hunger: This is a rather odd translation for the word *boulimos;* apparently, some editors see an etymological connection between this word and the Greek word for ox, *bous.* Others reject that interpretation. One of Plutarch's dinner-conversation dialogues (693F ff.) consists of a long conversation about the nature and causes of *boulimos,* including the notion that it is a cold-weather affliction.

Scythians: A nomadic people who lived in the Black Sea region, expert equestrians, as would be expected of a people who were often on the move.

and the empty and yawning cavity of the stomach, cause hunger. But when these are either filled with food or are contracted and brought together by continued fasting, then, since the place into which the food is received is either filled or made smaller, the impulse to take food, or to crave it, is destroyed." He declared that Erasistratus also said that the **Scythians** too, when it was necessary for them to endure protracted hunger, bound a very tight bandage around their bellies. That by such compression of the belly it was believed that hunger could be prevented.

These things and many others of the kind Favorinus said most entertainingly on that occasion. But later, when I chanced to be reading the first book of Erasistratus's *Distinctions,* I found in that book the very passage which I had heard Favorinus quote. The words of Erasistratus on the subject are as follows: "I reasoned therefore that the ability to fast for a long time is caused by strong compression of the belly; for with those who voluntarily fast for a long time, at first hunger ensues, but later it passes away . . . And the Scythians also are accustomed, when on any occasion it is necessary to fast, to bind up the belly with broad belts, in the belief that the hunger thus troubles them less. And one may almost say too that when the stomach is full, [people] feel no hunger for the reason that there is no vacuity in it, and likewise when it is greatly compressed, there is no vacuity."

In the same book, Erasistratus declares that a kind of irresistibly violent hunger, which the Greeks call *boulimos,* or "**ox-hunger,**" is much more apt to be felt on very cold days than when the weather is calm and pleasant, and that the reasons why this disorder prevails especially at such times have not yet become clear to him. The words which he uses are these: "It is unknown and requires investigation, both in reference to the case in question and in that of others who suffer from ox-hunger, why this symptom appears rather on cold days than in warm weather." [Tr. John C. Rolfe. *The Attic Nights of Aulus Gellius* (15.1–10). Volume III. LCL, 1927. Page numbers: 135, 137, 139.]

AFTERMATH

Although the date of Aulus Gellius's essay is unknown, the fate of his friend Favorinus is more certain. As mentioned earlier, Favorinus had somehow offended the emperor Hadrian (ruled 117–138 CE). As a result, statues of him that had been set up in Athens were

APICIUS'S COOKBOOK

The early first-century CE gourmand Apicius wrote extensively on foods, cooking, and recipes. These writings were later collected and published under the title *De Re Coquinaria* (*On Cooking*). The book is divided into 10 chapters and encompasses a wide variety of culinary themes, including wines; spices; minces; puddings; vegetables (such as asparagus, squash, beets, carrots, peas, and beans); duck, pheasant, goose, and chicken dishes; meats (including wild boar, venison, beef, veal, and hare); and seafood dishes (including shellfish, oysters, sardines, and mussels).

Several writers, including Seneca and Martial, report that Apicius spent 100,000,000 sesterces on fancy foods and other extravagances. When Apicius took an inventory of his finances and discovered a balance of "only" 10,000,000 sesterces, he reputedly poisoned himself (at a banquet, of course) because he believed that no gourmet worth his salt could possibly live appropriately on such a paltry sum.

removed by the Greeks. Nonetheless, he willed his extensive library, and his mansion in Rome, to the Greek rhetorician Herodes Atticus.

ASK YOURSELF

1. It makes sense that gorging oneself with food would destroy feelings of hunger, but why does Erasistratus claim that fasting can have the same effect?
2. How did the Scythians prevent hunger? Do you think their method would work?

TOPICS TO CONSIDER

ᐒ Aulus Gellius does not directly reveal to the reader whether he agrees with the descriptions of Favorinus (and by extension, Erasistratus) on the matters of stomach constriction and bulimia, but is it possible to read between the lines and speculate on his views?

A DIFFERENT KIND OF RAVENOUS HUNGER

The Greek historian Xenophon, when describing the hardships of a military march that he helped to lead and that he detailed in a famous historical work entitled *Anabasis* (*The Expedition*), relates a slightly different account of excessive hunger:

> [T]hey marched . . . through snow, and many of the men fell ill with hunger-faintness [the *boulimia* referenced in the document, and confirming the statement that this disorder tends to occur more often in cold weather]. And Xenophon . . . [in the rear] . . . did not know what the trouble was. But as soon as a person who was acquainted with the disease had told him that they manifestly had hunger-faintness, and if they were given something to eat would be able to get up, he went around among the baggage animals, and wherever he saw something that was edible, he would distribute it among the sick men, or send [here and there] people who had the strength to run along the lines, to give it to them. And when they had eaten something, they would get up and continue with the march. [Xenophon. *Anabasis* 4.5; tr. Brownson.]

> ☙ The English word "bulimia" derives from the Greek word *boulimos*, which is generally defined in Greek-English lexicons as "extreme hunger" or "ravenous hunger." However, John C. Rolfe, the translator of the Aulus Gellius essay, renders *boulimos* as "ox-hunger," which is the literal meaning of the Greek word. Can you discover what the connection might be between extreme hunger and oxen?

> ☙ Why do you think that *boulimos* was more common in cold weather than in warmer weather?

Further Information

Holford-Strevens, Leofranc. *Aulus Gellius: An Antonine Scholar and His Achievement.* Oxford, 2003.

Vehling, Joseph Dommers (ed./trans.). *Apicius: Cookery and Dining in Imperial Rome.* Chicago, 1936.

Website

Aulus Gellius. Biography. http://www.bookrags.com/biography/aulus-gellius-dlb/

Bibliography for Document

Brownson, Carleton L. (tr.) *Xenophon: Anabasis.* Volume III. [LCL.] London and Cambridge, 1922.

Matz, David. *Ancient World Lists and Numbers. Numerical Phrases and Rosters in the Greco-Roman Civilizations,* Jefferson, NC, 1995.

Rolfe, John C. (tr.) *The Attic Nights of Aulus Gellius.* Volume I. [LCL.] Cambridge and London, 1927.

HEALTH CARE

18. HIPPOCRATES AND THE ETHICS OF THE MEDICAL PROFESSION

INTRODUCTION

The most famous name in the history of ancient medicine is undoubtedly Hippocrates, from the island of Cos, off the coast of modern-day Turkey. Hippocrates (ca. 460–370 BCE) came from a family of physicians; both his father and his grandfather practiced medicine, and his father served as one of his instructors in the medical arts. Hippocrates is generally associated with a voluminous output of medical treatises, perhaps 60. However, modern scholars doubt that he himself wrote all, or even any, of these; rather, it is thought that the works attributed to him were probably authored by a consortium of later physicians and then collected together in an anthology today known as the *Hippocratic Corpus*. Some of the major topics in this collection of medical writings include air, wind, and water, and their effects on health; epidemics; nutriments; the art of prognosis; epilepsy; fractures and dislocations; medical aphorisms; and treatments for various diseases and disorders.

The noted Roman natural scientist Pliny the Elder certainly seemed to accept the historical reality of a physician named Hippocrates. He credits Hippocrates, during the time of the Peloponnesian War (431–404 BCE), with having revived the practice of medicine after a period of dormancy. He notes that Hippocrates hailed from the island of Cos, sacred to Asclepius, the god of medicine. In the temple dedicated to Asclepius there, it was customary for "patients recovered from illness to inscribe in the temple of that god an account of the help that they had received, so that afterward, similar remedies might be enjoyed [thus forming a sort of medical casebook]. Accordingly, Hippocrates . . . wrote out these inscriptions and . . . founded that branch of medicine called 'clinical.'" [Pliny the Elder. *Natural History* 29.5; tr. Jones.]

KEEP IN MIND AS YOU READ

1. The Hippocratic Oath is perhaps one of the most famous writings in all of ancient Greek literature, but a number of thorny questions surround the oath. Its date, for example, is unknown. Nor is it known whether all ancient physicians took the oath, or even subscribed to its principles. It is not certain whether physicians who violated one or more of the oath's injunctions would be punished in some way.
2. The oath is very short—only 250 words in Greek.

Document: The Hippocratic Oath

Apollo Physician, Asclepius, Health [*Hygiea*], Panacea: An invocation to the family of "healer deities" of Greek mythology: Apollo, the father of Asclepius, who was the god of medicine. Hygiea and Panacea, whose names mean "health" and "all-curing" respectively, were daughters of Asclepius.

indenture: The exact application or meaning of this word in the medical context is uncertain. The Greek word *syngraphia* (here translated as "indenture") literally means "a writing together," and is generally understood to refer to a contract. It may here denote an agreement between teacher and student: the student's main responsibilities are to respect the teacher and to be willing to share his medical knowledge with other students; the teacher's responsibility is to instruct the student, possibly free of charge.

partner: This probably refers to a continued sharing of knowledge and expertise, rather than a more narrowly defined, shared professional medical practice.

stone: Presumably bladder or kidney stones.

And whatsoever I shall see or hear: The translator of the passage, W. H. S. Jones, comments: "This remarkable addition is worthy of a passing notice. The physician must not gossip, no matter how or where the subject matter for gossip may have been acquired; whether it be in practice or in private life makes no difference."

I swear by **Apollo Physician, by Asclepius, by Health [*Hygiea*], by Panacea** and by all the gods and goddesses, making them my witnesses, that I will carry out, according to my ability and judgment, this oath and this **indenture**. To hold my teacher in this art equal to my own parents; to make him **partner** in my livelihood; when he is in need of money to share mine with him; to consider his family as my own brothers, and to teach them this art, if they want to learn it, without fee or indenture; to impart precept, oral instruction, and all other instruction to my own sons, the sons of my teacher, and to indentured pupils who have taken the physician's oath, but to nobody else. I will use treatment to help the sick according to my ability and judgment, but never with a view to injury and wrongdoing. Neither will I administer a poison to anybody when asked to do so, nor will I suggest such a course. Similarly, I will not give to a woman a [suppository] to cause abortion. But I will keep pure and holy both my life and my art. I will not use the knife, not even on sufferers from **stone**, but I will give place to such as are craftsmen therein. Into whatever houses I enter, I will enter to help the sick, and I will abstain from all intentional wrongdoing and harm, especially from abusing the bodies of man or woman, [slave] or free. **And whatsoever I shall see or hear** in the course of my profession, as well as outside my profession in my [dealings with individuals], if it be what should not be published abroad, I will never divulge, holding such things to be holy secrets. Now if I carry out this oath, and break it not, may I gain forever reputation among all men for my life and for my art. But if I transgress it and forswear myself, may the opposite befall me. [Tr. W. H. S. Jones. *Hippocrates* (11, 12). LCL, 1924.]

AFTERMATH

The impact of Hippocrates's work is well summarized by the entry in the *Oxford Classical Dictionary* (s.v. Hippocrates): "If one asks what Hippocrates meant to the Greeks, the Middle Ages, the Renaissance, what he means even today, the answer is that by a complicated historical process he has become the embodiment of the ideal physician."

HIPPOCRATES WAS NOT THE ONLY NOTABLE GREEK PHYSICIAN

The fifth-century BCE historian Herodotus relates a story about the powerful and much-feared (by the Greeks) Persian king Darius (sixth century BCE). It seems that Darius was out hunting one day, when he dismounted awkwardly from his horse and badly sprained his ankle. The Egyptian physicians who were called in to treat him only made matters worse by their inept methods. But someone in the royal entourage knew of a Greek captive by the name of Democedes, from the city of Croton, and that this Democedes was a skilled medical practitioner. Democedes was summoned, and, after some cajoling, he agreed to attend to the king, who soon recovered, thanks to the care he had received from his Greek doctor. According to Herodotus, "it was chiefly because of Democedes' success [not only in treating Darius, but in his medical practice on the islands of Aegina and Samos] that Crotoniate doctors came to have such a high reputation. Darius' accident happened during the period when the physicians of Croton were considered the best in Greece, and those of Cyrene the next best." [Herodotus. *The Histories* 3.131; tr.de Selincourt.] An interesting side note: Democedes married the daughter of Milo of Croton, who was the finest Olympic athlete of his era and one of the best in all of ancient Olympic history.

ASK YOURSELF

1. What differences do you notice between the ways in which ancient and modern physicians viewed the practice of medicine?
2. Why do you think there seemed to be such a strong link between medicine and religion in the ancient Greek world?

TOPICS TO CONSIDER

- Although the Hippocratic Oath is very short, it contains a fairly large number of principles relating to the practice of medicine. Which of these principles would still be doable by modern physicians? Which ones do you think that many modern physicians might avoid or even outwardly oppose?

- How many medical schools today still require graduating students to take the Hippocratic Oath? If this information is not readily available, try doing a random survey of select medical schools to see which ones require it.

- It was mentioned in the introduction that Hippocrates may not have written all of the entries in the *Hippocratic Corpus*, and that he perhaps did not author any of them. What evidence leads modern scholars to these conclusions? Does it seem likely that there never existed an ancient physician named Hippocrates, and that the medical texts bearing his name were actually written by a consortium of now-unknown doctors?

- The document contains fairly straightforward condemnations of both euthanasia and abortion. What were the attitudes of other ancient physicians and philosophers about these issues? In particular, find out what Plato, Socrates, and Aristotle might have written.

Further Information

Cantor, David, ed. *Reinventing Hippocrates*. Burlington, VT, 2002.
Jouanna, Jacques. *Hippocrates*. Baltimore, 1999.

Levine, Edwin Burton. *Hippocrates*. New York, 1971.
Smith, Wesley D. *Hippocratic Tradition*. Ithaca, NY, 1979.

Website

Hippocrates. http://www.notablebiographies.com/He-Ho/Hippocrates.html

Bibliography for Document

de Selincourt, Aubrey (tr.); revised by A. R. Burn. *Herodotus: The Histories*. Baltimore, 1954.
Jones, W. H. S. (tr.). *Pliny: Natural History*. Volume VIII. [LCL.] London and Cambridge, 1963.
Jones, W. H. S. (tr.). *Hippocrates*. Volume I. [LCL.] Cambridge and London, 1923.

19. A MEDICAL MIRACLE MAN WHO DECLINED TO GIVE AN ENCORE PERFORMANCE

INTRODUCTION

This document comes to us by way of the second-century CE Greek satirist and essayist Lucian, who authored works on rhetoric, literature, and philosophy, as well as numerous satirical dialogues. He was born in Syria, but as a young man, he immigrated to the Greco-Roman world, where he traveled widely, both in Greece and Italy. Eventually, he gave up his travels, settled in Athens, and focused on his literary career.

KEEP IN MIND AS YOU READ

1. Lucian wrote over 60 dialogues and sketches; *The Disowned Son* is one of these. The narrator is a young man who, after being disowned by his father, studied medicine and became a physician. Meanwhile, his father fell ill with a mental disease that puzzled the doctors who were summoned to treat him. The disowned son, however, was able to cure his father, who, in gratitude, revoked his son's expulsion from the family. But in a cruel twist of fate, the young man's stepmother (his father's wife) was also victimized by some sort of mental ailment. When the father commanded his son to work another miracle cure, the son refused, saying that in his medical opinion, his stepmother's illness was different than the one suffered by his father, and likely incurable. For that refusal, the father disowned his son a second time.
2. This fictitious sketch is cast in the form of a legal action, with the son pleading his case in court that his disownment is unjust. As far as is known, no formal disownment case ever reached Athenian law courts, but the philosopher Plato writes that provisions for such an action did exist: "Between fathers and their children, and children and their fathers, there arise differences greater than is right, in the course of which fathers, on the one hand, are liable to suppose that the lawgiver should give them legal permission to proclaim publicly by herald, if they so wish, that their sons have legally ceased to be their sons..." [Plato. *Laws* 11.928D; tr. Bury.]
3. In the modern world, the mantra to which the medical profession seems to pay homage is "medicine by template": each disease has certain symptoms, courses, and outcomes and must be treated in much the same way, regardless of the specific circumstances of the individual patient. The disowned son refused to be bound by such restrictions. He realized that there were subtle differences in the afflictions of

his father and stepmother, and that the remedies that worked in his father's case would be ineffectual in treating his stepmother.

Document: No Physician—Not Even a Miracle Worker—Can Cure All Ills

There is . . . something of a novelty in my present plight [i.e., his second disownment], in that I am under no personal charge, but am in jeopardy of punishment on behalf of my profession because it cannot in every particular obey [my father's demands]. But what could be more absurd than to give treatment under orders, in accordance, not with the powers of the profession, but with the desires of my father? I could wish, to be sure, that medical science had a remedy of such sort that it could check not only insanity but unjust anger, in order that I might cure my father of this disorder also. As things are, his madness has been completely assuaged, but his anger is growing worse, and (what is hardest of all) he is sane to everyone and insane towards me alone, his physician. You see, therefore, what fee I receive for my attendance. I am disowned by him once more and put away from my family a second time, as if I had been taken back for a brief space merely that I might be more disgraced by being turned out of the household repeatedly.

For my part, in cases which can be cured, I do not wait to be summoned. On the previous occasion, for instance, I came to his relief uncalled. But when a case is perfectly desperate, I am unwilling even to [take it on]. And in respect to this woman I am with good reason even less venturesome, since I take into consideration how I should be treated by my father if I were to fail, when without having so much as begun treating her, I am disowned. I am indeed pained . . . at my stepmother's serious condition (for she was a good woman), at my father's distress on her account, and most of all at my own apparent disobedience and real inability to do the service which is enjoined upon me, both because of the extraordinary violence of the illness and the ineffectiveness of the art of healing. I do not think, however, that it is just to disown a man who declines at the outset to promise what he cannot perform . . .

In the case of the medical profession, the more distinguished it is and the more serviceable to the world, the more unrestricted it should be for those who practice it. It is only just that the art of healing should carry with it some privilege in respect to the liberty of practicing it; that no compulsion and no commands should be put upon **a holy calling, taught by the gods** and exercised by men of learning; that it should not be subject to enslavement by the law, or to voting and judicial punishment, or to fear and a father's threats and a layman's wrath . . . The physician ought to be persuaded, not ordered. He ought to be willing, not fearful. He ought not to be hailed to the bedside, but to take pleasure in coming of his own accord. Surely his calling is exempt from paternal compulsion in view of the fact that physicians have honors, precedence, immunities, and privileges publicly

> **a holy calling, taught by the gods:** According to the Roman natural scientist Pliny the Elder, "to its pioneers, medicine [is] assigned a place among the gods and a home in heaven, and even today medical aid is in many ways sought from the oracle." [Pliny the Elder. *Natural History* 29.1; tr. Jones.]

bestowed on them by states. [Tr. A. M. Harmon. *Lucian.* (1–2; 23.) Volume V. LCL, 1936. Page numbers: 477, 479, 511, 513.]

AFTERMATH

The son concludes his case by stating that there is no cure on the horizon for his stepmother, not even if "she takes medicine a thousand times," and that therefore, it is imprudent to embark upon a course of treatment. He also pledges that if his father should have a relapse, that he (the son) would once again attempt to effect a cure, despite the one, and possibly two, disownments inflicted upon him by his father. Further, he reminds his father that it was through shouting, arguments, anger, and hatred that his first bout of insanity was triggered, and by continuing to display those maladaptive character traits, he might well bring on a second one.

Lucian does not reveal whether the disownment action was upheld by the court.

ASK YOURSELF

1. Do you think the disowned son was right to refuse treatment to his stepmother, or should he have at least tried to administer a remedy, in the hope that it might work?
2. If you were sitting on the jury in this case, would you have supported or denied the father's case for disownment? Why?

TOPICS TO CONSIDER

∽ In the modern world, it might be considered inappropriate or even unethical for a physician to deliver health care services to an immediate family

---

DIVINE HEALING FOR A BATTLE WOUND

The connection between the gods and the art of medicine is illustrated by the two physicians who accompanied the Greek forces during the Trojan War: Machaon and Podalirius, both sons of Asclepius, god of medicine. In Book 4 of the *Iliad*, the Greek warrior-king Menelaus has been shot by an arrow and is bleeding profusely; Machaon is hurriedly summoned:

And gaining the place where red-haired Menelaus
nursed his wound and a growing ring of warlords
pressed around him, striding into their midst
the godsent healer reached the captain's side
and quickly drew the shaft from his buckled belt –
he pulled it clear, the sharp barbs broke back.
He loosed the glittering belt and slipped it off
and the loin-piece and the plated guard below it,
gear the bronzesmiths made. When he saw the wound
where the tearing arrow hit, he sucked out the blood
and deftly applied the healing salves that Chiron,
friend of Asclepius, gave his father long ago. [Homer. *Iliad* 4; tr. Fagles.]

member. This does not appear to have been the case in the ancient world. Why not, do you suppose?

    ❧ We know very little about what might have constituted medical malpractice in the ancient world, but there seems to have been a tradition to hold physicians blameless in the event that their treatments failed. The disowned son apparently hints at that idea when he proclaims that the practice of medicine "should not be subject to enslavement by the law, or to voting and judicial punishment [i.e., no medical malpractice lawsuits should be allowed!], or to fear a father's threats and a layman's wrath." In the same section, the son argues that the medical profession should be "unrestricted . . . for those who practice it." Research ancient Greek law and judicial procedure, to see if you can find any examples of the prosecution of physicians for real or perceived incompetence.

Further Information

Baldwin, Barry. *Studies in Lucian*. Toronto, 1973.

Branham, Bracht. *Unruly Eloquence: Lucian and the Comedy of Traditions*. Cambridge, MA, 1989.

Jones, Christopher P. *Culture and Society in Lucian*. Cambridge, MA, 1986.

Website

Bibliography to Lucian: A Select and Evolving Guide. http://classics.uc.edu/~johnson/Lucian/bibliography.htm

Bibliography for Document

Bury. R. G. (tr.). *Plato. Laws*. Volume II. [LCL.] London and Cambridge, 1926.

Fagles, Robert (tr.). *Homer: The Iliad*. New York, 1990.

Harmon, A. M. (tr.). *Lucian*. Volume V. [LCL.] Cambridge and London, 1936.

Jones, W. H. S. (tr.). *Pliny: Natural History*. Volume VIII. [LCL.] London and Cambridge, 1963.

20. How to Obtain Good Health, and Keep It

INTRODUCTION

Aulus Cornelius Celsus (first century CE) wrote an encyclopedic work covering agriculture, medicine, military matters, oratory, and philosophy. But only the portion on medicine (*De Medicina*) survives intact. The treatise was so highly regarded that it earned its author such laudatory epithets as the "Roman Hippocrates" and the "Cicero of Physicians."

KEEP IN MIND AS YOU READ

1. The document is excerpted from portions of Book 1 of *De Medicina*; the material presented is introductory. In later chapters, the author covers more detailed and specific topics concerning the practice of medicine, including an overview of the major organs of the body and remedies for ailments that afflict them; a description of various kinds of drugs and antidotes; treatments for wounds and injuries; surgical procedures; and a general description of fractures and dislocations.
2. The Roman essayist Quintilian reveals that Celsus did not confine his writings to medicine, but also wrote treatises on agriculture and military matters. Quintilian considers Celsus to have been a reliable authority on all topics on which he wrote.

Document: Good Health . . . and How to Maintain It

A man in health, who is both vigorous and his own master, should be under no obligatory rules, and have no need, either for a medical attendant, or for a **[masseuse] and anointer**. His kind of life should afford him variety; he should now be in the country, now in town, and more often about the farm. He should sail, hunt, rest sometimes, but more often take exercise. For while inaction weakens the body, work strengthens it. The former brings on premature old age, the latter prolongs youth.

It is well also at times to go to the bath, at times to make use of cold waters; to undergo sometimes [anointing], sometimes to neglect that same; to avoid no

handball: Various kinds of throwing, catching, and bouncing ball games were popular with the Romans, perhaps none more so than *trigon*, apparently similar to three-sided catch, in which the players threw the ball to one another. Points could be earned or lost with catches or drops, respectively.

lamplight: Pliny the Younger informs us that his famous uncle, the natural scientist—and prolific author—Pliny the Elder, often worked at night, by lamplight, not with any view toward getting a head start on the next day's agenda, but simply to gain time for additional research. Sometimes, he would arise at midnight, or one or two o'clock in the morning, to study and write.

[masseuse] and anointer: The Latin term *iatralipta* ("masseuse/anointer") covers both procedures. In one of his subsequent chapters, Celsus details the role of massage in medical care, noting that it should be used whenever a weak body needs toning, or one that is too hard requires softening, or when a thin or sickly body needs nourishment.

redundant: In a famous passage from his now-fragmentary play *Autolycus*, Euripides lambasts overfed athletes: "Although there are myriads of evils throughout Greece, there is nothing worse than the race of athletes. First of all, they neither learn how to live a good life, nor could they possibly do so. For how could a man who is a slave to his jaw and obedient to his belly acquire wealth to surpass than of his father?" [tr. Robinson]

kind of food in common use; to attend at times a banquet, at times to hold aloof; to eat more than sufficient at one time, at another no more; to take food twice rather than once a day, and always as much as one wants, provided one digests it. But while exercise and food of this sort are necessaries, those of the athletes are **redundant**. For in the one class [i.e., the exercise regimen] any break in the routine of exercise, owing to necessities of civil life, affects the body injuriously, and in the other [i.e., the dietary regimen], bodies thus fed up in their fashion age very quickly and become infirm ...

On waking, one should lie still for a while, then, except in winter time, bathe the face freely with cold water. When the days are long, the siesta should be taken before the midday meal, when short, after it. In winter, it is best to rest in bed the whole night long; if there must be study by **lamplight**, it should not be immediately after taking food, but after digestion. He who has been engaged in the day, whether in domestic or on public affairs, ought to keep some portion of the day for the care of the body. The primary care in this respect is exercise, which should always precede the taking of food. The exercise should be ampler in the case of one who has labored less and digested well. It should be lighter in the case of one who is fatigued and has digested less well.

Useful exercises are: reading aloud, drill [à la soldiers], **handball**, running, walking, but this is not by any means most useful on the level, since walking up and down hill varies the movement of the body, unless indeed the body is thoroughly weak. But it is better to walk in the open air than under cover; better, when the head allows of it, in the sun than in the shade; better under the shade of a wall or of trees than under a roof; better a straight than a winding walk. But the exercise ought to come to an end with sweating, or at any rate [tiredness], which should be well this side of fatigue ... But in these matters, as before, the example of athletes should not be followed, with their fixed rules and immoderate labor. [Tr. W. G. Spencer. *Celsus: De Medicina*. (1.2.1,4–7.) Volume I. LCL, 1935. Page numbers: 43, 47, 49.]

AFTERMATH

Topics covered in the remainder of Book 1 include advice on the kinds and amounts of food that ought to be consumed; how to deal with the various changes in life, such as occupation, place of residence, and the aging process; how to gain or lose weight; purging and vomiting; lifestyle choices that should be made depending on age and time of year; instructions for people who are susceptible to various and specific kinds of ailments (such as headaches, stomach pains, muscular aches and pains); and how to remain healthy during epidemics.

W. G. Spencer, the translator of the document, proclaims that Celsus's work has been highly regarded by scholars and historians of all subsequent time periods, and that Celsus richly deserves to be favorably compared with Cicero.

ASK YOURSELF

1. What parts of Celsus's "prescriptions" for good health sound contemporary? Does he articulate any advice that seems injurious or outdated?
2. What do you think of Euripides's harsh assessment of overfed athletes? Can you think of any modern examples of the kind of athletes described by Euripides?
3. Why do you suppose Celsus recommends reading aloud as a "useful exercise"?

TOPICS TO CONSIDER

- Would it be possible to draw a parallel between the dietary excesses of ancient athletes (i.e., the sort of excesses about which both Celsus and Euripides complain) and the stories of steroid abuse by modern athletes? In other words, could the food overindulgences of ancient athletes have long-term consequences similar to those suffered by modern steroid users? (Euripides goes on to say that "in their prime, [the athletes] make a brilliant spectacle as they go about and are the pride of the state; but when bitter old age comes upon them, they are gone like coarse cloaks which have lost their nap.")
- Delve further into the writings of Hippocrates and Celsus, (most likely) the two most notable Greek and Roman physicians, respectively. Which of the two authors seems more authoritative? Which one covers the various areas of medical practice more thoroughly?

Further Information

Garrison, Fielding. *An Introduction to the History of Medicine.* Philadelphia, 1929.
Langslow, D. R. *Medical Latin in the Roman Empire.* Oxford, 2000.
Scarborough, John. *Roman Medicine.* Ithaca, NY, 1969.

Website

Celsus on Medicine. http://penelope.uchicago.edu/Thayer/E/Roman/Texts/Celsus/ Introduction*.html

Bibliography for Document

Robinson, Rachel Sargent. *Sources for the History of Greek Athletics.* Ann Arbor, MI, 1927.
Spencer, W. G. (tr.). *Celsus: De Medicina.* Volume I. [LCL.] London and Cambridge, 1935.

21. How the Mind Can Heal the Body

INTRODUCTION

Lucius Annaeus Seneca (a.k.a. Seneca the Younger, to distinguish him from his father, Seneca the Elder) flourished in the first century CE. He produced a wide variety of literary works, including philosophical treatises, moral essays, letters (all addressed to his friend Lucilius), and plays. He was also one of the wealthiest men of his time; his net worth was estimated at 300,000,000 sesterces.

Seneca undertook the potentially dangerous task of serving as a tutor for the crazed emperor Nero. As Nero's madness grew steadily worse, Seneca found himself increasingly unable to restrain him, and so he resigned his position and withdrew from Nero's court. Unfortunately, he was later implicated in a plot to assassinate Nero (in 65 CE) and forced to commit suicide.

The document is excerpted from one of his 124 letters to Lucilius. The letters detail Seneca's views on a massive range of topics, such as using time wisely; the advantages of mental training over physical; retirement; festivals; wisdom; scientific discovery; drunkenness; the simple life; and many more.

KEEP IN MIND AS YOU READ

1. The ancient Romans (and the ancient Greeks) strongly believed in the mind-body connection, and that one could not enjoy health in one realm without health also in the other. Seneca's letter reflects those beliefs.

2. The Romans recognized walking as a particularly healthful exercise. The Younger Pliny wrote a very interesting account [3.1] of a friend of his, one Vestricius Spurinna, a vigorous septuagenarian and a devotee of walking. "This is the rule strictly observed by Spurinna [writes Pliny]: . . . every morning . . . [he] calls for his shoes and takes a three-mile walk to exercise mind and body." [The mind-body connection again! After a brief rest, he takes a seven-mile ride in a carriage, and then embarks upon a second walk, this time for one mile. And later in the day:] "When summoned to his bath in mid-afternoon in winter, and an hour earlier in summer, he first removes his clothes and takes a walk in the sunshine if there is no wind, and then throws a ball briskly for some time, this being another form of exercise whereby he keeps old age at bay . . . The result is that Spurinna has passed

his seventy-seventh year, but his sight and hearing are unimpaired, and he is physically agile and energetic; old age has brought him nothing but wisdom." [Pliny the Younger. *Letters* 3.1; tr. Radice.] In other letters, Seneca expresses skepticism about strenuous exercises, such as weightlifting, running, or jumping. However, he seems to think that walking is an ideal form of physical activity.

Document: The Mind-Body Connection [Epistle 78]

That **you** are frequently troubled by the snuffling of **catarrh** and by short attacks of fever which follow after long and chronic catarrhal seizures, I am sorry to hear, particularly because I have experienced this sort of **illness** myself, and scorned it in its early stages. For when I was still young, I could put up with hardships and show a bold front to illness. But I finally succumbed, and arrived at such a state that I could do nothing but snuffle, reduced as I was to the extremity of **thinness** . . .

Now I shall tell you what consoled me during those days, stating at the outset that these very aids to my peace of mind were as efficacious as medicine. Honorable consolation results in a cure, and whatever has uplifted the soul helps the body also. My studies were my salvation. I place it to the credit of philosophy that I recovered, and regained my strength. I owe my life to philosophy, and that is the least of my obligations! My friends, too, helped me greatly toward good health; I used to be comforted by their cheering words, by the hours they spent at my bedside, and by their conversation. Nothing, my excellent Lucilius, refreshes and aids a sick man so much as the affection of his friends . . .

These, then, are the remedies to which you should have recourse. The **physician** will prescribe [how much your should walk and how much you should exercise]; he will warn you not to become addicted to idleness, as is the tendency of the inactive; he will order you to read in a louder voice and to exercise your lungs, the passages and cavity of which are affected; or to sail and shake up your bowels by a little mild motion. He will recommend proper food, and the suitable time for aiding your strength with wine, or refraining from it in order to keep your cough from being irritated and hacking . . .

This, too, will help [to overcome illness and pain]— to turn the mind aside to thoughts of other things, and thus depart from pain. Call to mind what honorable or brave deeds you have done; consider the good side of your own life. Run over in your memory those things

catarrh: *destillatio* in Latin, a word meaning congestion.

illness: Interestingly, the Latin word translated as "illness," *valetudo* (which is the word used here by Seneca), was neutral; it could mean either good or bad health.

physician: Our English word "doctor" comes directly from Latin, but the Latin word *doctor* does not refer to a medical practitioner. Rather, it is closely related to the verb *docere*, to teach. Hence, a Roman *doctor* was a teacher, or an instructor. The Latin word for physician was *medicus* (which is the term Seneca uses in his letter).

thinness: According to the historian Dio Cassius, the emperor Caligula (reigned 37–41 CE) envied Seneca's oratorical skills and considered having him executed. But the emperor's advisors talked him out of it, arguing that Seneca's fragile health would do him in soon enough.

you: A reference to the author's friend Lucilius.

which you have particularly admired. Then think of all the brave men who have conquered pain: of him who continued to read his book as he allowed the cutting out of varicose veins; of him who did not cease to smile, though that very smile so enraged his torturers that they tried upon him every instrument of cruelty. You may tell me now of whatever you like: of colds, hard coughing spells that bring up parts of our entrails, fever that parches our very vitals, thirst, limbs so twisted that the joints protrude in different directions; yet worse than these are [various instruments of torture, which Seneca graphically describes] . . . Nevertheless there have been men who have not uttered a moan amid these tortures . . . Can you not bring yourself, after an example like this, to make a mock at pain? [Tr. Richard M. Gummere. *Seneca: Ad Lucilium Epistulae Morales*. (78). Volume II. LCL, 1920. Page numbers: 181, 183, 185, 193.]

AFTERMATH

It might be argued that with Seneca's forced suicide, the final restraint on Nero's extravagant behavior snapped. Undoubtedly, the emperor's reign of terror accelerated once Seneca was out of the picture. In an ironic postscript to Seneca's death, his wife, Pompeia Paulina, who had vowed to die with him and had begun the process by opening her veins, was restored to life, by Nero's orders, when her wounds were bandaged by his attendants. Apparently, Nero suspected that public opinion would be badly enough inflamed against him as a result of Seneca's suicide, and that the ill-will created by that act would only become worse if it appeared that Paulina were also a victim of his madness.

ASK YOURSELF

1. Imagine that you were the recipient of this letter. What would your reactions be? Do you agree with Seneca that a study of philosophy could aid in the recovery from physical illness? And what about his claim that "nothing . . . refreshes and aids a sick man [or woman!] so much as the affection of his friends." Does that sound plausible?
2. What do you think about Seneca's description of the kinds of healthy lifestyle choices that a Roman physician might prescribe: walking; reading in a loud voice; taking a ride in a sailing ship, to "shake up the bowels"; and proper food and drink?

WHO WAS LUCILIUS?

Most of what we know about Lucilius comes from Seneca's letters to him. He was born in south central Italy, possibly in Naples or Pompeii. During his lifetime, he held a number of important government positions (including a governorship, possibly of Sicily). His interests included geography and philosophy, as well as writing; he is thought to be the author of a poem entitled "Aetna," about volcanic activity at the site of the famous Sicilian mountain. It is not known how, where, or when he and Seneca met, although Seneca's 124 letters to him are all believed to have been written between 63 and 65 CE.

ANIMALS AS MEDICAL INSTRUCTORS?

The Roman natural scientist Pliny the Elder relates some amazing stories about animals making use of cures and treatments that could be applied to humans. The hippopotamus, for example: "The hippopotamus stands out as an actual master in one department of medicine. For when its unceasing voracity has caused it to overeat itself, it comes ashore to reconnoiter places where rushes have been recently cut, and where it sees an extremely sharp stalk, it squeezes its body down on to it and makes a wound in a certain vein in its leg, and by thus letting blood unburdens its body, which would otherwise be liable to disease, and plasters up the wound again with mud." [Pliny the Elder. *Natural History* 8.96; tr. Rackham.] Pliny goes on to note that many other creatures, such as ibises, deer, lizards, swallows, tortoises, weasels, storks, goats, snakes, elephants, bears, ravens, and many others have all developed remedies for the various injuries and ailments that befall them.

TOPICS TO CONSIDER

- Seneca certainly had access to the halls of power in ancient Rome, considering that he knew personally at least two Roman emperors (Caligula and Nero). But even though Seneca was a cultured and thoughtful man, and not likely to overthrow an emperor or even embarrass one, it seems as if his relationship with both Caligula and Nero was uneven at best. Research these relationships, and see if you can discover why the two emperors (apparently) felt so threatened by Seneca that both of them wanted him out of the way—and in Nero's case, that is precisely what transpired.

- Check the following website in the "Further Information" section: http://www.egs.edu/library/lucius-annaeus-seneca/biography. There, you will find this sentence: "Seneca considered himself to be a Stoic, although his personal life seems to contradict the noble attitude of his texts." Research Stoicism, and read a few more of Seneca's letters. Do you think that the Internet statement is accurate? Based on what you know of Stoicism, are there any statements in the document that would reflect—or contradict—a Stoic point of view?

- As a follow-up to the previous question, read some—or all—of Marcus Aurelius's short book *Meditations*. Marcus Aurelius was a noted Roman emperor (reigned 161–180 CE) and a Stoic philosopher, and his book is considered a good example of Stoic principles and ideas. Do you find any sentiments expressed in *Meditations* that are comparable to Seneca's statements in the document?

- Harsh judgments: Many modern commentators take Seneca to task for what they see as a disconnect between his high-minded Stoicism and his behavior in the real world. Lillian Feder's assessment is typical: "Readers of Seneca's philosophy have been troubled by the disparity between the high ethical standards set forth in his philosophical writings and the many compromises of his life." Do you think that Seneca's views on health, illness, and tolerance for pain, as described in the document, reveal a disparity between what he preached and what he practiced?

Further Information

Share, Don, ed. *Seneca in English*. New York, 1998.
Strem, George G. *The Life and Teaching of Lucius Annaeus Seneca*. New York, 1981.

Website

Lucius Annaeus Seneca. Biography. http://www.egs.edu/library/lucius-annaeus-seneca/
biography

Bibliography for Document

Feder, Lillian. *Apollo Handbook of Classical Literature*. New York, 1964.
Gummere, Richard M. (tr.). *Seneca: Ad Lucilium Epistulae Morales*. Volume II. [LCL.]
London and Cambridge, 1920.
Rackham, H. (tr.). *Pliny: Natural History*. Volume III. [LCL.] London and Cambridge,
1940.
Radice, Betty (tr.). *Pliny: Letters and Panegyricus*. Volume I. [LCL.] Cambridge and London,
1969.

HOUSING

INTRODUCTION

The ancient Greeks and Romans, much like modern Americans, built and lived in a wide variety of houses, ranging from humble cottages, to sweltering apartment buildings, all the way to magnificent palaces. The documents of this chapter reflect that diversity.

Not too much is known about the specifics of the architecture of Greek private houses, so for information on that topic, we turn, in the first document, to the writings of the Roman architect Vitruvius. His book on Roman architecture provides facts and information on Greek architecture as well as Roman, including a detailed look at the floor plan of a typical Greek house.

22. Vitruvius's Description of an Elegant Home

INTRODUCTION

Ironically, our best written source of information about ancient Greek houses comes not from a Greek author but from a Roman: the architect Vitruvius, who lived in the early first century CE. Vitruvius wrote a book on architecture, the only one of its kind surviving from antiquity. In this treatise (which is divided into 10 books), he covers many components of the subject: building materials; construction methods; public buildings (e.g., theaters and baths); private homes; interior decoration; water and water quality; aqueduct construction; acoustics; and civil and military machines.

The document below has been excerpted from Book 6, where Vitruvius takes up the topic of private homes.

KEEP IN MIND AS YOU READ

1. In the document, Vitruvius is describing an upscale house, the kind that would have been owned by a wealthy person. Greeks of more modest income could not have afforded all of the refinements that Vitruvius mentions here.

2. Vitruvius is a Roman writing a description of Greek houses, so he occasionally uses Latin architectural terms in his descriptions such as *atria*, *triclinia*, and *exedrae*.

3. Ancient Greek men and women seem to have led almost separate lives. Women, for example, were not allowed to participate with men in political discussions or debates, or run for public office, nor were they typically to be seen outside the home unless accompanied by a male relative. This segregation of the sexes is even reflected in house architecture; note how many rooms or areas of the house were restricted to men or women only.

Document: Pricey Greek Houses, as Described by a Roman

The Greeks, not using **atria**, do not build [houses] as we do; but as you enter, they make passages of scanty width with stables on one side, and the porter's

amusements: In this context, "amusements" is a generic word that might refer to various board or ball games, or entertainments staged by actors, singers, dancers, or acrobats.

atria: The atrium (pl. atria) was, as Vitruvius implies, a very common feature in most Roman homes, although not in Greek. It served as a sort of vestibule or entry room to the house, where the owners could greet their guests or visitors. The word survives in English today as a term for the lobby area in large department stores, banks, and similar structures. Interestingly, the word atrium also refers to the two chambers of the human heart where the blood collects before proceeding to the ventricles; hence, a heart's atrium is a kind of cardiac entry room.

exedrae: An *exedra* was a small alcove, or perhaps a den, used for reading, relaxing, meditating, polite conversation, or perhaps even napping. In his treatise *On the Orator*, Cicero recounts a story about how the orator/lawyer Crassus would often enjoy noon-day quiet time in an *exedra*, where he would reflect on an upcoming speech that he would have to deliver or a court case in which he was involved. Cicero says that Crassus sometimes spent nearly two hours in this way.

gyneconitis: Literally, the "women's quarters." The exact nature and location of the women's quarters in a Greek house is uncertain and the cause of a fair amount of scholarly discussion. The consensus seems to be that it was located in the upper floor of the house (houses generally did not rise higher than one story) and that it was reserved exclusively for

rooms on the other; and these immediately adjoin the inner entrance. The space between the two entrances is called in Greek *thyroron*. You then enter the **peristyle**. This has colonnades on three sides. On the side which looks southward, there are two piers at a fair distance apart, on which beams are laid. The space behind is recessed two-thirds of the distance between the piers. The recess by some is called *prostas, pastas* by others.

As we pass in, there is the Great Hall in which the ladies sit with the spinning women. Right and left of the recess are the bedchambers, of which one is called the *thalamus*, the other the *amphithalamus*. Round the colonnades are the ordinary dining-rooms, the bedrooms and servants' rooms. This part of the building is called the women's quarter, **gyneconitis**.

Next to this is a larger block of buildings with more splendid peristyles; in these the colonnades are equal in height, or else the colonnade which looks to the south has loftier columns. The peristyle which has one colonnade higher is called Rhodian. These buildings have splendid approaches and doorways of suitable dignity. The colonnades of the peristyles are finished with ceilings of stucco, plaster, and fine wood paneling. In the colonnades which face north are ... **triclinia** and picture galleries; on the east the libraries, the **exedrae** on the west; halls and square entrances face the south, that there may be ample room for four triclinia, and for the servants who attend them and assist in the **amusements**.

In these halls men's banquets are held. For it was not customary for women to join men at dinner. Now these peristyles are called the men's block, for in them men meet without interruption from the women. Moreover, on the right and left, lodges are situated with their own entrances, dining-rooms and bedrooms, so that guests on their arrival may be received into the guest houses ... For when the Greeks were more luxurious and in circumstances more opulent, they provided for visitors on their arrival, dining rooms, bedrooms, and storerooms with supplies. On the first day, they invited them to dinner; afterwards, they sent poultry, eggs, vegetables, fruit, and other country produce. Therefore, painters, when they portrayed what was sent to guests, called them guest-gifts. Thus the heads of families in a guest-house do not seem to be away from home when they enjoy private generosity in the visitors' quarters. Now between the two peristyles and the visitors' quarters, there are passages ... [called] *Andrones*, the men's quarters ... [T]he Greeks call *andrones* the halls where the men's banquets take place, because women are excluded. [Tr. Frank

Granger. *Vitruvius on Architecture.* (6.7) Volume II. LCL, 1934. Page numbers: 45, 47, 49.]

AFTERMATH

The basic plan of the Greek house was incorporated by the Romans into their own house designs. The common components included: rectangular floor plan and open-air courtyards surrounded by colonnades and by the various rooms of the house, including bedrooms, a dining room or rooms, a library, quarters for guests or visitors, and servants' rooms.

ASK YOURSELF

1. Vitruvius makes it clear that certain parts of the house were strictly segregated by gender: women's areas and men's areas. Why do you suppose the Greeks built houses in this way?
2. Why do you think the Greeks (at least according to Vitruvius) oriented their homes so that "the colonnade which looks to the south has loftier columns," that the colonnades facing the north (i.e., the south end of the house) contain the dining rooms, with the libraries on the east, and the *exedrae* on the west, while the "halls and square entrances [on the north end of the house] face the south"? Is there a reason for these directional orientations, or is it likely that rooms were placed more or less randomly?
3. In his description of a Greek house, there are some rooms and areas you would expect to find in the house that Vitruvius does not refer to at all. What are some of these unmentioned rooms? Why do you suppose he omitted them?

women. However, there are scattered references in Greek literature to both genders occupying the space, at least under certain conditions (husband and wife, for example), so the true nature of the *gyneconitis* will probably remain a matter of uncertainty.

peristyle: The peristyle was a centrally located, rectangular, open courtyard, usually surrounded by colonnades and by the rooms of the house. The peristyle functioned as the ancient equivalent of the backyard, which is a feature of most American homes.

triclinia: The word *triclinium* (sg.) originally referred to a dining room arrangement in which three couches were arranged around a central table. Later, however, the word came to refer to the dining room itself, which is what it means in the passage from Vitruvius.

AN UNDERGROUND STUDY

The noted Athenian orator Demosthenes had a difficult childhood. His father died when he was only seven years old, and much of his father's fairly considerable estate was stolen by the legal guardians who were supposed to administer it. He was a sickly child; his perhaps overly solicitous mother refused to allow him to engage in physical exercise, with the result that he became even more frail and the butt of malicious jokes of the neighborhood children. If all this were not enough, he also had a stuttering problem.

But he managed to overcome all these obstacles by dint of his own hard work and self-discipline. The biographer Plutarch says that part of Demosthenes's strategy in developing his mental acuity was the construction of an underground study in his house, a quiet, private place where he could concentrate on his manuscripts, speeches, and court cases: "[Here] he would come constantly, every day, to form his action and to exercise his voice; and here he would continue, oftentimes without intermission, two or three months together, shaving one half of his head, that so for shame, he [would not leave his study, although he greatly desired to do so]." [Plutarch. *Demosthenes.* tr. Fuller.]

TOPICS TO CONSIDER

- It is sometimes said that the Romans borrowed heavily from the Greeks in many areas, including literature, mythology, art, and architecture. Consider whether Vitruvius would be considered an architectural "borrower" or an architectural "innovator." Is there any way to tell from the document alone?

- Although the ancient Greeks produced many skilled architects, whose names, in many cases, are known—the chief architects of the Parthenon, for example, were Callicrates and Ictinus—it seems unusual that we have no surviving architectural books or manuals written by a Greek architect. Given this reality, how is it possible to learn about Greek architectural principles or methods (other than from someone like Vitruvius)?

Further Information

Ault, Bradley A. and Lisa C. Nevett (eds.). *Ancient Greek Houses and Households: Chronological, Regional, and Social Diversity.* Philadelphia, 2005.

Coulton, J. J. *Ancient Greek Architects at Work.* Ithaca, NY, 1982.

Nevett, Lisa C. *House and Society in the Ancient Greek World.* Cambridge, 1999.

Website

Furniture and the Greek House. http://www.mlahanas.de/Greeks/Furniture/Furniture.htm

Bibliography for Document

Fuller, Edmund (tr.) *Plutarch: Lives of the Noble Greeks.* New York, 1968.

Granger, Frank (tr.). *Vitruvius on Architecture.* Volume I. [LCL.] Cambridge and London, 1934.

23. A Husband and Wife Discuss Their Domicile: A Place for Everything and Everything in Its Place

INTRODUCTION

The second document in this chapter comes to us by way of Xenophon (ca. 430–355 BCE), author of 14 books and treatises on a variety of subjects. His *Oeconomicus* is a narrative about the organization of an upscale Athenian household. In the excerpt from *Oeconomicus* quoted below, Xenophon relates a conversation between the famous philosopher Socrates and an Athenian gentleman named Ischomachus. The latter explains to Socrates how he and his wife came to an agreement about organizing their household goods efficiently and in the appropriate rooms of their home.

KEEP IN MIND AS YOU READ

1. This discussion represents something of a "role reversal" for Socrates. In many of Plato's Socratic dialogues, Socrates often dominates the conversation, while his students or friends merely assent to his comments. But here, Socrates assumes the role of the instructed instead of the instructor.

2. Ischomachus's inspiration for organizing his household in the manner he suggests comes from an opportunity he had to get a first-hand look at a Phoenician transport ship. He notes that such a vessel carries a vast array of equipment: ropes, rigging, weaponry, galley necessaries, and personal effects of the sailors, not to mention the cargo. And since there was very little storage space aboard the ship, the items enumerated above had to be carefully and logically organized and stored, so that each could be retrieved quickly and easily when needed, without a lot of fruitless searching. Ischomachus spoke to one of the ship's mates, who happened to be making an inventory of the on-board equipment; he asked the man what he was doing. The reply: He simply wanted to make certain that everything was stored properly, that nothing was out of place, because if a sudden storm should arise, there would be no time for hunting up any item that might be needed to help the ship ride out the storm. Ischomachus was very impressed with his tour, and with the knowledge gained, so he decided to propose to his wife that they organize their household goods along the same lines.

Document: Xenophon on Household Management

bolted door: In his history of the Peloponnesian War, the historian Thucydides describes an incident [2.4] where the Thebans had besieged the city of Plataea and successfully occupied it—or so they thought. Rather, they had been lured into the city, and once inside, they could not escape, because the one and only exit gate had been barred, with the bar secured by a javelin pin. Xenophon does not state whether a javelin was used to secure the door between the women's and men's quarters in Ischomachus's house, but some similar device was probably used.

decorations: This refers particularly to embroidered works of art, such as wall tapestries.

market: The Greek word that is universally translated as "market" is *agora*, which is the word Xenophon uses in this passage. The agora in most ancient Greek towns and cities was indeed a marketplace, but much more than that. Temples, shops, law courts, pickpockets, traffic, and more could all be found there. Ancient agoras were similar to the downtown areas of typical American cities.

troop of dancers about the altar: This is apparently an analogy drawn from Greek theater, where a "troop of dancers," or the chorus, would perform ritual dances around the altar of a god, especially Dionysus. Ischomachus seems to be comparing the precise dance moves of a well-trained chorus to the beauty and symmetry of a well-organized set of kitchen utensils.

[Ischomachus speaks to Socrates]: "And what a beautiful sight is afforded by boots of all sorts and conditions ranged in rows! How beautiful it is to see cloaks of all sorts and conditions kept separate, or blankets, or bronze vessels, or table furniture! Yes, no serious man will smile when I claim that there is beauty in the order even of pots and pans set out in neat array . . . There is nothing, in short, that does not gain in beauty when set out in order. For each set looks like a troop of utensils, and the space between the sets is beautiful to see, when each set is kept clear of it, just as a **troop of dancers about the altar** is a beautiful spectacle in itself, and even the free space looks beautiful and unencumbered.

We can test the truth of what I say . . . without any inconvenience and with very little trouble. Moreover . . . there is no ground for misgiving that it is hard to find someone who will get to know the various places and remember to put each set in its proper place. For we know . . . that the city as a whole has ten thousand times as much of everything as we have; and yet you may order any sort of servant to buy something in the **market** and to bring it home, and he will be at no loss; every one of them is bound to know where he should go to get each article. Now the only reason for this is that everything is kept in a fixed place . . . Such is the gist of the conversation I think I remember having with her about the arrangement of utensils and their use.

And what was the result? Did . . . your wife pay any heed to the lessons you tried so earnestly to teach her?

Why, she promised to attend to them, and was evidently pleased beyond measure . . .

And how did you arrange things for her, Ischomachus?

Why, I decided first to show her the possibilities of our house. For it contains few elaborate **decorations**, Socrates. But the rooms are designed simply with the object of providing as convenient receptacles as possible for the things that are to fill them, and thus each room invited just what was suited to it. Thus the storeroom, by the security of its position, called for the most valuable blankets and utensils, the dry covered rooms for the corn, the cool for the wine, the well-lit for those works of art and vessels that need light. I showed her decorated living rooms for the family that are cool in summer and warm in winter. I showed her that the whole house fronts south, so that it was obvious that it is sunny in winter and shady in summer. I showed her the women's quarters too, separated by a **bolted door** from the men's, so that nothing which ought not to be moved may be taken out." [Tr. E. C. Marchant. *Xenophon: Memorabilia and Oeconomicus*. (8.9) Volume IV. LCL, 1923. Page numbers: 437, 439, 441.]

AFTERMATH

Ischomachus went on to explain to Socrates the manner in which he directed that the specific household goods should be organized: vessels used in religious sacrifices, women's and men's formal attire, blankets and shoes for men and women, cloth-making equipment, cooking and bread-making utensils, and laundry supplies. He then suggested a sort of prioritizing system of dividing these goods into those that are more and less frequently used and calculating when each item might need to be replaced or replenished.

The next step was to ensure that the servants were familiarized with this system, and finally, that Ischomachus's wife understood that she was in charge of the whole enterprise, and that it would surely flounder if she did not exercise strict oversight of it.

After the detailed exposition on arranging the household and its contents, the couples' next task was to choose a (female) housekeeper who would oversee the day-to-day operations, under the supervision of Ischomachus's wife. The bar was set quite high for the prospective employee: she must be moderate in eating, drinking, and sleeping; she must be loyal, dependable, and have an excellent memory. Furthermore, she must be thoroughly knowledgeable about the management system, and be willing and able to suggest improvements.

Even so, Ischomachus emphasized to his wife that she was ultimately answerable for the smooth running of the household, and that she should not be insulted or annoyed that she bore a heavier responsibility in this regard than the servants. She responded that it would have been more difficult if she had no role to play instead of the leading role, and that it would be easier for her to care for the family's possessions than it would be to turn that job over to a servant.

ASK YOURSELF

1. How would you characterize Ischomachus's attitude toward his wife? Does she have any real role to play in making decisions about how the household goods are to be organized?
2. Do you think Ischomachus's system is workable? Why or why not? What factors or problems might arise that could cause the system to go awry? Is it a practical system, or does it seem that he is trying to unnecessarily micromanage the organization of the household?
3. Are there any statements in the document that would lead you to believe that the ancient Greeks tried to orient their houses in such a way that they could take advantage of natural ways to heat and cool the houses?

TOPICS TO CONSIDER

- ❧ Consider Ischomachus's statement that "you may order any sort of servant to buy something in the market and to bring it home, and he will be at no loss; every one of them is bound to know where he should go to get each article." What does this statement tell us about public marketplaces in Athens? What does it reveal about the expectations for household servants?

∽ Consider the author's (Xenophon) perspective. If you examine the list of his known written works, you can observe quite a surprising variety of topics. But mostly, he seems to have been a biographer and a historian, with particular emphasis on military matters. Is there any way to know what motivated him to write a book on household management? Does this book seem to have any connection to his other writings?

Further Information

Bartlett, Robert C. (tr./ed.), with Thomas Prangle and Wayne Ambler. *Xenophon: The Shorter Socratic Writings. Apology of Socrates to the Jury, Oeconomicus, and Symposium.* Ithaca, NY, 1996.

Strauss, Leo. *Xenophon's Socratic Discourse: An Interpretation of the Oeconomicus.* Ithaca, NY, 1970.

Waterfield, Robin H. *Conversations of Socrates*, by Xenophon. New York, 1990.

Websites

Xenophon. http://www.crystalinks.com/xenophon.html

Xenophon's *Oeconomicus.* http://bingweb.binghamton.edu/~clas382a/study_guides/03-05_xenophon_oecnomicus.htm

Xenophon—Introduction. http://www.enotes.com/classical-medieval-criticism/xenophon

Bibliography for Document

Marchant, E. C. (tr.). *Xenophon: Memorabilia and Oeconomicus.* [LCL.] Cambridge and London, 1923.

24. You Take Your Life in Your Hands if You Live in Rome

INTRODUCTION

One of the difficulties facing those interested in finding out information about how the ancient Greeks and Romans lived their lives is the relative lack of written source material on ordinary people. We have a plethora of writings that provide biographical detail on the famous politicians, military leaders, emperors, and other high-profile people of the ancient civilizations, but not so much source material on the less prominent, but far more numerous, members of society.

The literary output of the poet/satirist Juvenal (ca. 60–ca. 130 CE) is an exception to that general rule. Perhaps because he himself came from a small town (Aquinum, about 80 miles southeast of Rome) from an apparently comfortable, but undistinguished, family background, he tends to feature in his written works people who shared his lot in life. Not surprisingly, then, much of what we know about housing in antiquity comes from descriptions of upscale homes, as we saw in the two Greek documents in this chapter. Juvenal provides us with a glimpse of how "the other half" lived in the document below, an excerpt from his third *Satire*.

KEEP IN MIND AS YOU READ

1. Juvenal, as noted above, was a satirist, and satirists (whether ancient or modern) must employ exaggeration as a key element in making their points. Therefore, we should probably keep that fact in mind as we read the document.
2. The Romans, unlike the Greeks, tended to build dwellings "vertically." That is, most Greek houses (regardless of the owner's financial circumstances) seldom rose higher than two stories, whereas the Romans built high-rise structures that sometimes topped five or six stories. These *insulae* ("apartments"; literally, "islands"), as the buildings were called, were the domiciles of the less affluent; they were often poorly built, because there were no codes or regulations governing their construction. Noise from other tenants and from the city streets below was a constant annoyance; flash fires were a constant danger.
3. Although we do not possess a host of specific details about Juvenal's life, it is known that he was exiled from Rome sometime during the reign of the emperor Domitian (reigned 81–96 CE), and that after the death of the emperor, he returned to Rome both bitter and impoverished. This downturn in his circumstances undoubtedly

influenced the angry and sarcastic tone of much of his satirical writing. His dour attitude toward life in general and Rome in particular is well summarized by a famous line from his first *Satire*: *Difficile est satiram non scribere*. "It is difficult *not* to write satire."

4. The insurance industry was unknown in ancient Rome, so when a person's house or apartment burned down (or was destroyed by any other natural or man-made event), the owner or renter had no recompense for his/her loss, except through the generosity of friends.

5. Although this document focuses on the danger of flash fires breaking out in the *insulae*, fire was not the only problem faced by urban tenants. Noise from the street was another. The Romans from time to time attempted to pass regulations prohibiting the use of wagons and draft animals in the city streets during certain hours. However, these regulations were apparently not very effective in curtailing the noise, with the result that apartment dwellers often found themselves awakened in the middle of the night by the racket emanating from the streets below. A rich man, as Juvenal wryly notes, could afford a more expensive domicile in a quieter part of the city, where uninterrupted sleep was more of a reality than a goal.

Document: Juvenal's Take on Life in Rome

In cool **Praeneste** or the verdant hills
of **Volsinii**, who
Has ever feared his house would
Collapse as we all do –
Or in simple **Gabii** or **Tivoli's** craggy

Digitally-rendered illustration of an ancient Roman city with apartment buildings called *insulae*, and an aqueduct in the background. Based on archaeological excavations at Pompeii and Herculaneum. (Dreamstime.com)

Heights? But here
We live in a city held up for the
greater part by mere
Toothpicks, for thus the **janitor** props
the tottering beams
And patches up the old walls at cracks
and gaping seams,
And tells the tenants to rest in
peace—well said, "R.I.P.,"
With rafters ready to cave in on their
heads! Not for me!
I must live where there are no fires
and no alarms in the night.
Below, some **Ucalegon** already is shouting
in fright
For water and moving his stuff. From
your **attic room**, smoke pours,
But you don't know it; for if the fire
starts on the lower floors,
The last one to burn will be the man
with nothing to keep
Him from the rain but the roof tiles,
beneath which, in a heap,
The soft rock-doves lay eggs. The one
bed that **Codrus** owned
Was too small for a dwarf, his cupboard
boasted six mugs, a lone
Pitcher, a **Chiron** reclining, made of
the same soft stone,
With an old chest of Greek books, whose
lovely poems were chewed
By illiterate mice. Poor Codrus had
nothing—isn't it true? –
But he still lost the whole nothing.
The straw on the camel's back
Is this: although he's stripped of all
and begging a snack,
No one will give him a paltry
handout, no one a bed,
Or even offer him shelter, a roof above
his head.
But let the great house of **Asturicus**
catch and burn,
The matrons mourn, the nobles wear
black, the courts adjourn.
Oh, then we bewail the city's disasters
and hate its fires!
The palace is still in flames and
someone runs up and desires

Asturicus: Just as the name "Codrus" was used to refer to a poor man, so the name "Asturicus" symbolizes a man of wealth.

attic room: The Latin phrase used by Juvenal, *tabulata tertia*, literally means "third floor," which was apparently the top floor in the burning apartment building.

Chiron: One of the centaurs—hybrid, half-man, half-horse creatures—of Greek mythology. Chiron was always portrayed as a wise, cultured, and gentle being, and a tutor of some of the most famous figures in Greek and Roman legend, including Achilles, Hercules, and Aeneas. It would have been appropriate if Codrus had indeed placed the statue of Chiron on top of his chest of Greek books.

Codrus: Here, probably a generic name referring to any impoverished person.

Euphranor or Polyclitus. Both were famous Greek sculptor/artists, who lived in the fourth century BCE and the fifth century BCE, respectively.

games: A reference to chariot races in the Circus Maximus. The implication seems to be that one of the advantages of living in Rome is that one can easily frequent the Circus Maximus, whereas residence in one of the outlying towns requires some inconvenient travel to get to the games. However, living in one of these towns, like **Sora** or **Frusino**, can have a major benefit, too: more affordable housing.

Persicus: Another rich man, whose wealth is due to his childlessness and also to the suspicion that he may have torched his own house in order to receive gifts from sympathetic friends, not to mention the presents from legacy hunters who hoped to be recompensed, and then some, by being named heirs in Persicus's will. The poet Martial (3.52) relates the story of a certain Tongilianus, whose house burned to the ground, but who received monetary contributions from friends that totaled *five times* the value of the gutted house.

Praeneste: Praeneste was a small town nestled in the hills about 20 miles southeast of Rome. It was a desirable place for retirees, offering the pleasures and comforts of a small town, combined with easy accessibility to Rome. The downside? Real estate there was very pricey, so only the richest Romans could afford to buy a home in Praeneste.

Tivoli: Tibur, in Latin. Tivoli, like Praeneste, was a fashionable community for well-to-do Romans. Juvenal calls it "craggy"; the poet Horace, in one of his *Odes*, refers to it as "sloping." Both are references to Tivoli's location on the side of a hill. Juvenal cites all four of these towns (Praeneste, Volsinii, Gabii, and Tivoli) as examples of safe and pleasant places to live. Compare them, he suggests, to the dangers of residing in Rome: houses that collapse; roof and ceiling beams supported by mere "toothpicks"; a **janitor**—the Latin word employed by Juvenal is *vilicus*, perhaps better translated as "apartment manager"—makes a few cosmetic repairs, and then assures the tenants that their rooms are sound and that they should all "rest in peace."

The sloppy construction and maintenance methods that were rampant in these inner-city apartments contrast vividly to the care

To give him marble or building funds, another is pleased
To offer shining nude statues, another a masterpiece
Of **Euphranor or Polyclitus** or figures of bronze from nooks
In ancient Asian temples. And others will give him books,
Bookshelves, a bust of Minerva, or silver in coin or plate.
This is how **Persicus**, most refined and most fortunate
Of the childless, restores his loss with more and richer things.
No wonder that he's suspected of arson—look what it brings!
If you can be torn from the **games**, you can buy a fine house and stay
In **Sora**, **Frusino**, or anywhere else for what you now pay
In Rome to rent a dark hole one year. You'll have a small lawn,
A garden, a shallow well from which water is easily drawn,
With no need of ropes, to wet your tender plants. Live in peace
With a hoe as companion there, grow a truck garden fit to feast
A Vegetarian convention. Remote though your farm may be,
It's something to be the lord of one green lizard—and free . . .
what rented flat
Allows you to sleep? Only rich men in this city have that.

[Tr. Hubert Creekmore. *The Satires of Juvenal.* (*Satire* 3.) Mentor Classic, 1963. Page numbers: 55, 56, 57, 58.]

AFTERMATH

Juvenal apparently wrote his satires—16 in all—after his return from exile. After a period of unknown duration, during which he occupied himself with the hard work of writing the satires, he was able to acquire a country farm home and at least some financial stability. The source of this largesse is a mystery; it may have been a generous literary patron, or perhaps even the emperor, the enlightened Hadrian (reigned 117–138 CE).

Life in Rome generally was undoubtedly better after the death of Domitian. That despotic ruler was followed by the so-called Five Good Emperors (Nerva, Trajan, Hadrian, Antoninus Pius, and Marcus Aurelius), who collectively reigned from 98 to 180 CE. The historian Edward Gibbon famously referred to this era with these glowing words: "If a man were called to fix the period in the history of the world during which the condition of the human race was most happy and prosperous, he would, without hesitation, name that which elapsed from the death of Domitian to the accession of Commodus."

ASK YOURSELF

1. Juvenal writes, somewhat enviously, about pleasant but pricey retirement communities like Praeneste. Would it be accurate to compare Praeneste to a place like Palm Springs, California, a well-known retirement destination for the rich and famous?
2. It was mentioned in "Keep in Mind as You Read" that Juvenal, as a satirist, often relied on exaggeration to help him make his points or convey his message. Do you notice any passages or descriptions in the document that seem like they might be exaggerated? Which one(s), and why?
3. What do you make of the passage where Juvenal chides an apartment dweller for being unwilling to move to inexpensive housing in one of the small country towns near Rome, because of the allure of attending chariot races in Rome? Might there be a desire on the part of a city resident to be "where the action is"? Is the same true today?

TOPICS TO CONSIDER

- The Romans enjoyed gardens and gardening in the same way as many contemporary Americans. Juvenal suggests that living in a small town, away from Rome, would enable the occupant to have a garden, but only a small one. (The word in Latin for garden is *hortus*; Juvenal uses the diminutive, *hortulus*, a "little garden," to describe the typical small-town garden.) Consider and research the topic of Roman gardens. In addition to size, how was a standard garden (*hortus*) different from a little garden (*hortulus*)? Are there any similarities between Roman and American gardens?
- The Romans excelled in the area of civil engineering (the construction of public works such as roads, bridges, and aqueducts), but they never seemed to be able to solve the problem of congestion and noise in the streets of their big cities, especially Rome. Consider the topic of street construction and usage in ancient Rome. What specific measures did they take to try

that was taken in the building of upscale homes. In his treatise on architecture, Vitruvius recounted at some length the importance of properly fabricated walls, piers, columns, arches, and other weight-bearing components that contributed to the structural integrity of the house.

Ucalegon: Ucalegon is the (probably fictitious) name of one of the tenants on a lower floor. However, in the *Aeneid*, the epic poet Virgil also refers to a certain Ucalegon, a resident of the doomed city of Troy: "Even now, the spacious house of Deiphobus has fallen, as the fire-god towers above; even now his neighbor, [the house belonging to] Ucalegon, blazes." [2.310–312; tr. Fairclough.] Perhaps Juvenal had in mind the Virgilian Ucalegon, another house-fire victim, when he wrote these lines.

Volsinii; Gabii: Both were towns in central Italy.

with nothing to keep him from the rain but the roof tiles: The implication seems to be that apartment fires often start on the lower floors, in which case the tenant on the top floor will be "the last one to burn." Roof tiles (*tegulae*) were constructed of flat sheets of stone joined together by curved, raised connectors.

A SLUMLORD AND FINANCIAL PROFITEER EXTRAORDINAIRE

The first-century BCE politician Marcus Licinius Crassus amassed a fortune that would have been the envy of a Gates or a Trump . . . or even an Alex Rodriguez. One of his favored ways of maintaining and augmenting his bottom line was to buy up properties in lower-income neighborhoods in Rome and then rent them out at exorbitant rates. He was especially aggressive in purchasing properties that had been destroyed by fire; according to the biographer Plutarch, destructive house and apartment fires were frequent in Rome because of the height and physical proximity of these buildings. Plutarch relates that Crassus bought about 500 slaves who were knowledgeable about building and architecture, and then when a conflagration was raging in some residential district in Rome, Crassus would appear on the scene and offer the distraught owner a bargain basement price for his property. The owner, figuring that something was better than nothing, usually agreed to the price. In this way, says Plutarch, Crassus acquired on the cheap a large number of burned-out houses and apartments, which his 500 slaves subsequently rebuilt, and from which Crassus profited greatly through the excessive rental fees he charged.

Oddly, Rome had no organized, government-sanctioned fire brigade until early in the first century CE, when the emperor Augustus placed throughout the city some 7,000 *nocturnae vigiles*—literally, "night watchmen"—whose primary job was to guard against the outbreak of fires and to assist in extinguishing them when needed. These *vigiles* probably also had some law enforcement responsibilities, thus making them kind of a hybrid combination of police officers and firefighters.

The biographer Suetonius has an interesting, albeit rather cryptic, comment on firefighting, in his *Life of Nero*. [16.1] He states that Nero ordered porticos to be constructed in front houses and apartments in Rome; these porticos had flat roofs, from which residential fires could be battled. However, Suetonius does not mention the methods that could be employed by rooftop brigades in containing fires. It was also during Nero's reign that the great fire of 64 CE swept through Rome, for six days and seven nights, according to Suetonius. Whether Nero himself set the conflagration, and whether he "fiddled while Rome burned," are both open to debate.

---

to deal with the noise-pollution problem? How successful were they in doing so? Are there any parallels between ancient Roman cities and modern American cities in the way(s) in which they handled these kinds of problems?

Further Information

Green, Peter. *Juvenal: The Sixteen Satires*. Baltimore, 1967.
Highet, Gilbert. *Juvenal the Satirist: A Study*. New York, 1954.

SATIRE: A ROMAN INVENTION

The ancient Romans, rightly or wrongly, are often accused of "borrowing" large portions of their culture—mythology, literature, art, and architecture, to name a few—from the Greeks. But one literary niche was totally Roman: satire. A famous line from the first-century CE orator Quintilian attests to Roman ownership of this genre: *Satira quidem tota nostra est*: "Satire, at least, is all ours." [10.1.93] This line occurs within the context of a lengthy defense of Roman authors and their sometimes implied, sometimes stated, equivalence or even superiority to their Greek counterparts.

Websites

Juvenal. http://www.nndb.com/people/055/000097761/
Sample Plan of a Roman house. http://vroma.org/~bmcmanus/house.html

Bibliography for Document

Creekmore, Hubert (tr.). *The Satires of Juvenal*. New York, 1963.
Fairclough, H. Rushton (tr.). *Virgil: Eclogues; Georgics; Aeneid*. Volume I. [LCL.] Cambridge
    and London, 1916.

25. Ah! At Last I Can Live Like a Human Being!

INTRODUCTION

For an egregious contrast to the conditions under which denizens of the *insulae* passed their days in Rome, we need look no further than the spectacular *Domus Aurea*, or Golden House, built for the emperor Nero in the first century CE. The biographer Suetonius (ca. 70–140 BCE) provides the details of this monument to excess.

KEEP IN MIND AS YOU READ

1. Nero had an obsession with over-the-top behavior, if Suetonius is to be believed. Some examples: There must have been a constant turnover in his closet, because he wore none of his clothing more than once. When he went fishing, he used a gilded net that was equipped with purple and red drawstrings. When he went on a trip, he was accompanied by a thousand carriages (minimum!), all drawn by mules with silver shoes, with drivers wearing expensive woolen clothing, and horsemen and messengers all attired with finely wrought jewelry. It is hardly surprising, then, that his Golden House would exceed all boundaries of propriety.

2. Suetonius is occasionally accused of something approximating "tabloid journalism": that is, an inordinate interest in reporting gossip, scandal, and indecorous behavior. This charge, however, seems a little unfair, since the purpose of a biographer is to present a picture of the complete person, including that person's eccentricities and improprieties.

3. Although the exact square footage of the Golden House is unknown, it must have been built on a vast scale, since it was large enough to encompass a one-mile long colonnade and sprawling enough to fill the entire space in between two of Rome's famous Seven Hills, the Esquiline and the Palatine. So ambitious were Nero's construction projects that the comedians of the time joked that the buildings would eventually stretch in a continuous line all the way from Rome to the town of Veii, 10 miles away. Suetonius writes that Nero ordered all prisoners, anywhere in the Empire, should be brought to Italy to provide the unskilled labor for the projects, and that even those guilty of capital crimes would live to see their sentences overturned. Working for Nero, apparently, was sentence enough!

4. The Golden House received its name not because it was literally a house made of gold (although Nero's housing proclivities would undoubtedly have tended in that direction!), but most likely because—as Suetonius explains—much of its wall and ceiling space was overlaid with gold.

Document: Suetonius's Account of Nero's Golden House

colossal statue of the emperor: Nero, never one to be too modest about his self-image as a larger-than-life authority figure, believed himself worthy of both adulation and commemoration in the form of a colossal statue, 120 feet tall, as Suetonius records. The statue, designed by the first-century CE Greek architect Zenodorus, was made of bronze, with gold and silver overlays. Some historians doubt that it actually ever stood in the Golden House. Suetonius states only that the vestibule was large enough to accommodate a statue of that size, but it seems probable, given the immensity of Nero's ego, that an equally immense colossus did reside in his home. The statue is no longer in existence.

After Nero's death, his Golden House was demolished, and construction began on the Flavian Amphitheater, which was built on the site formerly occupied by the house. It is widely believed that this amphitheater, better known today as the Coliseum, derived its popular name from its proximity to the original location of Nero's colossus.

enormous wealth ... queen Dido: Dido was a legendary queen of Tyre (a city of Phoenicia, on the eastern shore of the Mediterranean Sea). She had a rather unusual family background. She was married to her uncle, Sychaeus, reportedly a

There was nothing, however, in which he [Nero] was more ruinously prodigal than in building. He made a palace extending all the way from the **Palatine** to the **Esquiline**, which at first he called the House of Passage, but when it was burned shortly after its completion and rebuilt, the Golden House. Its size and splendor will be sufficiently indicated by the following details. Its vestibule was large enough to contain a **colossal statue of the emperor** a hundred and twenty feet high; and it was so extensive that it had a **triple colonnade** a mile long. There was a pond, too, like a sea, surrounded with buildings to represent cities, besides tracts of country, varied by tilled fields, vineyards, pastures and woods, with great numbers of wild and domestic animals. In the rest of the house all parts were overlaid with gold and adorned with gems and mother-of-pearl. There were dining rooms with fretted ceilings of ivory, whose panels could turn and shower down flowers and were fitted with pipes for sprinkling the guests with perfumes. The main banquet hall was circular and constantly revolved day and night, like the heavens. He had baths supplied with sea water and sulphur water. When the edifice was finished in this style and he dedicated it, he deigned to say nothing more in the way of approval than that he was at last beginning to be housed like a human being...

He was led to such mad extravagance, in addition to his confidence in the resources of the empire, by the hope of a vast hidden treasure, suddenly inspired by the assurance of a **Roman knight,** who declared positively that the **enormous wealth** which **queen Dido** had taken with her of old in her flight from Tyre was hidden away in huge caves in Africa and could be recovered with but trifling labor. [Tr. John C. Rolfe. *Suetonius. Nero* (31). Volume II. LCL, 1914. Page numbers: 135, 137, 139.]

AFTERMATH

Nero's short and out-of-control life came to an ignominious end at age 31, in 68 CE, when he was toppled in a military coup engineered by one of his generals, Servius Sulpicius Galba. Apparently, Nero never saw it coming; he had been assured by a prophecy from the renowned Delphic Oracle that he need only fear the seventy-third year. Since he was a young man when he received that news, he felt certain that many long and "ruinously prodigal" years lay before him. It never occurred to him that the "seventy-third year" might apply to something or someone else. Galba's age when he deposed Nero? Seventy-three!

When the coup was underway, and Nero realized that his situation was hopeless, he began making preparations for his own demise, all the while, according to Suetonius, saying over and over: *Qualis artifex pereo!*: "What an artist is dying!" This was perhaps a reference to his expensive appreciation for works of art, or perhaps to his own efforts at composing music and presenting recitals.

Shortly after his death, his Golden House was almost completely demolished by the emperor Vespasian (Galba's eventual successor, after the very short reigns of Otho and Vitellius), although vestiges of the house still remain. The Flavian Amphitheater was built on the spot where the house once stood. Some say that this amphitheater derived its more famous name—the Coliseum—because of its location near the site of the former colossus of Nero. Guilt by association!

ASK YOURSELF

1. Suetonius's account of the early years of Nero's reign indicates that the emperor (and he became emperor at age 17) was sensible and just. He showed great respect to his elders, he was generous to those in need, he was approachable and friendly, and he had a knack for remembering the names of people he met and then greeting them by name when he saw them. He was a supporter of the arts, patronized chariot races and gladiatorial shows, and established contests in music, oratory, and poetry. Why, then, do you suppose that the later years of his reign were marked by cruelty, greed, licentiousness, and extravagance, as exemplified by the Golden House?

2. As mentioned in the "Keep in Mind as You Read" section, Suetonius is sometimes accused of a sort of tabloid journalism in his biographies: reporting the salacious gossip about an individual while ignoring or downplaying the less scandalous but more serious aspects of that individual's life. Do you think the description of the Golden House falls

man of great wealth. Dido's brother, Pygmalion, murdered Sychaeus in order to get his hands on Sychaeus's money. In the confusion following the murder, Dido and a group of her friends and supporters fled from Tyre, eventually landing in North Africa, where she became the founder and ruler of the famous city-state Carthage. In her flight, Dido supposedly took her uncle's considerable fortune with her; the rumor persisted—more than a millennium after the event—that this treasure trove was hidden somewhere in the area and "could be recovered with but trifling labor." Nero, at least, hoped so!

Dido is a principal character in the first four books of Virgil's *Aeneid*. When Aeneas and his friends are shipwrecked on the coast of North Africa, Dido welcomes them hospitably and even prepares a banquet in their honor. After the feast, she prevails upon Aeneas to tell her the story of the Trojan War and its aftermath. As the days go by, Dido becomes increasingly enamored of Aeneas, to the point where a marriage seems both logical and inevitable. However, Aeneas realizes that his destiny lies elsewhere, and so he and the Trojans sail away from her kingdom. From a watchtower, she sees the departing Trojans, and in her despair and anger prays to the gods that they will at some time bring forth an avenger to destroy the progeny of Aeneas. She then commits suicide.

Later generations of Romans will hark back to this tragic story and interpret it as a harbinger of the bitter Punic Wars (Rome versus Carthage) of the third and second centuries BCE, even suggesting that the intractable Carthaginian general Hannibal was the "avenger" for whom Dido prayed.

Palatine/Esquiline: Two of Rome's famous Seven Hills (although the city actually encompassed more than a dozen named hills and ridges. The other five: the Aventine, the Caelian, the Capitoline, the Quirinal, and the Viminal. The Palatine Hill (*Mons Palatinus*, in Latin) was home to a number of palatial residences; indeed, our word "palace" derives from *Palatinus*.

Roman knight: The equestrian class, sometimes called "knights," comprised Rome's thriving upper middle class. Suetonius does not name the particular knight who provided Nero with this assurance.

triple colonnade: The vestibule's roof was supported by three rows of columns. It defies speculation or imagination to calculate how many individual columns would be required for a mile-long roof.

into the category of "salacious gossip"? Could this description have been omitted entirely from the biography and still leave us with a more or less complete picture of the sort of life that Nero lived?

TOPICS TO CONSIDER

- Consider the topography of ancient Rome. Find out approximately how far it was between the Palatine and Esquiline Hills. Would it have been practical, or even possible, to have built a house that occupied that much space? Was the house constructed entirely in the valley formed by those two hills, or were parts of the house built into or on the hills?

- Consider the information in the "Aftermath" section. Can you think of other examples in both ancient and recent history of iconoclasm: the intentional destruction of statues, paintings, or other graphic representations of previous rulers by successor regimes?

- Consider the immense scale on which the Golden House was built. Can you think of any contemporary examples of rulers or heads of state who dwell in comparably plush and extravagant living quarters?

BUILD 'EM BIG: COLOSSAL STATUES IN THE ANCIENT GREEK AND ROMAN WORLD

Nero's remarkable colossal statue was not a one-of-a-kind creation; there were precedents. Perhaps the most famous of these was the Colossus of Rhodes, one of the Seven Wonders of the Ancient World. Built ca. the early third century BCE in honor of the god Apollo, it soared skyward some 100 feet and overlooked the harbor at Rhodes. According to the naturalist and historian Pliny the Elder, the circumference of its thumbs was greater than the span of an average man's hand. Legend has it that it straddled the harbor so that ships entering and leaving would sail directly beneath it; however, this is a largely discredited account. The Colossus did not long survive; it was destroyed by an earthquake about 75 years after it was erected.

The fifth-century BCE Athenian sculptor/architect Pheidias created some of the ancient world's most beautiful and noteworthy colossal statues. His statue of Zeus at Olympia—like the Colossus of Rhodes, ranked as one of the Seven Wonders—was reputedly 40 feet tall, and made of gold and ivory. Pheidias's statue of Athena in the Parthenon in Athens was also about 40 feet tall, and also crafted of gold and ivory; the gold alone was supposedly worth some 44 talents, the equivalent of perhaps $15 million. Pheidias sculpted another noted statue of Athena—the Athena Promachos—which was situated on the Acropolis, the high hill overlooking Athens. This statue, including the base, was about 70 feet tall; according to the second-century CE travel writer Pausanias, the sunlight's reflections off the statue's helmet crest and the point of the spear in its hand could both be seen by sailors on ships rounding Cape Sounion, about 40 miles from Athens.

Further Information

Ball, Larry F. *The Domus Aurea and the Roman Architectural Revolution.* Cambridge, 2003.
Grant, Michael. *Nero.* New York, 1989.

Website

Domus Aurea. http://en.wikipedia.org/wiki/Domus_Aurea

Bibliography for Document

Rolfe, John C. (tr.). *Suetonius.* Volume II. [LCL.] Cambridge and London, 1914.

INTELLECTUAL LIFE

26. AN INTELLECTUAL ON TRIAL

INTRODUCTION

When we ponder the array of intellectuals who added color and controversy to ancient Athenian life, we would be hard pressed to come up with a more famous name than Socrates (469–399 BCE). For three decades, he wandered the streets of Athens, teaching, asking questions, forcing his audiences to think. His annoying (to the authorities!) habit of investigating and sometimes casting doubts upon established modes of governance, religion, and education eventually caused him to be put on trial and ultimately condemned to death. The transcript of that trial, written by his disciple Plato, remains one of the most famous documents that has come down to us from antiquity.

KEEP IN MIND AS YOU READ

1. The Greek title of Plato's recounting of Socrates's trial, *Apologia*, is often translated as *The Apology*. However, we must be careful to remember that the word *apologia* neither connotes nor denotes an expression of regret or sorrow. Rather, it means "defense," and that definition precisely applies to the words Socrates spoke at his trial.

2. Modern juries are traditionally composed of "12 good men (and women) and true," but ancient juries—both Greek and Roman—regularly featured much higher numbers. The jury that convicted Socrates, for example, had 501 members; many jurymen were elderly citizens who depended on the stipends they received for jury service as part of their retirement income. An odd number of jurors was selected to preclude tie votes. However, if some extenuating circumstance caused the absence of one or more jurors, thus creating an even number, a tie vote went to the defendant, and the case would be dismissed.

3. Stating the case against Socrates were three accusers, Meletus, Anytus, and Lycon. Apparently, they were very good at what they did; Socrates himself admitted that he was "almost carried away by them; their arguments were so convincing."

gentlemen: In the original Greek, Socrates refers to the jurors as *andres Athenaioi,* "men of Athens."

god at Delphi: The "god" is Apollo, who had an important shrine at Delphi, a remote location in the mountains, north of Athens. But why would Socrates call Apollo as a witness? According to translator Hugh Tredennick, the "explanation of its reply about Socrates is that it was well aware of his true character and ideals and thoroughly approved of them."

priestess: Apollo's pronouncements were conveyed via the priestesses who tended his temple.

professor of wisdom: The term is not to be taken literally; the Greek word that Socrates uses, *sophos,* simply means "a wise man."

wisdom: *Sophia* in Greek, one of the elements of our word "philosophy," which etymologically means the "love of wisdom."

Document: The Trial of Socrates

[O]ne of you might interrupt me and say "But what is it that you do, Socrates? How is it that you have been misrepresented like this [i.e., that his accusers' charges were baseless]. Surely all this talk and gossip about you would never have arisen if you had confined yourself to ordinary activities, but only if your behavior was abnormal. Tell us the explanation, if you do not want us to invent it for ourselves." This seems to me to be a reasonable request, and I will try to explain to you what it is that has given me this false notoriety; so please give me your attention. Perhaps some of you will think that I am not being serious, but I assure you that I am going to tell you the whole truth.

I have gained this reputation, **gentlemen** [i.e., the jurors], from nothing more or less than a kind of **wisdom**. What kind of wisdom do I mean? Human wisdom, I suppose. It seems that I really am wise in this limited sense. Presumably the geniuses whom I mentioned just now [other noted scholars, philosophers and teachers, including Georgias of Leontini, Prodicus of Ceos, and Hippias of Elis] are wise in a wisdom that is more than human; I do not know how else to account for it. I certainly have no knowledge of such wisdom . . . Now, gentlemen, please do not interrupt me if I seem to make an extravagant claim, for what I am going to tell you is not my own opinion. I am going to refer you to an unimpeachable authority. I shall call as witness to my wisdom . . . the **god at Delphi**.

You know Chaerephon . . . a friend of mine from boyhood . . . [O]ne day he actually went to Delphi and asked this question of the god: . . . whether there was anyone wiser than myself. The **priestess** replied that there was no one."

[At this point, Socrates relates that he went on a sort of pilgrimage, to test the god's response to determine whether it was actually true that no one was wiser than he. He interviewed a number of people, including politicians, poets, craftsmen, and other professionals, and he came to the conclusion that indeed he could not find anyone who surpassed him in wisdom. He also discovered, much to his surprise, that some people who had great reputations as intellectuals failed to live up to those lofty reputations, whereas others, who did not enjoy similar esteem, were "much better qualified in practical intelligence."]

"The effect of these investigations of mine . . . has been to arouse against me a great deal of hostility, and hostility of a particularly bitter and persistent kind, which has resulted in various malicious suggestions, including the description of me as a **professor of wisdom**. This is due to the fact that whenever I succeed in disproving another person's claim to wisdom in a given subject, the bystanders assume that I know everything about that subject myself. But the truth of the matter . . . is pretty certainly this: that real wisdom is the property of God [i.e., Apollo], and this oracle is his way of telling us that human wisdom has little or no value. It seems to me that he is not referring literally to Socrates, but has

ARISTOPHANES'S SATIRICAL PORTRAYAL OF SOCRATES

One of the 11 surviving plays of the Athenian comic playwright Aristophanes (ca. 445–380 BCE) was entitled *Clouds*, a satirical critique of the sophists in general and Socrates in particular. In the play, Socrates was portrayed as accepting money for his teachings, founding a school, and corrupting his students by instructing them in deceptive methods of argumentation. None of these representations was strictly accurate; rather, they were exaggerations used to create an effective satirical portrayal.

Some historians think that the audiences interpreted the satire too literally, and therefore, they formed a distorted image of Socrates and his ideas. This, in turn (so the critics say), nurtured the climate of persistent and bitter hostility that Socrates claims surrounded him. However, the play was produced around 423 BCE, and Socrates was not put on trial until nearly a quarter century later; so it is difficult to imagine that *Clouds* had any direct impact on the decision to prosecute him. Furthermore, Socrates himself was reportedly in the audience during a production of the play, and by all accounts, he laughed heartily at the scenes in which he was portrayed. Apparently, he "got it."

merely taken my name as an example, as if he would say to us, 'The wisest of you men is he who has realized, like Socrates, that in respect of wisdom he is really worthless.'" [Tr. Hugh Tredennick. *Plato: The Last Days of Socrates.* (21–22.) Penguin Books, 1954. Page numbers: 49, 52.]

AFTERMATH

The conviction of Socrates could well have had a depressing effect on free speech and intellectual inquiry in Athens. A few years earlier (404 BCE), the city's democracy had been temporarily suspended, while a cabal of dictators—the Thirty Tyrants—held sway. Although the democracy was soon restored, the experience may have encouraged the harassment, and even prosecution, of free thinkers like Socrates. In any event, Socrates's famous student Plato left Athens shortly after the trial and did not return until some years later.

ASK YOURSELF

1. Do Socrates's words and arguments at his trial convey the impression that he really did surpass all others in wisdom and knowledge?
2. Socrates claims that his displays of knowledge inspired jealousy and even hostility toward him, because other people then assumed that he knew everything there was to know about a particular subject. He tried to deflect this hostility by claiming that "real wisdom is the property of God," and that "human wisdom has little or no value." Are these arguments sensible? Believable?
3. Socrates was overwhelmingly condemned by the "men of Athens" who formed the jury. Why do you suppose he was unable to persuade them that he was innocent of the charges brought against him?

TOPICS TO CONSIDER

- ☙ Investigate further Apollo's oracle at Delphi. How long had it been in the business of supplying answers and information to pilgrims who visited it with questions? What accounted for its credibility? How did the process actually "work"? That is, how did the priestesses gain the information they relayed to the questioner? Do you suppose that pilgrims truly believed this information came directly from the god, or were they at least somewhat skeptical?

ɘ In his speech, Socrates mentions the reasons why he is being prosecuted: "corrupting the minds of the young, and of believing in deities of his own invention instead of the gods recognized by the state." How plausible do these charges seem? Could an argument be made that Socrates's accusers were jealous of his intellectual acuity and therefore his ability to attract large and interested audiences to hear his teachings?

Further Information

Allen, Reginald F. *Socrates and Legal Obligation.* Minneapolis, 1880.
Brickhouse, Thomas C. *Socrates on Trial.* Princeton, NJ, 1989.
Reeve, C. D. C. *Socrates in the Apology.* Indianapolis, 1989.
West, Thomas G. *Plato's Apology of Socrates.* Ithaca, NY, 1979.

Website

Commentary on Plato's *Apology of Socrates.* http://www.friesian.com/apology.htm

Bibliography for Document

Tredennick, Hugh (tr.). *Plato: The Last Days of Socrates.* Baltimore, 1954.

27. AN INTELLECTUAL WHO INVENTED MANY INGENIOUS DEVICES

INTRODUCTION

Archimedes, a resident of Syracuse (in Sicily), was one of the most brilliant intellectuals of the ancient world and certainly a foundational individual in the history of mathematics. He filled his long life (ca. 287–211 BCE) with remarkable accomplishments in geometry, engineering, and physics. He was an ingenious inventor who devised many offensive and defensive military weapons, as well as a device to help drain fields that had been flooded. His sudden insight into a difficult problem in physics occasioned his famous cry of *Eureka!* (literally, "I have found [it]."), a word that he reportedly yelled as he ran home through the streets of Syracuse from the bathing establishment where the epiphany had occurred.

Archimedes famously boasted that if he were given a pole long enough, and a place to stand, he could move the world. If anyone could perform such a feat, Archimedes would have been that person.

KEEP IN MIND AS YOU READ

1. The document is excerpted, oddly enough, from Plutarch's biography of the Roman general Marcus Claudius Marcellus (d. 208 BCE). During the Second Punic War (218–201 BCE), Marcellus commanded a Roman fleet that was besieging Syracuse, then under the control of the Carthaginians, the bitter enemy of the Romans in that war. Plutarch devotes a fairly lengthy section of the biography to the exploits of Archimedes in that conflict, as well as the famous mathematician's other achievements.

2. Archimedes's fame had spread far and wide by the time of the Second Punic War. Marcellus had heard of him and had given orders that his life was to be spared once Syracuse fell, even though it was largely thanks to Archimedes's war machines that it had taken the Romans so long (about two years) to capture the city.

Voices of Ancient Greece and Rome

Document: Archimedes, a Man of "Lofty Spirit" and a "Wealth of Scientific Theory"

King Hiero: King Hiero enjoyed a long reign as the king of Syracuse, from 270 to 216 BCE. The city flourished under his leadership, especially in the latter decades. He was also an author, having written several books on agriculture.

merchantman: The essayist Athenaeus [5.40] provides the description of a famous ship built for King Hiero, under the general supervision of Archimedes. The ship contained enough wood to construct 60 triremes, no small feat considering that triremes were large and menacing battleships. Three hundred carpenters and their assistants were hired. Building materials were imported from Italy, Spain, and Germany. It was ultimately outfitted with amenities such as promenades, a gymnasium, gardens, and even a mosaic floor depicting scenes from Homer's *Iliad*. The huge ship was constructed on dry land, and when the job was finished, the problem remained of how to move such a large and cumbersome object from land to sea. To solve this problem, Archimedes designed a windlass that required only a small number of people to operate it. Athenaeus says that the device was an original invention of Archimedes.

And yet even Archimedes, who was a kinsman and friend of **King Hiero**, wrote to him that with any given force it was possible to move any given weight. And emboldened ... by the strength of his demonstration, he declared that, if there were another world, and he could go to it, he could move this. Hiero was astonished, and begged him to put his proposition into execution, and show him some great weight moved by a slight force. Archimedes therefore fixed upon a three-masted **merchantman** [i.e., a cargo vessel] of the royal fleet, which had been dragged ashore by the great labors of many men, and after putting on board many passengers and the customary freight, he seated himself at a distance from her, and without any great effort, but quietly setting in motion with his hand a system of compound pulleys, drew her towards him smoothly and evenly, as though she were gliding through the water. Amazed at this, then, and comprehending the power of his art, the king persuaded Archimedes to prepare for him offensive and defensive engines to be used in every kind of siege warfare. These he had never used himself, because he spent the greater part of his life in freedom from war and amid the festal rites of peace; but at the present time his apparatus stood the Syracusans in good stead, and with the apparatus, its fabricator.

[Plutarch next describes the "offensive and defensive engines": large showers of stones and missiles, which fell from the sky with ear-piercing noise and speed. Shields were useless against these projectiles; they were relentlessly destructive. Huge, weighted wooden beams were catapulted at the Roman ships. When one of these beams hit a ship, its force and weight immediately sank the vessel. Other weapons seized ships by the prow, with massive iron claws that pulled them up into the air, and then, when the ships were vertical to the water, they were released and sank when they crashed into the water. Still other ships were smashed against the cliffs when they were grasped by various kinds of machines. Another device could lift a ship completely out of the water and into the air, where it would be twirled around until all its crew had been flung out of it, whereupon it was allowed to fall back into the water.

Marcellus tried to counter all this carnage by bringing forward a *sambuca*, a tall, water-borne structure that enabled soldiers to deploy on steep cliffs, towers, or other lofty landing points without having to climb them. The device was placed on top of a platform supported by eight large warships, lashed together.

138

Marcellus was confident that the intimidation factor would be sufficient to discourage an attack on the *sambuca*, but he had not taken into account the genius of Archimedes, who had invented machines that could launch 50-pound boulders; three of these sent flying toward the *sambuca* scored either direct or near hits, such that the tower was shattered and torn loose from the ships.

Marcellus's next ploy was a nocturnal attack, with soldiers stealthily creeping toward the city walls, the hope being that Archimedes's long-range weapons would be ineffective against soldiers at such close proximity. But once again, Archimedes had outsmarted the Roman general, by directing volleys of stones and arrows thrown and shot down at the soldiers who were attempting to breach the walls.]

At last the Romans became so fearful that, whenever they saw a bit of rope or a stick of timber projecting a little over the wall, "There it is," they cried, "Archimedes is training some engine upon us," and turned their backs and fled. Seeing this, Marcellus desisted from all fighting and assault . . .

And yet Archimedes possessed such a lofty spirit, so profound a soul, and such wealth of scientific theory, that although his inventions had won for him a name and fame for superhuman sagacity, he would not consent to leave behind him any treatise on this subject [of designing military weapons or any kind of practical invention, considering such things unworthy] . . .

And therefore, we may not disbelieve the stories told about him, how, under the lasting charm of some familiar and domestic Siren, he forgot even his food and neglected the care of his person; and how, when he was dragged [forcefully], as he often was, to the place for bathing and anointing his body, he would trace geometrical figures in the ashes, and draw lines with his finger in the oil with which his body was anointed, being possessed by a great delight, . . . a captive of the Muses. And although he made many excellent discoveries, he is said to have asked his kinsmen and friends to place over the grave where he should be buried a cylinder enclosing a sphere, with an inscription giving the proportion by which the containing solid exceeds the contained. [Tr. Bernadotte Perrin. *Plutarch's Lives.* (*Marcellus* 14, 17). Volume V. LCL, 1917. Page numbers: 473, 479, 481.]

AFTERMATH

Archimedes could rightly be called a casualty of the Second Punic War, a victim of the collateral damage that occurred during that devastating conflict. Several ancient authors, notably Livy, Cicero, Valerius Maximus, and Pliny the Elder—in addition to Plutarch— provide accounts of what happened. Livy writes: "[After the Roman blockade finally succeeded in the capture of Syracuse] the city was turned over to the troops to pillage as they pleased . . . Many brutalities were committed in hot blood and the greed of gain, and it is on record that Archimedes, while intent upon figures that he had traced in the dust, and regardless of the hideous uproar of an army let loose to ravage and despoil a captured city, was killed by a soldier who did not know who he was. Marcellus was distressed by this; he had him properly buried and his relatives inquired for . . ." [25.31; tr. de Selincourt] It appears that Archimedes was so focused on the mathematical problem that occupied him at the time that he was unaware of the approach of an armed and hostile soldier.

ASK YOURSELF

1. What do you think of the various weapons that Archimedes invented for the defense of Syracuse? Do they seem practical?
2. Archimedes lived and worked in Syracuse, on the island of Sicily, nowhere near Greece. Why, then, is he usually called a Greek mathematician?
3. What do you think of Archimedes's famous claim that, if given a place to stand and a pole long enough, he could move the world? Is that really practical, or rather, an empty boast?
4. What were the circumstances of Archimedes's death? What lessons are to be learned from that tragic event?

TOPICS TO CONSIDER

- Do some additional investigative work on King Hiero's famous ship. The dimensions seem so outlandishly gigantic as to be impractical; the statement that it contained 60 triremes' worth of lumber, in particular, appears incredible. Triremes were large, imposing ships; even one of them would have made an impression. Do you think that it would have been possible to build a ship as large and as heavy as one that Athenaeus describes?
- What were the specific circumstances under which Archimedes cried out the now-famous Greek word *eureka*? *Eureka* is also the state motto of California. Why is that word an appropriate motto for California?
- It has been said that Archimedes's mathematical theories and discoveries formed the basis for the branch of mathematics that today is called calculus. Is this statement accurate? Why or why not?
- What is the Archimedes Palimpsest? What is its significance?

Further Information

Boyer, Carl Benjamin. *A History of Mathematics*. New York, 1991.
Pickover, Clifford A. *Archimedes to Hawking: Laws of Science and the Great Minds behind Them*. Oxford, 2008.
Stein, Sherman. *Archimedes: What Did He Do Besides Cry Eureka?* Cambridge, 1999.

Website

Death of Archimedes. http://www.cs.drexel.edu/~crorres/Archimedes/Death/Histories.html

Bibliography for Document

Perrin, Bernadotte. *Plutarch's Lives*. Volume V. [LCL.] London and Cambridge, 1917.
de Selincourt, Aubrey. *Livy: The War with Hannibal, Books XXI-XXX*. Baltimore, 1965.

28. An Intellectual Defends the Study of Literature

INTRODUCTION

Marcus Tullius Cicero (106–43 BCE) was the preeminent Roman lawyer of his time, or of all time, as some might argue. His career as an advocate spanned almost 40 years, and during that time, he argued many noted and controversial cases.

His courtroom speech on behalf of the poet Aulus Licinius Archias ostensibly turned on the twin issues of immigration and citizenship: Was Archias, a Greco-Syrian poet, living in Rome illegally, without Roman citizenship? (The case came up in 62 BCE, a couple of years after a law had been passed evicting all noncitizens from the city.) Cicero used a two-pronged argument in his defense. The first argument was based on purely legal grounds: Archias held citizenship in the southern Italian town of Heraclea, and a treaty agreement between Rome and that town specified that any Heraclean citizen was thereby also a Roman citizen.

The second argument was more abstract. Cicero pointed out that Archias, as a poet and an intellectual, should hold a place of honor in Rome, and even if he were not a citizen, he should be granted citizenship on the basis of his literary attainments alone. Cicero noted that creators of literature had almost universally been held in high esteem, and that it would be absurdly illogical for the Romans to spurn a great poet who was already in their midst and desired to remain there.

KEEP IN MIND AS YOU READ

1. Before addressing Archias's situation, Cicero reminds the jury that he himself would never have attained his lofty status as a top-shelf lawyer without a keen interest in literary pursuits, and that it is to these literary studies that he owes his success. The unspoken conclusion: If literature can nourish and inspire Ciceronian-style attainments, it then makes eminently good sense for Rome to attract and retain as many skilled writers and thinkers as possible, including, of course, Archias.
2. This courtroom speech is unconventional by Roman legal standards. As noted above, Cicero divided it into two major sections. The strictly legalistic arguments presented in the first section would probably have sufficed for Cicero to make his case. The defense of literary pursuits in the second half may well have had more

to do with Cicero's own self-image and intellectual lifestyle choices than it did with the case on behalf of Archias.

3. The classical scholar N. H. Watts has described Cicero's speech in the following glowing terms: "[The speech] contains what is perhaps the finest panegyric of literature that the ancient world offers us: a panegyric that has been quoted and admired by a long series of writers from Quintilian, through Petrarch, until today, when it has lost none of its luster."

Document: Cicero's Unconventional Speech

as brief and simple as usual: An ironic statement, considering that Cicero's cases were almost never brief nor simple.

chairman: The presiding judge (*praetor*) in this case is thought to have been Cicero's brother, Quintus Tullius Cicero. Apparently, a question of conflict of interest was not raised.

encore: Most likely, Cicero is referring to an informal public recitation, in which Archias, at the conclusion of his performance, was recalled by the audience for additional readings. During the first century CE and beyond, such public recitations (*recitationes*, in which both budding and established authors would read their works aloud) became both common and fashionable. Pliny the Younger remarks in one of his letters [1.13] that in one particular year "there was scarcely a day throughout the month of April when someone was not giving a public reading." [tr. Radice.]

Ennius: Quintus Ennius (239–169 BCE), the "father of Roman poetry," was a playwright, historian, satirist, philosopher, and poet, highly regarded in his own time and in later times, as the Ciceronian description of him indicates. He referred to himself as a man of three hearts, because he knew Greek,

[E]ven if their [literary studies] aim were pure enjoyment and nothing else, you [the jurors, and perhaps others in the courtroom] would still, I am sure, feel obliged to agree that no other activity of the mind could possibly have such a broadening and enlightening effect. For there is no other occupation upon earth which is so appropriate to every time and every age and every place. Reading stimulates the young and diverts the old, increases one's satisfaction when things are going well, and when they are going badly provides refuge and solace. It is a delight in the home; it can be fitted in with public life; throughout the night, on journeys, in the country, it is a companion which never lets me down.

And indeed even if we ourselves were not capable of any inclination or taste for these pursuits, we ought all the same to feel admiration when we see such gifts exemplified in others. No one can have been so boorish and insensitive that he remained unaffected when **Roscius** recently died. Although he was an old man at the time of his death, we had a feeling that such a superb and attractive artist ought somehow to have been exempted from our common fate. And if such a man's mere physical comportment on the stage was enough to win the hearts of us all, surely we cannot be left indifferent by genius of a purely intellectual kind, with all its enigmatic motions and scintillations ...

Many is the time ... that I have listened to this Archias ... many is the time I have listened to him improvising quantities of admirable verses about topics of the day without having written down one single letter before he spoke. Many times I have also heard him respond to demands for an **encore** by repeating the same subject matter in an entirely new set of words and phrases. And as for his written works, the products of meticulous care and cogitation, I have seen them accorded a degree of appreciation in no way inferior to the reverence felt for writers of ancient times. Should I not love and admire such a man, and deem it my duty to defend him by every means in my power?

... whereas **other arts** need to be based upon study and rules and principles, poets depend entirely on their own inborn gifts and are stimulated by some internal force, a sort of divine spark with the depths of their own souls. Our great **Ennius** was therefore right to call poets holy, because they seem to bring to us some special gift and endowment which the gods have accorded them as a passport for this world. Even the most barbarous of races has never treated the name of poet with disrespect. How imperative therefore it is that **you yourselves, with all your noble culture**, should regard it as holy indeed! The very rocks and deserts echo the poet's song. Many is the time when ferocious beasts have been enchanted and arrested in their tracks as these strains come to their ears. Shall we, then, who have been nurtured on everything that is fine, remain unmoved at a poet's voice?

[Next, Cicero reminds his audience that many communities—at least seven—claimed that Homer was their own native son, and that Archias had already written several histories that celebrated the accomplishments and conquests of the Roman armies. Achilles's name would have been buried in the dusts of history had Homer not penned the *Iliad*, and Alexander the Great would never have been famous were it not for the Archiases of his own time, poets and historians who could record his deeds for posterity; immortality comes via the written word.]

Cicero's concluding words: "I have made the statement of my case **as brief and simple as usual;** and I have the feeling that it has gained your approbation. I hope my digression ... to tell you something about my client's talent and about literary studies in general, has been to your taste. To the **chairman** of this tribunal—I venture to express the conviction—it has proved acceptable enough." [Tr. Michael Grant. *Selected Political Speeches of Cicero (Pro Archia Poeta)*. Penguin Books, 1977. Reprinted in *The Intellectual Journey*. Simon & Schuster Custom Publishing, 1998. Page numbers: 12, 13, 16.]

AFTERMATH

Oddly, it is not known if Cicero won the case, but most scholars who have studied his arguments have assumed that he did indeed triumph. It seems to be an eminently reasonable assumption. Cicero was evidently hoping that Archias would reward him for his legal efforts by writing a laudatory poem about him, but that

Latin, and a local dialect, Oscan. The famous Roman general Scipio Africanus, conqueror of Hannibal, ordered that a statue of Ennius be placed on his own tomb.

other arts: By "other arts," Cicero presumably means other intellectual activities and/or working within other literary genres. It is almost as if he is suggesting that poets are born, not made.

Roscius: Full Roman name: Quintus Roscius Gallus. Roscius, who died in the same year in which Cicero presented his defense of Archias, was considered the best comic actor of his time. He was a close friend of Cicero, who always spoke of him in the most complimentary terms. His name became proverbial in the acting profession, so much so that any actor who attained prominence was called a "Roscius."

Cicero had defended Roscius in a court case a number of years earlier; the exact year is uncertain, with dates of 76, 68, and 66 BCE suggested. The gist of the case: a certain Gaius Fannius Chaerea owned a slave by the name of Panurgus. This Fannius entered into an agreement with Roscius, which contained three clauses: that they would jointly own Panurgus; that Roscius would train Panurgus to act; and that Fannius and Roscius would share in any earnings that Panurgus might subsequently generate through his work as a professional actor. Panurgus was indeed an apt pupil, and this, along with his innate talent, soon translated into success on the stage. Unfortunately, Panurgus was later murdered by a certain Quintus Flavius, whose motive for so doing was never determined. Roscius sued Flavius, whose homicidal act had deprived Roscius of a profitable source of income. But an out-of-court settlement was reached: Roscius agreed to accept a farm from Flavius as compensation; this farm, which Roscius astutely managed, soon became a money-maker. But in another twist, Fannius, the co-owner of the actor Panurgus, demanded half the proceeds of the farm, arguing that the settlement was not on behalf of Roscius alone but the partnership, and that therefore half the value of the farm belonged to Fannius. Cicero now entered the picture to defend Roscius against the claims of his partner.

you yourselves, with all your noble culture. A direct address to the jury. Cicero was a master at flattering the members of Roman juries, and especially in suggesting that they were men of learning and culture, which presumably, they often were not.

seemingly did not happen. "Archias has not written anything about me," Cicero wrote in a letter to his friend Atticus. "I am afraid, now [that] he has written his Greek poem on the Luculli [a prominent Roman family who had befriended Archias], he is turning to . . . drama" [Cicero. *Letters to Atticus* 1.16; tr. Winstedt.].

ASK YOURSELF

1. Do you agree with Cicero's claim that "there is no other occupation [other than literary pursuits] upon earth which is so appropriate to every time and every age and every place"?
2. What do you think of Cicero's belief that writing poetry successfully relies more on inborn talent and divine inspiration than it does on training and study?

TOPICS TO CONSIDER

- Cicero admits that that portion of his speech in which he defends literary pursuits is unconventional, not the kind of approach that would be expected in a courtroom oration. Research Roman legal procedure to determine what form a conventional speech would take. Was there anything in Roman legal tradition that would prohibit Cicero's approach?
- Most authorities agree that polite Roman society scorned actors and treated them with contempt. Comporting in public (as actors obviously did, by the nature of their profession), and receiving payment for it, was frowned upon. Why, then, do you suppose an elegant and sophisticated Roman

HOMER'S HOMETOWN

One of the enduring questions about the famous epic poet Homer is his place of origin. No one seems to know where he was born. And so there arose a kind of competition among many cities in the ancient world, all claiming to be Homer's birthplace. A famous epigram lists the front-runners for the honor as the following seven cities: Smyrna, Rhodes, Colophon, Salamis, Chios, Argos, and Athens. Of these, Salamis, Argos, and Athens are in Greece; the rest are situated on or near the western coast of modern Turkey. In his speech, Cicero specifically mentions Colophon, Chios, Salamis, and Smyrna, and notes that the people of the latter city were so certain of their claim that they even constructed a building in Homer's honor, called the Homereum.

Cicero's point is that citizens of all seven of these communities, and also of others that were not named, knew that the fame and prestige of their town could be enhanced by virtue of the town's status as the birthplace and hometown of a famous poet. So it would follow that Rome could receive similar boost by accepting Archias as one of its own.

gentleman like Cicero would have had such high regard for the actor Roscius and even have defended him in a legal matter?

Further Information

Gutoff, Harold. *Cicero's Elegant Style: An Analysis of the Pro Archia*. Chicago, 1979.
Sherwin-White, Adrian. *The Roman Citizenship*. Oxford, 1973.
Wood, Neil. *Cicero's Social and Political Thought*. Berkeley, CA, 1988.

Website

Bibliography: Cicero's "Pro Archia Poeta." http://www.uga.edu/juro/2004/patrickbib.htm

Bibliography for Document

Grant, Michael (tr.). *Selected Political Speeches of Cicero*. New York, 1977.
Watts, N. H. (tr.) *Cicero: The Speeches*. [LCL] London and New York, 1923.
Winstedt, E. O. (tr.) *Cicero. Letters to Atticus*. Volume I. [LCL] Cambridge and London, 1912.

29. AN INTELLECTUAL PAYS TRIBUTE TO HIS UNCLE'S LITERARY OUTPUT

INTRODUCTION

Pliny the Younger (62–114 CE) was a noted diplomat, statesman, author, and epistler. Still extant are 247 letters that he wrote to friends. An additional 121 letters also remain, written to and received from the emperor Trajan while Pliny was serving as his representative in the province of Pontus-Bithynia.

The document consists of the introductory portions of a letter that he wrote to his friend Baebius Macer. This friend had asked Pliny for a "complete list" of all the books that his illustrious uncle, Pliny the Elder, had written. The document is the Younger Pliny's response to this request.

KEEP IN MIND AS YOU READ

1. Many of the letters of Pliny the Younger are not written in a chatty, informal mode, but are more like informational essays. The letter about his uncle's literary accomplishments clearly falls into the latter category.
2. Pliny, of course, did not have available to him any of the modern technologies that writers make use of today. Books always had to be written out longhand, either by the authors themselves or by scribes to whom they dictated their words.
3. As an educated and well-traveled civil servant, Pliny had many friends and acquaintances throughout the Roman world, and so it should come as no surprise that his surviving letters reflect a great deal of variety. Many of the individuals to whom he addressed letters are known to us, but Baebius Macer (the recipient of the letter that provides the text for the fourth document) is unknown to us. This is the only one of the 247 letters that was written to Macer.

Document: How Pliny the Elder Was Able to Write So Many Books

I am delighted to hear that your close study of my uncle's books has made you wish to possess them all. Since you ask me for a complete list, I will provide a

Aufidius Bassus: This historian lived during the time of the emperor Tiberius, and wrote a history that covered the end of the Roman Republic, down to the reign of the emperor Claudius (reigned 41–54 CE). This was the book that Pliny apparently completed. Quintilian [10.1.103] admired the dignity that Bassus brought to the writing of history and said that he was "always praiseworthy."

Drusus Nero: The stepson of the emperor Augustus (reigned 27 BCE–14 CE), and brother of the emperor Tiberius (reigned 14–37 CE); Drusus died in 9 BCE.

friendship: It became customary for Roman emperors to gather about them the so-called *amici principis*—"friends of the emperor"—who constituted a *consilium*, or "advisory council"; this council offered advice to the emperor on legal and judicial matters, and perhaps on other issues as well. It was a mark of the high esteem in which Pliny the Elder was held that he was selected for this *consilium* by several emperors.

his official duties: The nature of Pliny's official duties is not known.

junior officer: The *praefectus alae*. The word *ala* literally means "wing"; in military parlance, it referred to the wing of an army. So a *praefectus alae* was in charge of one wing of an army, usually composed of cavalry, as indicated in the document.

Pomponius Secundus: He was "the most important tragedian of the time of the Empire, probably the last who wrote for the stage" [*Harper's*]. He also served as a politician (as consul in 44 CE) and as a military general. Both Tacitus and Quintilian respected his work.

bibliography, and arrange it in chronological order, for this is the sort of information also likely to please scholars.

Throwing the Javelin from Horseback . . . a work of industry and talent, written when he was a **junior officer** in the cavalry.

*The life of **Pomponius Secundus*** . . . My uncle was greatly loved by him and felt he owed this as an act of homage to his friend's memory.

The German Wars . . . covering all the wars we have ever had with the Germans. He began this during his military service in Germany, as the result of a dream; in his sleep he saw standing over him the ghost of **Drusus Nero**, who had triumphed far and wide in Germany and died there. He committed his memory to my uncle's care, begging him to save him from the injustice of oblivion.

The Scholar . . . in which he trains the orator from his cradle and brings him to perfection.

Problems in Grammar . . . This he wrote during Nero's last years [Nero died in 68 CE] when the slavery of the times made it dangerous to write anything at all independent or inspired.

*A Continuation of the History of **Aufidius Bassus*** . . .

A Natural History [Pliny's only surviving work]—thirty-seven volumes, a learned and comprehensive work as full of variety as nature itself.

You may wonder how such a busy man was able to complete so many volumes, many of them involving detailed study, and wonder still more when you learn that up to a certain age he practiced at the bar, that he died at the age of fifty-five [in 79 CE, in the eruption of Mount Vesuvius], and throughout the intervening years his time was much taken up with the important offices he held and his **friendship** with the Emperors. But he combined a penetrating intellect with amazing powers of concentration and the capacity to manage with the minimum of sleep.

From the fest of **Vulcan** onwards he began to work by lamplight, not with any idea of making a propitious start, but to give himself more time for study, and would rise halfway through the night; in winter, it would often be at midnight or an hour later, and two at the latest. Admittedly, he fell asleep very easily, and would often doze and wake up again during his work. Before daybreak, he would visit the Emperor Vespasian [in his role as one of the "friends of the emperor"] (who also made use of his nights), and then go to attend to **his official duties**. On returning home, he devoted any spare time to his work. [More of his work habits are described next, including an incident that illustrated his near-obsession with using time wisely. It seems that on one occasion, a passage from a book was being read to Pliny and some of his friends; Pliny took copious notes during the recitation At one point, the reader mispronounced a word, whereupon one of the hearers asked him to go back and correct himself. Pliny asked his friend whether he had understood the word the first time, and the man replied in the affirmative. "Then why make him go back?" said Pliny. "Your interruption has lost us at least ten lines."] [Tr. Betty Radice. *Pliny: Letters and Panegyricus* (3.5). Volume I. LCL, 1969. Page numbers: 173, 175, 177.]

Problems in Grammar: Quintilian [3.1.21] had a favorable opinion of Pliny's book on grammar, writing that Pliny's book ranks highly because of its accuracy.

Vulcan: "The 23rd of August, when sunrise is about a quarter past five; the date chosen for the first lighting lamps before daylight, because Vulcan was the god of fire. This was with most persons merely a ceremony...but Pliny really began to study." [Westcott, p. 178]

AFTERMATH

In the remainder of the letter, Pliny informs us that his uncle's gift of focused concentration enabled him to work on his writing in almost any circumstance: while in the country; while traveling from place to place; while being rubbed down after a bath—he dictated to a scribe in that instance! Pliny relates that his uncle often chided him for walking, instead of being transported in a litter, because walking wasted time that could have been devoted to writing. He claims that compared to his uncle, even the most industrious person would seem like an unabashed slacker.

In conclusion, he expresses the hope that the friend to whom he addressed the letter would be motivated to try to "produce something similar."

ASK YOURSELF

1. What is your impression of the list of the Elder Pliny's published works? Do you notice any similarities among them, or does each one seem quite different and distinct? Is there any way to categorize or classify the letters?
2. What do you think of Pliny's work schedule? Does it seem reasonable? Doable? A little bit extreme?

HOW MUCH MONEY FOR A BOOK?

At one point in his letter, Pliny writes that his uncle had left him 160 notebooks, with all text written in very small letters and on both sides of the page—unusual, given that most manuscripts were written on one side only. He also claims that had his uncle wished to sell those notebooks, he would have been able to command a sale price of 400,000 sesterces for them. But how would that figure compare with the sale prices for other works of literature at various times in the history of the ancient world?

The essayist Aulus Gellius writes that although the philosopher Plato was hardly a wealthy man, he once paid 10,000 denarii (the equivalent of 40,000 sesterces) for three books written by the Pythagorean philosopher Philolaus. He also reports that Aristotle bought "a very few books of the philosopher Speusippus" for the equivalent of 72,000 sesterces. [3.17]

On the other hand, John C. Rolfe, in his translation of the essays of Aulus Gellius, states that "the first book of [the Roman poet] Martial's *Epigrams*, 700 lines, in an elegant form, cost only [20 sesterces], and cheaper editions could be bought for from 6 to 10 sesterces."

TOPICS TO CONSIDER

- ☙ The survival rate of the works of ancient authors often presents modern readers with some interesting questions. In the case of Pliny the Elder, for example, why do you suppose that out of his vast array of multivolume books, only one of them, *Natural History*, survives to the present day? Was this mere coincidence? Or could there be other reasons for the disappearance of his other written works?

- ☙ Pliny seems to have mastered the art of time management, which in part accounts for his ability to produce so many lengthy books. Do you know of any contemporary, or near-contemporary, prolific authors who observe similarly strict time management rules? (Hint: Research the writing schedules of Mark Twain or Charles Dickens for starters.)

- ☙ Letter writing is a generally accepted literary genre. Should it be? How would Pliny's letters compare with the letters written by other famous epistlers of the ancient world, such as Cicero or St. Paul?

Further Information

Bell, Albert. *All Roads Lead to Murder: A Case from the Notebooks of Pliny the Younger.* Boone, NC, 2002.

Sherwin-White, A. N. *The Letters of Pliny: A Social and Historical Commentary.* Oxford, 1966.

Websites

Ancient History Sourcebook: Pliny the Younger (61 or 62–113 CE): Selected Letters, c. 100 CE). http://www.fordham.edu/halsall/ancient/pliny-letters.html

The Letters of Pliny the Younger. http://www.vroma.org/~hwalker/Pliny/

Bibliography for Document

Radice, Betty (tr.). *Pliny. Letters and Panegyricus.* Volume I. Cambridge and London, 1969.

Westcott, J. H. (ed.). *Selected Letters of Pliny, with an Introduction and Notes.* Norman, OK, new edition 1965.

POLITICS

Political campaigning, speechmaking, lawyering ... these were the lifeblood of the public arena in both ancient Greece and Rome. Oratorical skills were highly prized essentials for anyone desiring a career in the sometimes topsy-turvy world of ancient politics. Lawyers and politicians abounded in both societies; we have numerous sources and documents attesting to that fact. The four documents selected for this chapter will hopefully be representative of the many that are still available to us.

30. Out with Him! An Athenian Method of Ridding the City of Tiresome Politicians

INTRODUCTION

The ancient Athenians had a unique method of dealing with politicians who became too egotistical, or who seemed dangerously inclined toward dictatorship, or who were viewed as displaying some other seriously inappropriate attitude or behavior pattern: ostracism. Under the Athenian system, ostracism meant something far more severe than simply social isolation, which, of course, is what the word suggests today. An ostracized politician was required to leave the city—to be exiled—for a period of 10 years. A preliminary vote on whether to conduct an ostracism was held every year; if a majority of voters assented, the vote itself was held. As long as at least 6,000 votes were cast, the one politician who received the most was considered ostracized.

The practice was reportedly introduced somewhere around 509 BCE, by the lawgiver Cleisthenes, and first employed early in the fifth century. The last known ostracism occurred in 417.

The intent of an ostracism may have been noble—to protect Athenian democracy from unscrupulous politicians or military leaders who might seek to undermine it—but sometimes, decent and honest politicians fell victim to an ostracism vote conducted by an electorate with less than honorable motives. Such was the case of the fifth-century BCE politician Aristides. In his biography of Aristides, Plutarch provides not only the details surrounding the ostracism of Aristides, but also a most concise and understandable explanation of how the system worked.

KEEP IN MIND AS YOU READ

1. In the fifth century BCE, the Athenian democracy was in full flower, and great political debates occurred frequently. The heart of the democracy was the Assembly, which met about 40 times per year; all Athenian citizens were permitted to attend and participate in Assembly meetings. In the Assembly, the major issues of the day were discussed and voted upon, including ostracisms.
2. In ancient Greek (and Roman) times, punishment for criminal behavior was quite different than punishments meted out today. Nowadays, felonious lawbreakers are usually sentenced to prison terms. But although the Greeks and Romans both had places of confinement for criminal defendants, incarceration was generally used only

to keep these accused persons in custody prior to their trials; prison sentences, as punishments, were virtually unknown. Much more often, a convicted defendant would be executed or fined, or, as in the case with the "winner" of an ostracism vote, exiled.

3. Plutarch, our source for this document, habitually included much anecdotal information in the biographies he wrote. This kind of information helps to give us a complete picture of the true nature of the individual. The story of Aristides writing his own name on the ostracism ballot—in effect, voting for his own exile!—is an example of how he came to be given the nickname The Just. Most people, in a similar situation, probably would have greeted such a request with an expletive, or worse. A truly just person, however, would comply with the request.

Document: The Ostracism of a Just Man

Alcibiades and Nicias: As Plutarch notes, these individuals were two of the major players on the Athenian political stage in the late fifth century. In 415—just two years after the ostracism of Hyperbolus—the two of them locked horns over the question of whether to send an Athenian military expedition to the island of Sicily. Alcibiades was in favor, Nicias opposed. They engaged in a very heated debate about this in the Assembly. Alcibiades prevailed, and the expedition proceeded. The invasion of Sicily turned out to be a major disaster for the Athenians; most of the some 50,000 soldiers whom they sent to Sicily never returned.

Plutarch's biographies of Alcibiades and Nicias are both extant.

archons: The Greek word *archon* literally means "ruler," or "commander." Later, it came to refer to the chief magistrate, or administrative officer, of a Greek polis; one of their functions, as indicated by the document, was to preside over ostracism votes. In fifth-century Athens, there were nine archons. As democracy took hold in Athens, the power and

This **sentence of ostracism** was not in itself a punishment for wrongdoing. It was described for the sake of appearances as a measure to curtail and humble a man's power and prestige in cases where these had grown oppressive; but in reality, it was a humane device for appeasing the people's jealousy, which could thus vent its desire to do harm, not by inflicting some irreparable injury, but by a sentence of ten years' banishment. Later on the penalty came to be inflicted on various ignoble creatures, the scum of the political world, and it was then abandoned, the last man to be ostracized being **Hyperbolus** [in ca. 417 BCE]. Hyperbolus's banishment is said to have been brought about in this way. **Alcibiades and Nicias**, the two most powerful men in the state, were the leaders of the two **opposing parties**. So when the people were on the point of carrying out an ostracism and were obviously going to vote against one or the other, the two men came to terms, combined their rival factions and so arranged matters that Hyperbolus was ostracized. The people were enraged at this and felt that the institution of ostracism had been abused and degraded, and so they not only ceased to resort to it but formally abolished the practice.

The procedure, to give a general account of it, was as follows: Each voter took an *ostrakon*, or piece of earthenware, wrote on it the name of the citizen he wished to be banished and carried it to a part of the **market-place** which was fenced off with a circular paling. Then the **archons** first counted the total number of votes cast, for if there were less than six thousand, the ostracism was void. After this they sorted the votes and the man who had the most recorded against his name was proclaimed to be exiled for ten years, with the right, however, to receive the income from his estate.

The story goes that on this occasion, while the votes were being written down, an illiterate and uncouth **rustic** handed his piece of earthenware to Aristides and asked him to write the name Aristides on it. The latter was astonished, and asked the man what harm Aristides had ever done him. 'None whatever,' was the reply, 'I do not even know the fellow, but I am sick of hearing him called The Just everywhere!' When he heard this, Aristides said nothing, but wrote his name on the *ostrakon* and handed it back. At the last, as he was leaving the city, he lifted his hands to heaven and uttered a prayer, which, it appears, took the opposite form to **the prayer of Achilles**; in it he begged that no crisis might befall the Athenians which would force them to remember Aristides. [Tr. Ian Scott-Kilvert. *Plutarch: The Rise and Fall of Athens; Nine Greek Lives.* (*Aristides* 7.) Penguin Classics, 1960. Page numbers: 116, 117.]

AFTERMATH

Sometimes, under certain circumstances, ostracism votes could be reversed, and this fortunate outcome befell Aristides. His ostracism began around 483 or 482 BCE, but less than three years later, the mighty Persian army had advanced westward, with the goal of overrunning Greece. The Athenians realized that at this critical moment, they needed all their best citizens, so Aristides was recalled from exile and given an important leadership position in the Athenian army. In 479, he found himself leading the Athenian forces in the decisive Battle of Plataea, in which the Persians were turned back.

Little is known of Aristides's life after that famous battle. It is thought that he may have died around 468, apparently in the depths of poverty. Plutarch records that his estate did not even cover his funeral expenses. Still, Aristides was held in such high esteem that when his daughters married, each received a dowry of 3,000 drachmas from the public treasury, and his son, Lysimachus, was given 100 minas, 100 acres of vineyard farmland, and a four-drachma per day pension.

ASK YOURSELF

1. The "official" explanation (according to Plutarch) for the abolition of ostracism votes was that they were being imposed upon degenerate characters like Hyperbolus. But the story of the ostracism of Aristides—not to mention other ostracism victims like Themistocles—implies that

influence of the archons gradually diminished.

Hyperbolus: Ironically, ostracism was often viewed as a dignified penalty, reserved for prominent citizens who had strayed, perhaps inexplicably, from appropriate patterns of behavior. The ostracism of Hyperbolus, a low-born demagogue, was apparently viewed as having trivialized the process; Hyperbolus, it seems, was not altogether worthy of such a punishment! He was exiled to the island of Samos, where, a few years later, he met his end in the unrest caused by pro- and antidemocracy factions there. The fifth-century historian Thucydides writes that Hyperbolus was ostracized because he was a totally disreputable character, not because the Athenian citizens feared his political status or objectives. In his biography of Alcibiades, Plutarch claims that Hyperbolus was such a buffoon that the local satirists of the time used him unceasingly as ready material for their jokes, but that Hyperbolus did not mind at all because of his total disregard for any criticism, humorous or otherwise.

market-place: The Greek word *agora* is almost universally translated as "market-place," a somewhat misleading rendering. Nearly every ancient Greek city had an *agora*, and the *agora* was much more than a section of town devoted merely to shops and markets, as the word "market-place" implies. A better translation would be "downtown"; the *agora* of a Greek city was home to law courts and public squares, meeting halls and shops, streets with sometimes snarled traffic, conmen and muggers . . . in other words, much the same kinds of phenomena that one would find in the downtown area of a modern city.

opposing parties: Care must be taken not to understand "opposing parties" in the modern sense, like Democrats and Republicans. The Greek word used by Plutarch, and here translated as "party," is *stasis*, which refers more accurately to factions or voting blocs within the political system. The word seems to have a slightly pejorative meaning, with overtones of sedition or gang activities.

***ostrakon*:** As Plutarch states, an *ostrakon* was a "piece of earthenware," or a broken piece of poverty, a potsherd. These *ostraka* served as ballots in ostracism votes; voters scratched or carved (not really "wrote") on the potsherd the name of the person whom they wished to see ostracized. Archaeologists have discovered hundreds of these sherds.

the prayer of Achilles: In Book 1 of Homer's *Iliad*, the mighty Achilles bitterly complained to his mother, the goddess Thetis, about how greatly he had been disrespected and humiliated by Agamemnon, king of the Greeks. He ended his entreaty to her with a plea that she ask Zeus to aid the Trojans (against the Greeks!) in the Trojan War. By contrast, the just Aristides prayed just the opposite kind of prayer, that the Athenians might be safe during his period of exile.

rustic: The Greek word *agroikos*, translated as "rustic," can have a negative connotation, as it probably does here, akin to our words "hick" or "hillbilly."

sentence of ostracism: Notable victims of ostracism votes (in addition to

there may have been additional reasons for its discontinuation. What might some of these reasons be?

2. Talk about a political comeback! To be the "winner" of an ostracism vote—as happened to Aristides around 482—was probably not an event that any ancient Athenian politician would want to list on his resume. And yet three years later, Aristides experienced a huge upturn in his fortunes; not only was his ostracism revoked (long before the 10-year requirement had expired), but he was placed in a position of great authority, as the Athenian leader at the Battle of Plataea. Can you think of any modern parallels in American politics where a political leader's career seemed to be over, perhaps because of a scandal of some kind, only to see that individual rise to prominence once again?

TOPICS TO CONSIDER

- The Athenian ostracism procedure has rightly been called an "unpopularity contest." Is there anything comparable to it in the modern American political system? Do you think Athenian-style ostracism would work today? Why or why not?

- Alcibiades and Nicias were two of the more colorful characters in fifth-century Athenian history; Alcibiades, especially, seemed to be an unpredictable man of many moods. Briefly research the lives of these two individuals; Plutarch's biographies would be a good place to start. Why do you suppose they were such intractable political enemies? Can you find any instances (other than the one cited in the document) where they cooperated with one another?

- Plutarch uses some pretty uncomplimentary terms—illiterate, uncouth, and rustic (as mentioned in the notes above, "rustic" was a word equating to "hick")—to describe the farmer who asked Aristides to write his own name on the *ostrakon*. The farmer's level of ignorance is reinforced by the fact that he did not even know Aristides by sight. Do you suppose that Plutarch here is at least subtly hinting that democracy has its flaws, and that maybe the worst of these is that even the most uninformed or unintelligent citizens are allowed to vote in elections? Or would that be reading too much into the text?

Further Information

Hansen, Mogens Herman. *The Athenian Democracy in the Age of Demosthenes*. Oxford, 1987.

Thomsen, Rudi. *The Origins of Ostracism: A Synthesis*. Copenhagen, 1972.

Vanderpool, Eugene. *Ostracism at Athens*. Cincinnati, 1970.

Website

Ostracism. http://www.livius.org/on-oz/ostracism/ostracism.html

Bibliography for Document

Scott-Kilvert, Ian. *Plutarch: The Rise and Fall of Athens; Nine Greek Lives*. New York, 1960.

Aristides) included: Xanthippus, the father of Pericles; Themistocles, the Athenian general whose leadership in the Battle of Salamis (480 BCE) helped turn the tide against the invading Persians; Cimon, another Athenian general who achieved many military successes in the 470s and 460s.

31. Women in Politics? In Ancient Athens?

INTRODUCTION

For the second document in this chapter, we turn once again to the biographer/essayist Plutarch. Although we will find no women as the subjects of any of the 50 biographies that Plutarch wrote, there was at least one who certainly could have occupied that niche: Aspasia, a woman from Miletus, which was a powerful city located in what is now southwestern Turkey. Aspasia immigrated to Athens, where she became a force to be reckoned with in both the political and social life of the city. She regularly rubbed elbows with some of the most noteworthy politicians and philosophers of the time, including Pericles and Socrates. The second document is excerpted from Plutarch's biography of Pericles, in which the biographer provides us with a considerable amount of information about Aspasia.

KEEP IN MIND AS YOU READ

1. It was a fact of ancient Athenian life that women generally did not play a prominent role in public life. Women never held any of the political offices in the government, and they were not even allowed to participate in the proceedings of the Assembly, which was the focal point of Athenian democracy. And since, therefore, women do not appear prominently in the writings of historians and biographers, it is not surprising that the lives of Athenian women are not as well attested as the lives of their male counterparts. But if any ancient author would be likely to tell us anything about the topic, that author would be Plutarch, a man whose wide-ranging mind was not constrained by the social expectations of the time.

2. Even though the western world's first functioning democracy arose in fifth-century Athens, it was not without its shortcomings. There was a lingering sense of entitlement on the part of rich and influential politicians from prominent families, which made it difficult for men from humble or impoverished backgrounds to ascend too high in Athenian politics. One exception to this general rule might have been Aspasia's husband Lysicles, whom Plutarch identifies as "a man of low birth and character"; Lysicles eventually gained an important post in the Athenian army, but only with a considerable boost from his influential wife.

Document: Aspasia: Teacher of Rhetoric, and Much More

according to some writers: Unlike many ancient nonfiction authors, Plutarch is very generous with information about his sources, especially when we consider that he was writing in a time when conventions like bibliographies, footnotes, and works cited lists were unknown, and never created or utilized. Often, Plutarch will mention his source(s) by name, as he does with Aeschines, a few lines below. Other times, he might refer to sources with a more generic phrase such as the one highlighted here: "according to some writers."

Aeschines: Aeschines (393–322 BCE) was a Greek orator and rival of Demosthenes. Three of his speeches are extant, but unfortunately, the Socratic dialogue he wrote featuring Aspasia does not survive. His speech *Against Ctesiphon* (330 BCE) was directed against Demosthenes, whose friend Ctesiphon had proposed that Demosthenes be awarded a golden crown for his many years of service to Athens. The offended Aeschines took the matter to court, and made his speech; Demosthenes's response (*On the Crown*) so effectively demolished Aeschines's arguments that, having badly lost his case, he eventually retired to the island of Rhodes. The story goes that he once gave an encore performance of his *Against Ctesiphon* for the Rhodians, whereupon they marveled that he did not prevail against his famed opponent. "You would not be surprised," replied Aeschines, "if you had heard Demosthenes."

[T]his is perhaps a suitable place to consider the extraordinary art or power which this woman exercised, which enabled her to captivate the leading statesmen of the day, and even provided the philosophers with a theme for prolonged and elevated discussions. It is generally agreed that she was Milesian [i.e., from Miletus] by birth and that her father was Axiochus, and she is said to have set out to rival the career of Thargelia, an **Ionian woman** of earlier times, in marking down for her conquests only men of great power. Thargelia came to be a great beauty and possessed at the same time exceptional charm and intelligence. She had many lovers among the Greeks, all of whom she won over to the Persian interest, and in this way, since they were all men of high position and influence, the seeds of sympathy for the Persians were sown throughout the Greek cities [in Ionia]. In the same fashion, Pericles, too, **according to some writers**, was attracted to Aspasia mainly because of her rare political wisdom. Socrates visited her from time to time with his disciples and some of his close friends brought their wives to listen to her conversation, even though she carried on a trade that was anything but honorable or even respectable, since it consisted of keeping a house of young courtesans. **Aeschines** says that Lysicles the sheep-dealer, a man of low birth and character, came to be the leading figure in Athens because of his marriage to Aspasia after **Pericles' death**. And in Plato's dialogue, the *Menexenus*—even though the first section is written partly as a parody of the rhetoricians—there is certainly this element of truth, namely, that the woman had the reputation of being associated with a whole succession of Athenians, who came to her to learn rhetoric. However, Pericles' attachment to Aspasia seems to have been a more passionate affair. His own wife was closely related to him; she had been married first of all to Hipponicus, to whom she bore **Callias**, who was nicknamed "the rich," and her children by Pericles were **Xanthippus and Paralus**. Afterwards, when they found each other incompatible, Pericles legally handed her over to another man with her own consent and himself lived with Aspasia, whom he loved dearly. The story goes that every day, when he went out to the [agora] and returned, he greeted her with a kiss. [Tr. Ian Scott-Kilvert. *Plutarch: The Rise and Fall of Athens, Nine Greek Lives* (Pericles 24). Penguin Classics, 1960. Page numbers: 190, 191.]

AFTERMATH

Pericles's political opponents found it very difficult to oppose him directly, so they often adopted the strategy of trying to weaken his popularity and influence by attacking his friends and associates. For example, they contrived to put on trial the famous sculptor Pheidias, a close friend of Pericles, on a charge of impiety, because he had allegedly carved his own likeness into a shield held by a statue of the goddess Athena. Pheidias was convicted and died soon thereafter. Likewise, Aspasia was tried, for impiety and also for "procuring free-born Athenian women for Pericles and receiving them into her house." Pericles was able to come to her rescue and win her an acquittal by addressing the jury personally, and with great emotion.

Six months after Pericles's death, Aspasia married the sheep dealer Lysicles, who, despite his low birth, was chosen as a general of the Athenian army in 428. Some suggest that he owed his newfound prominence to the machinations of Aspasia. Shortly after his military appointment, he and four other generals, along with a contingent of soldiers, were sent out to the hinterlands of Caria, in southwestern Ionia, to do some fund-raising from among the cities allied to Athens. (This was during the initial stages of the Peloponnesian War, when Athens was trying to enhance its military capabilities and required money from outside sources to do so.) The Carians did not appreciate these efforts, and in the end, they attacked and killed Lysicles, along with a large number of his soldiers.

Aspasia continued to live on in Athens after her husband's death. It is thought that she died sometime during the last decade of the fifth century.

ASK YOURSELF

1. Plutarch says that the Ionian woman Thargelia was instrumental in sowing "the seeds of sympathy for the Persians . . . throughout the Greek cities." And yet it is known that there was widespread resentment and resistance to Persian rule on the part of the cities in Ionia. So why do you suppose Thargelia, from Ionia, was apparently trying to advance the Persian cause in her home region?

2. "Power couples." We hear the phrase quite often these days. Do you think that Pericles and Aspasia could have been considered a "power couple"? What do you suppose Pericles's rival politicians thought when they heard the news that Pericles and Aspasia were "together" (although they apparently never married, because Aspasia was foreign-born)?

Callias: Callias owned an imposing home in Athens, which he often made available to philosophers and sophists for their discussions and social gatherings. The philosophical discussion reported in Plato's *Protagoras* (see chapter 2, on education) took place at the home of Callias, as did an elaborate banquet described in the historian Xenophon's dialogue, entitled, logically enough, *Banquet*. (Plato recounts an amusing vignette about the arrival of Socrates and a couple of his friends at Callias's front door. The group was in the midst of a serious discussion on some question that had arisen as they were walking to Callias's house, so before knocking, they continued their discussion. But from inside the house, the butler overheard the talking—according to Plato, "very likely the great number of sophists . . . made him annoyed with callers at the house"—and so when Socrates did finally knock, the butler opened the door, immediately told the new arrivals to get lost, and slammed the door in their faces. They knocked again. This time, the butler did not even open the door but repeated his earlier instruction to them, through the closed door. Finally, after many entreaties, including Socrates's claim that they were *not* sophists, the butler reluctantly admitted them.)

Ionian woman: Ionia was a sort of generic place-name, applied to the western coast of Asia Minor, modern Turkey. Generic place-names are still used today; for example, the northeastern United States is often collectively called "New England." Since Aspasia's hometown of Miletus was located in Ionia, Thargelia obviously came from the same region.

Pericles' death: Pericles was a victim of the plague that ravaged Athens in the 420s. Pericles died in 429.

Xanthippus and Paralus: Plutarch records that both Xanthippus and Paralus died from the plague and that both predeceased Pericles. Even though Pericles had thus lost both sons, as well as his sister and many other relatives and friends, he always kept his composure at their funerals. Always, that is, until the death of Paralus, his last remaining legitimate son, during whose funeral, Plutarch says, Pericles "broke into a passion of tears and sobs."

TOPICS TO CONSIDER

- One of the books cited in the "Further information" section below is Madeleine Henry's *Prisoner of History: Aspasia of Miletus and Her Biographical Tradition*. In the publisher's description of the book, there appears this sentence: "[C]ontinued uncritical reception of her depiction in Attic [i.e., Athenian] comedy and naïve acceptance of Plutarch's account of her in his Life of Pericles prevent us from understanding who she was and what her contributions to Greek thought might have been." Plutarch was a thorough and careful researcher, whose credibility has stood the test of time. Why, then, do you suppose some contemporary critics consider it "naïve" to accept his account of Aspasia? Do you see anything in the document that would lead you to believe you are being "prevent[ed] . . . from understanding who she was and what her contributions to Greek thought might have been"?

- Plato's dialogue *Menexenus* is relatively short, and most of it is comprised of the funeral oration that (according to Plato) Aspasia wrote and Socrates recited. Read Aspasia's speech. Does it sound convincing? Is it well organized? Based only on this speech, would you say that Aspasia deserved her apparently solid reputation as a philosopher and rhetorician?

- As mentioned above, ancient historians, biographers, and other nonfiction authors never cited their sources in formats with which we are familiar today: bibliographies, footnotes, quotation marks, parenthetical citations, and the like. And they certainly never asked, formally or otherwise, for permission to use or quote material from another author's books in their own work. Apparently, these authors, and the scholarly community in general, believed that no one could "own" words, ideas, and information, and therefore, it would be ludicrous to ask permission of, or to offer payment to, another author for the use of his written material. Things are different these days, where copyright laws and antiplagiarism

ASPASIA AS A MATCHMAKER

Among her many other talents, Aspasia was a noted matchmaker. According to the historian Xenophon (in *Memorabilia*), Socrates once solicited her thoughts on this topic. She responded by stating that above all, a matchmaker has to be certain that she does not misrepresent the qualities or personalities of the people whom she is trying to match. For if she conveys inaccurate or false information, not only will the poorly matched couple hate each other; they will hate the matchmaker, too, which in turn, obviously would damage the matchmaker's reputation.

ASPASIA AS AN AUTHOR

Aspasia was reputedly the author of not one, but two, funeral orations, including perhaps the most famous such oration of all: the one that Pericles delivered after the first year of fighting in the Peloponnesian War, in which, among other things, he declared that Athens was the "school of Greece." She receives credit for authoring the second one by no less an authority than Plato, in his dialogue *Menexenus*. The title character and Socrates are discussing the art of crafting and delivering such a speech: "*Menexenus*: And do you think that you yourself would be able to make the speech, if required . . . *Socrates*: That I should be able to make the speech would be nothing [surprising], Menexenus. For she who is my instructor is by no means weak in the art of rhetoric. On the contrary, she has turned out many fine orators, and amongst them one who surpassed all other Greeks, Pericles, the son of Xanthippus. *Menexenus*: Who is she? But you mean Aspasia, no doubt. *Socrates*: I do." [Plato. *Menexenus* 235 E; 236 A. tr. Bury.] Socrates goes on to explain that on the previous day, he had heard Aspasia rehearsing a funeral speech that she was preparing. Some of it she had already written; other parts of it she was making up on the spot, and she was doing all of this at the same time she was working on Pericles's funeral oration. Socrates apparently had a copy of the first speech, and Menexenus prevailed upon him to recite it. The rest of the dialogue is taken up with Socrates's presentation of Aspasia's speech.

---

guidelines have combined to form rigid citation and permission rules to which nonfiction authors must adhere. Which system do you think is superior? Why?

⮞ Plutarch says that Pericles persuaded the Assembly to pass a decree authorizing Athenian military action against the island of Samos (off the western coast of Ionia), because the Samians had disobeyed an Athenian order to end their war against the city of Miletus. (The two of them were fighting over possession of Priene, another city in Ionia.) Some Athenians believed that Aspasia was responsible for fomenting Athenian involvement in this conflict. Why would that suspicion have arisen? Does it make sense?

Further Information

Henry, Madeleine M. *Prisoner of History: Aspasia of Miletus and Her Biographical Tradition.* Oxford, 1995.
Radice, Betty. *Who's Who in the Ancient World* (s.v. "Aspasia"). Baltimore, 1973.

Websites

Aspasia. http://www.newworldencyclopedia.org/entry/Aspasia
Aspasia biography. http://www.yourdictionary.com/biography/aspasia
Aspasia of Miletus. http://penelope.uchicago.edu/~grout/encyclopaedia_romana/greece/hetairai/aspasia.html

Bibliography for Document

Bury, The Rev. R.G. (tr.). *Plato: Timaeus; Critias; Cleitophon; Menexenus, Epistles.* [LCL.] London and Cambridge, 1929.
Scott-Kilvert, Ian (tr.). *Plutarch: The Rise and Fall of Athens: Nine Greek Lives.* New York, 1960.

32. Homegrown Terrorism?

INTRODUCTION

First-century BCE Roman politics was as well documented as it was muddled. We have more first-hand literary sources of information about that century than any other in Roman—or Greek—history. It was a time of egomaniacal military and political leaders, whose goals seemed to include domination of the Roman government, and also a time of idealistic individuals determined to stop them. It was a time of shifting political alliances and shifting friendships, changes that seemed to happen weekly . . . or daily . . . or even hourly. The dynamic of the century could be well summarized by one of its most famous events: the assassination of Julius Caesar, in 44 BCE As the circle of almost two dozen conspirators closed around him on the Ides of March, and each one delivered a knife thrust, the mortally wounded Caesar recognized the faces of several men whom he thought were his friends, including Brutus. Young Brutus, his protégé. No wonder Caesar was struck with disbelief—"even you, Brutus?"—at being stabbed in the back, both literally and figuratively, by a friend. Or was he a friend? First century Roman politicians who wanted to survive needed to know who their friends were.

One of the most famous—or infamous—Roman politicians of the time was the disappointed office-seeker Lucius Sergius Catilina, better known today as Catiline. Catiline had been a provincial governor (in Africa) in 66, and at the close of his tenure there, he returned to Rome, hoping to run for election to the top office in the Roman government, the consulship. However, irregularities in his African administration precluded his candidacy. He was put on trial for provincial mismanagement, acquitted, and again decided to run for the consulship, this time in 64. He lost. He tried again the next year, and lost again. Now, in effect a three-time loser, Catiline began to search for a more direct, less constitutional, method to gain power: a military coup, which he began organizing toward the end of the year 63. He eventually amassed a large army of followers, over 10,000, and his plot might have worked had not one man gotten in the way, one of the duly elected consuls for 63, the famous orator, lawyer, and statesman Marcus Tullius Cicero.

Cicero found out about Catiline's plot, and exposed it in a memorable series of four speeches, delivered near the end of 63. The document consists of the first several paragraphs of his first speech against Catiline, on November 7, 63.

KEEP IN MIND AS YOU READ

1. The Roman Senate was not an elected, legislative body, like the United States Senate, but instead was composed of nonelected statesmen and politicians, drawn from the ranks of former officeholders, who remained senators for life. Its numbers fluctuated, but generally hovered around 300. The Senate's primary role was advisory (although its advice was taken seriously, given the composition of its membership), but it also exercised some control over financial matters and foreign policy issues. The Senate met when convened by a consul, and Cicero had good reason to call a meeting for November 7: he had been the target of a failed assassination plot engineered by Catiline!

2. Catiline himself had the audacity to attend the November 7 Senate meeting, even though he must have known, or at least suspected, that he was about to be denounced by one of the most eloquent orators of all time. It is uncertain whether Catiline delivered a rebuttal; there is some indication that he made an effort to deny the charges. Or, as some believe, he may have simply walked out of the temple where the meeting took place without attempting to make a reply. It does seem clear, however, that he was shunned by the senators and took a seat by himself during Cicero's speech, well apart from the others.

3. One of the interesting, if unanswerable, questions about Cicero's speech is whether he had a written text of it or simply delivered it extemporaneously. It seems unlikely that he carried a manuscript, or even notes, with him to address the Senate; Roman (and Greek) orators always used elaborate and vigorous arm and hand gestures during their speeches, and it is difficult to envision an orator encumbered by sheets or rolls of paper being able to perform the appropriate gestures. Cicero probably had prepared and rehearsed the speech in advance, rather than making it up as he went along, but he almost certainly did not read it.

4. Like modern attorneys, Cicero bases many of his arguments on legal and historical precedents.

Document: When Cicero Speaks, People Listen!

In the name of heaven, Catiline, how long do you propose to exploit our patience? Do you really suppose that your lunatic activities are going to escape our retaliation for evermore? Are there to be no limits to this audacious, uncontrollable swaggering? Look at the garrison of our Roman nation which guards the **Palatine** by night, look at the patrols ranging the city, the whole population gripped by terror, the entire body of loyal citizens massing at one single spot!

Look at this meeting of our Senate behind **strongly fortified defenses**, see **the expressions on the countenances** of every one of these men who are here! Have none of these sights made the smallest impact on your heart? You must be well aware that your plot has been detected. Now that every single person in this place knows all about your conspiracy, you cannot fail to realize it is doomed. Do you suppose there is a single individual here who has not got

A group of senators outside the Temple of Jupiter, Roman, fourth century CE. (Louvre, Paris, France/ Alinari/The Bridgeman Art Library)

the very fullest information about what you were doing **last night and the night before**, where you went, the men you summoned, the plans you concocted?

What a **scandalous commentary on our age and its standards!** For the senate knows all about these things. The **consul** sees them being done. And yet this man still lives! Lives? He walks right into the Senate. He joins in our national debates—watches and notes and marks down with his gaze each one of us he plots to assassinate. And we, how brave we are! Just by getting out of the way of his frenzied onslaught, we feel we are doing patriotic duty enough.

But yours was the death which **the consul should have ordered** long ago. The calamity which you have long been planning for each one of us ought to have rebounded on to yourself alone. The noble **Publius Scipio Nasica**, who was **chief priest** but held no administrative office, killed Tiberius Gracchus, although his threat to the national security was only on a limited scale [unlike the much more serious danger posed by

chief priest: As the title suggests, the *pontifex maximus* (chief priest) was in charge of official religious functions and supervisor of all priests in Rome. Although the responsibilities of the chief priest were mostly religious, there was also a political dimension: the chief priest had to be elected, which necessitated a political campaign—but only once, because he held the position for life.

consul: Remember, there were two consuls each year. It is not totally clear whether Cicero is referring to himself here or to the other consul for the year, Gaius Antonius Hybrida. (Interestingly, Hybrida was once thought to have Catilinarian symphaties, but Cicero gained his support by promising to help him obtain a desirable province to govern after his term as consul had expired.)

the consul should have ordered: Here, Cicero seems to be referencing himself, not his colleague Hybrida. In October 63, the Senate had passed a resolution conferring wide-ranging powers upon the consuls for the protection of the state in an emergency. (This was the *senatus consultum ultimum*, often abbreviated as *S.C.U.*, or "final decree of the Senate," somewhat similar to martial law in our own times. Such a decree empowered the consuls to order executions of individuals deemed to pose a serious danger to the state.)

decree of the Senate: The *senatus consultum ultimum*, mentioned above.

the expressions on the countenances: According to Ciceronian commentator Albert Harkness, Cicero is here referring to the "looks of surprise and indignation with which the senate received Catiline as he took his seat . . ."

Gaius Servilius Ahala: As he himself admits, Cicero is reaching far back into Roman history for this precedent: 439 BCE. Spurius Maelius was a wealthy plebeian who, at a time of famine and food shortages, was able to devote his own resources to the provision of cheap corn for his starving fellow countrymen. This altruistic action stirred suspicions among the leaders of the Roman government that Spurius was in reality trying to court popular favor, so as to position himself for a run at royal power. Accordingly, the government sent their representative Ahala to deal with Spurius, and deal

Catiline]. Shall we, then, who hold the office of consuls, tolerate Catiline when he is determined to plunge the world into fire and slaughter? Upon precedents that go too far back into antiquity, such as the act of **Gaius Servilius Ahala** who with his own hand slew Spurius Maelius for plotting a revolution, I shall not dwell, except to say that at former epochs, in this country of ours, brave men did not lack the courage to strike down a dangerous Roman citizen more fiercely even than they struck down the bitterest of foreign foes. Moreover, we have in our hands, Catiline, a **decree of the Senate** that is specifically aimed against yourself, and a formidable and stern decree it is. From this body, then, the state has no lack of counsel and authority. I tell you frankly, it is we, the consuls, who are not doing our duty. [Tr. Michael Grant. *Selected Political Speeches of Cicero. (Against Lucius Sergius Catilina.* I.1–3.) Penguin Classics, 1969. Page numbers: 76, 77.]

AFTERMATH

Catiline stormed out of the Senate meeting after the speech and left Rome to join up with his revolutionary army, which was quartered not far away. The next day, November 8, Cicero made a speech to the general population outlining the situation and trying to prevent panic. Meanwhile, the conspirators who remained in Rome after Catiline's abrupt departure on the 7th imprudently divulged their plans to some ambassadors from Gaul (modern France) who happened to be in the city; apparently, the conspirators were hoping that the ambassadors would provide them with additional manpower and supplies. But instead, the Gauls reported the information to Cicero, replete with written documentation. It was precisely the break he needed!

Five of the ringleaders of the conspiracy were apprehended and detained. On December 3, Cicero delivered his third Catilinarian oration, directly to the Roman people, in which he explained the most recent developments in the case against Catiline. Two days later, the Roman Senate debated the issue; during this debate, Cicero brought forth his fourth and final oration against Catiline. The Senate voted for execution, and the sentence was carried out immediately, with Cicero's support and supervision. (Although the Senate's vote did not have the force of law, such was that body's influence in Roman politics that Cicero, and others, would have felt comfortable in interpreting a senatorial decree as tantamount to legal sanction for his actions.)

For the next 20 years of his life, until he was killed in 43, Cicero looked back with pride on his role in suppressing the

Catilinarian conspiracy as the time when he almost single-handedly saved the Roman state. But his political enemies condemned him for his actions in this case, because he ordered the summary execution of the five men without giving them an opportunity to appeal their death sentences, as required by Roman law.

ASK YOURSELF

1. Why do you suppose Catiline showed up at this meeting of the Roman Senate when he very likely knew that his plot was going to be exposed, and that he himself might be in physical danger?
2. Cicero refers to Publius Scipio Nasica as a *vir amplissimus*—a very distinguished man. Can we infer from those complimentary words that Cicero approved of Nasica's actions in leading the crowd of senators who struck down Tiberius Gracchus? Would that incident be sound precedent for Cicero to push ahead for the death penalty for the five conspirators?
3. Could Catiline be aptly described as a "home-grown terrorist"? Why or why not?

TOPICS TO CONSIDER

- Although Catiline's conspiracy certainly posed an imminent threat to the Roman government, and its leading officeholders, especially Cicero, some historians have argued that Cicero's speech against Catiline contains elements of exaggeration. Could you identify any places in the document where Cicero seems to be going a bit overboard in what he says?
- Cicero argued dozens of court cases and made dozens of public speeches during his long career as a lawyer and orator. In court, he excelled both as a prosecutor and as a defense attorney, but he was probably more sharp-tongued when on the offensive, as he is in the speech against Catiline. Can you find examples in the document where Cicero seems to be sarcastic? Or instances where he engages in personal attacks?
- When the Senate engaged in its momentous December 5 debate on the fate of the five captured conspirators, the first 16 speakers all argued in favor of the death penalty. The 17th speaker, however, suggested that they simply be imprisoned for life, and such was his eloquence that

he did: he killed him. Spurius's true motives, therefore, are unknown. But Cicero makes it clear what *he* thought Spurius was up to.

last night and the night before: Cicero may be referring, in part, to a meeting of the conspirators in which they discussed the details of assassinating him.

Palatine: The Palatine Hill, one of Rome's famous Seven Hills, was home to some of the city's wealthiest residents, who lived in exquisite mansions; our English words "palace" and "palatial" derive from Palatine. The fact that the Palatine had to be patrolled by armed guards indicates the seriousness of the situation caused by Catiline's conspiracy.

Publius Cornelius Scipio: Nasica was one of the consuls in 138 BCE. A short time later, in the turbulent year of 133, when the tribune Tiberius Gracchus had proposed a highly controversial land redistribution measure, Nasica was a leader of the opposition. When Gracchus announced that he would run for reelection to the tribunate—a very nontraditional decision, given that the tribunes were term-limited to one year—Nasica demanded that the consuls take action to stop him. When they refused, Nasica led a band of senators, who were equipped with clubs and heavy sticks, to one of Gracchus's campaign rallies, with the apparent intention of taking matters into their own hands. Things quickly turned ugly; violence broke out, and Gracchus was killed. The biographer Plutarch writes that this was the first time in all of Roman history that the blood of citizens was shed in a civil disturbance.

scandalous ... standards: This is the translation given for one of Cicero's most famous utterances: *O tempora! O mores!*, more succinctly rendered as "Oh, the times! Oh, the morals!"

strongly fortified defenses: This Senate meeting took place in the Temple of Jupiter Stator ("Protector"), which was located on the Palatine Hill, and which was guarded even in normal times. But in this situation, the temple guards were augmented by the patrols that Cicero had previously mentioned.

the Senate was at least temporarily inclined to go along with that proposal. That speaker's name: Julius Caesar. There has been speculation—although no solid proof—that Caesar was at least a covert supporter of Catiline. Could this be true? If so, what reasons might Caesar have had for backing someone like Catiline?

> ❧ Imagine that you were given the assignment of defending Catiline in court. What arguments on his behalf could you present?

> ❧ Investigate the *senatus consultum ultimum* (S.C.U.), "the final decree of the Senate." Under what kinds of circumstances in Roman history had it been invoked prior to the trial of Catiline? What would be the modern equivalent of the S.C.U.? Are there any similarities between ancient and modern usages of a decree like this?

Further Information

Hutchinson, L. *The Conspiracy of Catiline.* New York, 1967.

Kaplan, A. *Catiline: The Man and His Role in the Roman Revolution.* New York, 1968.

Odahl, Charles M. *Cicero and the Catilinarian Conspiracy.* New Haven, CT, 1971.

Scullard, H. H. *From the Gracchi to Nero: A History of Rome from 133 B.C. to A.D. 68.* London, 1959.

THE ULTIMATE ANCIENT AUTHORITY ON CATILINE'S CONSPIRACY

Gaius Sallustius Crispus (86–34 BCE), commonly known today as Sallust, wrote a detailed historical account of the Catilinarian conspiracy. The treatise, which survives intact, contains 61 sections and covers all the important events: a description of Catiline's character; his plot and all its ramifications; the arrest of the five ringleaders; the debate over their punishment; their execution; the activities of Catiline's revolutionary army and its defeat; and the death of Catiline.

In addition to his writing career, Sallust was also a politician, orator, and lawyer. Interestingly, he was once matched up against Cicero, in a court case (52 BCE) involving Titus Annius Milo, on trial for murdering a political opponent; Cicero was the defense lawyer, Sallust assisted in the prosecution. The story goes that Sallust had a personal motive for joining in with the prosecution: some time before, he had been discovered *in flagrante* with Milo's wife, whereupon Milo publicly horse-whipped him for his adulterous behavior and, in addition, laid a heavy fine upon him.

As for the outcome of Milo's court case . . . the situation was so politically charged—the courtroom was surrounded with heavily armed guards—that Cicero never actually delivered any speeches in defense of his client, although the transcript still survives of the speech he would have made. Milo fled to Massilia (modern Marseilles in southern France) and enjoyed a brief "retirement" from the hurly-burly of Roman politics, until once again reprising his involvement, and ultimately being executed (48 BCE) for fomenting violence.

Websites

Catiline Biography. http://www.bookrags.com/biography/catiline
Catiline Conspiracy. http://www.unrv.com/roman-republic/catiline-conspiracy.php

Bibliography for Document

Artwork: The cover of this book displays a very famous painting that depicts Cicero excoriating Catiline before the Roman Senate. Catiline sits off to one side, alone, depressed, and sulking. The painting is entitled *Cicero Denounces Catiline*, by Cesare Maccari (1840–1919), who created it in 1888.

Grant, Michael (tr.). *Selected Political Speeches of Cicero*. New York, 1969.

33. THE WOMEN OF ROME REFUSE TO BACK DOWN

INTRODUCTION

Roman women were probably as politically disadvantaged as Greek women: they could not vote; they could not hold public office; they could not attend and participate in the gatherings of the legislative bodies. And they usually could not take collective action to show their support for or displeasure with legal or political issues . . . usually.

But in 195 BCE, a striking exception occurred to the stay-at-home status to which most Roman women were restricted most of the time. In that year, a political debate was occurring about the possibility of repealing the Oppian Law of 215 BCE. This law, which was passed just after the disastrous Battle of Cannae (216) in the Second Punic War, placed severe restrictions on women's finery; specifically, it mandated that: (1) no woman could own more than a half ounce of gold; (2) no woman could wear multicolored clothing, especially that which was trimmed with purple; (3) no woman could ride in horse-drawn carriages, except during religious processions. The rationale for the passage of this law in 215 was probably that since Rome was in the midst of a desperate war against their bitter rival the city-state of Carthage, luxury goods had to be regulated, and perhaps even contributed to help fund the war effort. But by 195, the war was over, and so there was a concomitant longing for repeal of some of the restrictive wartime measures that had been enacted, including the Oppian Law. Accordingly, two tribunes, Marcus Fundanius and Lucius Valerius, proposed removing the law from the books. But two other tribunes, Marcus Junius Brutus and Publius Junius Brutus, threatened to veto the repeal effort, and that is when the sparks began to fly!

Our source for this chapter's fourth document, the historian Titus Livius (better known today as "Livy"), reports that when news of the veto threat spread, crowds of people flocked to the streets, both supporters and opponents of the repeal, to raucously make known their views. A large portion of the assemblage—astonishingly—was comprised of women! Angry, aggressive women. Livy says that they streamed out of their houses, even when forbidden by their husbands to do so, and blocked the streets. They accosted the men who opposed repeal, bitterly complaining that since better times had returned with the end of the war, the need for sumptuary laws had vanished. Day after day, the street demonstrations continued, and even grew larger and more vocal as women from the countryside and nearby towns joined in. Their boldness increased commensurately; they took their arguments directly to the leading officeholders of the government. The stage was set for a major public debate, filled with emotion and rancor.

KEEP IN MIND AS YOU READ

---

1. The Oppian Law was named for the politician who proposed it in 215, the tribune Gaius Oppius.
2. Although the crowds in the streets were both large and noisy (if Livy is to be believed), the formal debate about the fate of the Oppian Law involved only Marcus Porcius Cato (anti-repeal), Lucius Valerius (pro-repeal), and short, unrecorded speeches by the two tribunes who had threatened to veto the repeal.
3. Cato, the chief proponent and spokesman for the Oppian Law, was a formidable force in Roman politics for most of his adult life (he lived into his eighties). To openly oppose him on any issue would require a powerful mixture of fortitude, assertiveness, oratorical skill, and intelligence, and so it must have been a daunting task for someone like a mere tribune to take him on in a public debate. But Lucius Valerius seemed to be up to the task.

Document: Women in Roman Politics

angered plebeians once did: See the sidebar.

authority: The Latin word *auctoritas*, here translated as "authority," connotes more than simply authority, but also an aura of leadership, prestige, and influence that commands respect. No one would doubt Cato's *auctoritas*, which means that his views on the Oppian Law would be taken very seriously. As Valerius admits, Cato's *auctoritas*, even if "unexpressed would have had enough of weight."

Aventine: One of the famous Seven Hills of Rome.

Forum: A word equivalent to the Greek *agora*, referring to the downtown section of Rome. It is a generic word that referred to the downtown section of any Roman city or town.

Marcus Porcius Cato: Cato (234–149 BCE; also known as "Cato the Elder" and "Cato the Censor")

Amid the anxieties of [a recently-ended great war], an incident occurred, trivial to relate, but which, by reason of the passions it aroused, developed into a violent contention. Marcus Fundanius and Lucius Valerius, tribunes of the people, proposed to the [legislative] assembly the abrogation of the Oppian Law . . . [O]ne consul [remained] adamant, **Marcus Porcius Cato**, who spoke thus in favor of the law whose repeal was being urged.

"If each of us, citizens, had determined to assert his rights and dignity as a husband with respect to his own spouse, we should have less trouble with the sex as a whole. As it is, our liberty, destroyed at home by female violence, even here in the **Forum** is crushed and trodden underfoot, and because we have not kept them individually under control, we dread them collectively."

[Cato next argues that the magistrates of the city need to rein in the women, and that the assembly must defeat the repeal movement; for if the women were to win on this issue, it would set a dangerous precedent, and encourage them to take collective action again in the future.] "For myself, I could not conceal my blushes a while ago, when I had to make my way to the Forum through a crowd of women." [Cato follows up this condescending comment with a short history lesson—back in the day, women *never* behaved like this!—and then returns to an earlier point: if they are allowed to get away with this sort of behavior now, then heaven help us in the future!]

"If they win in this, what will they not attempt? Review all the laws with which your forefathers restrained their licentiousness and made them subject to their husbands. Even with all these bonds, you can scarcely control them. What of this? If you allow them to seize these bonds one by one and wrench themselves free and finally to be placed on a parity with their husbands, do you think that you will be able to endure them? The moment they begin to be your equals, they will be your superiors."

[Cato next defends the Oppian Law as reasonable and effective; what would be the point of discarding sound legislation? He argues that the law has yet to be passed which will please all of the people, all of the time. He then complains about what he sees as an objectionable and dangerous trend in Roman society toward luxury, extravagance, and wealth, things which will undermine the values of hard work, self-discipline, and moderation in which he believes so staunchly. He concludes by stating that the Oppian Law should by no means be repealed. Next, the tribunes who promised to veto the repeal effort made short speeches in support of Cato's position, and then Lucius Valerius, one of the tribunes who proposed the repeal, came to the speaker's platform.]:

"If only private citizens had come forward to support or oppose the measure which we have placed before you, I too, since I judged that enough had been said on each side, should have waited in silence for your ballots. Now, since that most influential man, the consul Marcus Porcius [Cato], has attacked our proposal not only with his **authority**, which unexpressed would have had enough of weight, but also in a long and carefully prepared speech, it is necessary to make a brief reply. And yet he used up more words in reproving the [women] than he did in opposing our bill . . ."

[Valerius next asserts that he will defend the legislative initiative rather than defending himself and Marcus Fundanius, whom Cato had accused of instigating the street demonstrations undertaken by the women. He repeats the argument that wartime legislation, like the Oppian Law, often has no relevance during times of peace. He reminds his listeners that the women's collective action is not without precedent, and that there are many notable examples in both distant and recent Roman history of women taking an active role in public life. Furthermore, failure to repeal this law would create an uncomfortable double standard: that Roman men would be permitted to wear multicolored clothing (including purple), but women would not. And then there is the matter of the women of Italian cities allied to Rome; the prohibition against owning or wearing gold or jewelry did not apply to them, so how would Roman women feel when they observed their near neighbors enjoying a privilege that was denied to

was one of the most famous individuals in all of Roman history. He wore many hats: farmer, soldier, politician, orator, author, defender of traditional Roman customs and values. Strict and rough-hewn, he would be remembered by later generations as one of the Romans of the old school, who lived his life by the disciplined codes he constantly preached. One of the traditional values he espoused was the notion that the husband/father was the unquestioned ruler of the household. (Note the first sentiment that Cato articulates in his speech: that if only the men of Rome had asserted their rights as husbands and kept their wives under control, this whole messy business could have been avoided.) As one of the consuls in 195 BCE, it would have come as absolutely no surprise to anyone that he stepped forward to defend the Oppian Law, and to sternly reprimand the women who came to demonstrate in favor of its repeal.

Sacred Mount: *Mons Sacer* in Latin, a country hill about three miles from Rome.

them? Finally, he makes the interesting argument that repealing the law would actually help to *restore* paternal control of a private household—a nice rebuttal to Cato's general complaint about the erosion of traditional Roman family values!—because matters of women's clothing, jewelry, and transportation in public could then be decided by individual husbands and fathers, and not by laws or politicians.]

"They [wives and daughters] prefer to have their finery under your [husbands' and fathers'] control and not the law's; you too should keep them in control and guardianship and not in slavery, and should prefer the name of father or husband to that of master. The consul a while ago used words intended to create prejudice when he spoke of female 'sedition' and 'secession.' For the danger, he tells you, is that they will seize the **Sacred Mount** or the **Aventine**, as the **angered plebeians once did**. In reality, their frail nature must endure whatever you decree. The greater the authority you exercise, the greater the self-restraint with which you should use your power." [Tr. Evan T. Sage. *Livy.* (34.1–5, 7.) Volume IX. LCL, 1935. Page numbers: 413, 415, 417, 419, 427, 439.]

AFTERMATH

According to Livy, after the last speech in the debate had been concluded, and it was time for the legislative assembly to begin its formal vote on the measure on the following day, "an even greater number of women appeared in public." Then, as if about to initiate siege operations, they marched directly to the doors of the two tribunes who had threatened to veto the repeal and did not leave until the two agreed to back off on their obstructive intentions. The voting then took place without incident, and the law was repealed.

WE ARE OUT OF HERE!

In the earliest days of the Republic (especially the fifth century BCE), Roman society was plagued by disputes between the ruling upper class—the patricians—and the subservient nonruling class—the plebeians. The patricians controlled much of the wealth and all of the political offices in those early days; the plebeians fought against this obvious (obvious to them, at any rate) injustice. The inequities seemed particularly acute given the fact that in military emergencies, when some foreign invader was threatening the city's safety, the plebeians were always the ones called upon to serve as soldiers. Because of their sacrifices for the common good, they desired and demanded political and legal equality with the patricians. The patricians, ever contemptuous of those whom they did not consider to be social equals, resisted.

One of the most effective weapons the plebeians employed in what might be called their civil rights struggle was the *secessio*, a withdrawal from the city, in which all the plebeians would march out of Rome in a group, often to the Aventine Hill, or perhaps the Sacred Mount. There they would remain, refusing to serve as soldiers or cooperate in any other way with the patrician-led government until they gained concessions of one sort or another. There were five known secessions between 494 and 287 BCE (although some scholars doubt the historical authenticity of the earliest ones).

The possibility that such a radical action might be used by the women must have been pure anathema to politicians like Cato. He apparently thought that by referencing plebeian secessions in his anti-repeal speeches, and capitalizing on the fear such a reference could generate, he might be able to sway enough votes in the legislative assembly to prevent the repeal effort from succeeding.

A similar "group effort" undertaken by women occurred many years later, in 42 BCE, during the time when civil war had broken out after the assassination of Julius Caesar. The cash-strapped triumvirate in charge of the government had decided to impose a war tax on 1,400 of the richest women in the city. These women were enraged over this decree and ultimately marched to the Forum to make known their displeasure. They had chosen as their spokesperson Hortensia, the daughter of one of the foremost orators in Roman history, Quintus Hortensius. She made a very persuasive speech in which she pointed out the injustice of requiring women to pay a war tax of any amount, arguing that it was unfair for women to pay such a tax when they had no voice generally in the government or in military affairs, and considering that the women did nothing to initiate hostilities in this instance, and had neither share nor say in how the war was conducted. The triumvirs (Mark Antony, Octavian [the future emperor Augustus], and Lepidus) backed off; they reduced the number of women affected by the decree from 1,400 to 400, and they placed a similar tax on all men of wealth. The first-century CE author and orator Quintilian remarked that Hortensia's speech was still being read and studied in his time.

ASK YOURSELF

1. Why do you suppose Livy uses the words "trivial to relate" to describe the controversial events surrounding the repeal of the Oppian Law?
2. What do you think were Cato's strongest arguments for retaining the Oppian Law? What were Valerius's strongest arguments for repealing it?
3. In his biography of Cato, Plutarch states that Cato was a kind and considerate husband and father who thought it was nothing short of a sacrilege for a man to beat his wife or his children. The biographer also writes that Cato considered it more important to be a good husband than a great political leader. Given these attitudes, does there seem to be a disconnect between Cato's love and respect for his wife and the perhaps antifemale slant of his speech? Why or why not?

TOPICS TO CONSIDER

- One of the enduring problems for modern historians studying ancient texts involves the analysis and interpretation of speeches. In many cases, an ancient historian who recorded a speech was not present when the speech was made; often, he was not even alive at the time. Livy, for example, was born about 135 years after the debate over the Oppian Law, and some modern historians have questioned the accuracy of his accounts of the speeches of Cato and Valerius. Since there is probably no way to know for certain about the reliability of the information in these speeches, how are we to interpret them? Do we discount them entirely? Take them with the proverbial grain of salt? Assume that the general outline of the speeches is accurate, while acknowledging that Livy has not given us verbatim accounts (since the original, complete texts of the speeches from 195 likely were not available to him)? Or is there some other approach we could take?
- Cato expresses great concern, and even trepidation, about these women "taking it to the street" to express their displeasure over the possible defeat of the repeal. He is fearful that if they are not stopped here and now, there will be no limit to their outrageous behavior in the future. As Livy tells us,

the repeal was passed. Did Cato's fears come true? In the subsequent decades and centuries of Roman history, were female uprisings common?

⤶ Cato refers to "all the laws with which your forefathers restrained their [i.e., the women's] licentiousness and made them subject to their husbands." Unfortunately, he does not cite any specific laws. Research this issue, and see if you can find information about any of these laws. Were they as restrictive as Cato claims?

⤶ One of the main arguments put forth by Lucius Valerius for the repeal of the Oppian Law is that laws passed under the duress of wartime conditions are often unneeded once peace has returned. Can you think of any examples of the same situation (i.e., restrictive wartime legislation, later repealed) in American history, especially during World War II?

Further Information

Bauman, Richard A. *Women and Politics in Ancient Rome.* New York, 1992.

Pomeroy, Sarah B. *Goddesses, Whores, Wives, and Slaves: Women in Classical Antiquity.* New York, 1975.

Website

"The Roman Matron of the Late Republic and Early Empire," by Sarah B. Pomeroy: http://www2.stetson.edu/~psteeves/classes/pomeroy.html

Bibliography for Document

Sage, Evan T. (tr.). *Livy.* Volume IX. [LCL.] London and Cambridge, 1935.

RELIGION

34. Squabbling among the Gods Was a Major Headache for Zeus

INTRODUCTION

What percentage of human life is the result of divine intervention, and the plans and will of a god, and what percentage is a consequence of free will, and the choices that humans make? To what degree, if any, are divine beings involved in human events? These are questions that interested the ancient Greeks, and they are questions that still resonate. Homer would probably have come down on the side of "activist" gods, as the document below suggests.

KEEP IN MIND AS YOU READ

1. The document is drawn from Book 20 of Homer's *Iliad*, his epic poem about the final days of the Trojan War, Greeks against Trojans.
2. Throughout the *Iliad*, Homer makes it clear that the gods took sides in the war, with a majority favoring the Greeks but some supporting the Trojans. Disputes among the gods over the events of the war were frequent; it was the responsibility of Zeus, king of the gods, to mediate these disputes. Often, Zeus himself was the focus of bitter criticism from the other gods, usually because of his real or perceived bias favoring or opposing the Greeks, or the Trojans, or some of the gods over others.
3. In Book 8 of the *Iliad*, Zeus had forbidden the gods to engage in direct involvement in the war. But here in Book 20, he is summoning a council of the gods, in which he will retract his former prohibition and allow them once again to interfere as they please.

Document: Disputatious Greek Gods and Goddesses

Zeus ordered **Themis**, from the summit of rugged Olympus, to call the gods to Assembly, and she went the rounds and summoned them to his Palace. Excepting **Ocean**, not a single River stayed away, nor did any of the Nymphs

Achaeans: Homer never refers to the Greeks as "Greeks" in the *Iliad*. Instead, he uses the more or less interchangeable terms Achaeans, Argives, and Danaans; Achaeans is the most common.

Aphrodite: Goddess of love and marriage.

Ares: The god of war, disliked by the other divinities.

Artemis: Hunter goddess, and twin sister of Apollo.

Callicolone: A word that literally means "beautiful hill." References to this hill appear only twice in the entire *Iliad*, and both in Book 20: here and a few lines later. The exact location of Callicolone is unknown.

Cloud-compeller: One of the many sky- and weather-related epithets associated with Zeus.

from which I can enjoy the spectacle: There has been some scholarly discussion about Zeus's intent here, but the consensus seems to be that he is referring not to the upcoming battle between Greeks and Trojans, but rather to the inevitable squabbles among the gods and goddesses.

Hephaestus: The lame, limping blacksmith god, and the god of fire. Homer often depicts Hephaestus as a skilled builder and artisan. It was Hephaestus who fabricated Achilles's magnificent shield (see above).

Hera and Pallas Athena: Hera was the wife of Zeus and perhaps the most partisan of the pro-Greek divinities. Athena was a warrior goddess and the patron of the city of Athens.

Hermes: The wing-footed messenger of the gods.

Leto: Mother of Artemis and Apollo.

Ocean: According to Greek mythology, Ocean, or Oceanus, was a

that haunt delightful woods, the sources of streams, and the grassy water-meadows. They all came to the **Cloud-compeller's** house and sat down in the marble gallery that **Hephaestus** the great Architect had made for Father Zeus.

When all had foregathered in the Palace, the Earthshaker **Poseidon** . . . inquired what purpose Zeus might have in mind. "Lord of the Lightning Flash," he said, "why have you ordered the gods to assemble? Are you concerned for the Trojans and **Achaeans**, who at this moment are about to come to grips once more?"

"Lord of the Earthquake," replied Zeus, "you have read my mind aright and know why I have summoned this gathering. They do concern me, even in their destruction. Nevertheless, I propose to stay here and seat myself in some Olympian glen **from which I can enjoy the spectacle**. The rest of you have my permission to join the Trojans and Achaeans, and to give your help to either side as your sympathies dictate." . . . These words from the Son of Cronos unleashed the dogs of war. The immortals at once set out for the scene of action in two hostile groups. **Hera and Pallas Athena** made their way to the Achaean fleet. So did Poseidon, the Girdler of the World, and **Hermes**, the Bringer of Luck and the cleverest wonder-worker of them all. Hephaestus followed them, exulting in his enormous strength, for though he limped he was active enough on his slender legs. To the Trojan side went **Ares** in his flashing helmet, **Phoebus** of the Flowing Hair, **Artemis** the Archeress, **Leto**, the **River Xanthus**, and laughter-loving **Aphrodite**.

Up to the moment when the gods came down among the men, the Achaeans carried all before them . . . But the scene changed when the Olympians reached the field and **Strife** the great Battle-maker rose in all her strength. For though Athena raised the war cry . . . she was answered on the other side by Ares, who raged like a black squall and incited the Trojans by the piercing cries he gave, at one moment from the heights of the citadel, and at the next from the banks of **Simois**, as he ran along the slopes of **Callicolone**.

Thus the blessed gods threw the two forces at each other's throats and at the same time opened a grievous breach in their own ranks. Up on high the Father of men and gods [i.e., Zeus] thundered ominously, and down below, Poseidon caused the wide world and the lofty mountain-tops to quake . . . Thus they went to war, god against god. [Tr. E. V. Rieu. *Homer: The Iliad.* (*Iliad*, Book 20.) Penguin Books, 1950. Page numbers: 366, 367, 368.]

AFTERMATH

The remainder of Book 20 features successive battles between perhaps the Trojans' two best fighters—Aeneas and Hector—and the "best of the Achaeans," the mighty warrior Achilles. The first confrontation pitted Aeneas against Achilles. Achilles would have defeated him, had it not been for the god Poseidon, who feared for Aeneas's safety and, at a critical moment, whisked him away from the battlefield.

Hector next took on the fierce Achilles. Hector's first move was to cast a spear at his adversary, but once more, divine intervention came into play; the goddess Athena blew on the spear in its flight and caused it to boomerang back to Hector and land at his feet! Achilles then took the offensive and charged at Hector, spear in hand, but this time, Apollo was the Olympian who blunted the attack, by hiding Hector in a mist. Four times, Achilles unsuccessfully attempted to dispatch his Trojan opponent; each time, Apollo's mist prevented a direct hit.

As Book 20 ends, Achilles contented himself by embarking on a violent onrush against the Trojans whom he *could* see, and killed many of them.

ASK YOURSELF

1. Homer writes that nearly all the gods and goddesses participated in the council. Which ones does he name? Which of these sided with the Greeks? Which with the Trojans?
2. In the council, the first one to speak to Zeus was Poseidon. Is there any significance to this? Many powerful gods and goddesses attended—all of them, in fact—so why did Poseidon have the distinction of speaking first?
3. Note the following epithets: Girdler of the World (for Poseidon); Bringer of Luck (Hermes); Flashing Helmet (Ares); Flowing Hair (Phoebus [Apollo]); Archeress (Artemis); Laughter-loving (Aphrodite). In what way is each epithet appropriate to the god or goddess to whom it applies?

great stream of water that surrounded the world. In his famous description of Achilles's shield, in Book 18, Homer portrayed Oceanus as encircling the rim of the shield.

Phoebus: A common epithet for the sun-god, Apollo. Gods and goddesses are sometimes (as here) referenced by their epithets instead of their names.

Poseidon: God of the sea and earthquakes, and the brother of Zeus.

River Xanthus: The name of the river that flows past Troy. Homer says that the name Xanthus is used by the gods but that mortals refer to it as the Scamander. Xanthus is also the name of the god of this river.

Simois: A river near Troy in whose vicinity many battles were fought. The god of this river was also called Simois.

Strife: The goddess Eris, who rolled the famed Golden Apple, inscribed with the phrase "For The Most Beautiful," in among the wedding guests at the marriage of Peleus and Thetis. This sparked the quarrel among Aphrodite, Athena, and Hera over which of them was the rightful claimant to the apple.

Themis: Daughter of Zeus and a goddess of prophecy.

TOPICS TO CONSIDER

- Why do you suppose Oceanus was the only deity, out of all of the gods and goddesses, not to attend the council?
- Homer does not explain, at least in Book 20, why some gods favor the Greeks and others the Trojans. Sometimes, the reason is clear. Aphrodite, for example, is the mother of Aeneas, a Trojan warrior, so it comes as no surprise that she sides with the Trojans. But what about the others? Is there any way to discover the reasons for their loyalties?

- ❧ What do you make of the idea that even the rivers had gods specifically assigned to them (e.g., Xanthus and Simois)? What seems to be the primary role(s) of these river gods? It will probably be necessary to read the remainder of Book 20 in order to formulate an answer to these questions.
- ❧ Why do you suppose Zeus is content to simply sit back and "enjoy the spectacle" of battle, without taking part?
- ❧ The god Hephaestus has kind of a checkered reputation in Greek mythology. He is certainly respected for his blacksmithing and metal-working skills, and yet, he is often the butt of many a joke, a kind of buffoonish character. How does Homer delineate him in the *Iliad*, both in the document and elsewhere, especially in Book 18?

Further Information

Edwards, Mark W. *The Iliad: A Commentary*. Volume V: Books 17–20. Cambridge, 1991. (A heavy-duty commentary, but worth looking at.)

Fagles, Robert (tr.). *Homer: The Iliad*. New York, 1990. (This translation offers a lengthy and informative introduction.)

Wace, A. J. B. and F. H. Stubbings. *A Companion to Homer*. London, 1962.

Website

Summary of Iliad Book 20. http://ancienthistory.about.com/od/trojanwarinlit/a/IliadXX.htm

Bibliography for Document

Rieu, E. V. (tr.). *Homer: The Iliad*. Baltimore, 1950.

35. King Croesus Consults—and Bribes? —the Delphic Oracle

INTRODUCTION

Oracles were always an important part of Greek (and Roman) religion. The word "oracle" is related to the Latin word for "mouth" or "speech," and those associations capture the essence of what an oracle was: a god's reply to a question posed by a believer. Oracular shrines, housing priests or priestesses who would assist in the relaying of the divine response to mortal ears, were common throughout the Greco-Roman world and much referenced in ancient literature. The most famous of these oracular shrines was undoubtedly the one located in the remote mountain town of Delphi, in Greece. The Delphic Oracle, sacred to the god Apollo, attracted pilgrims from all over the ancient world over the course of many centuries. The first document in this chapter provides an account of one of these pilgrimages.

KEEP IN MIND AS YOU READ

1. The Greek historian Herodotus (490–425 BCE) is our source for this document.
2. Croesus, the sixth-century BCE proverbially wealthy ruler of the kingdom of Lydia, in Asia Minor, had a problem. His land was facing an onslaught led by the powerful king of the Persians, Cyrus the Great, and Croesus was not quite certain about how to combat the threat. So he sent messengers to the Oracle at Delphi and to five other Greek oracles as well: "to Abae in Phocis, to Dodona, to the oracles of Amphiaraus and Trophonius, and to Branchidae," according to Herodotus, as well as to the Libyan oracle of Ammon, hoping for help and information.
3. The Delphic Oracle had something of an international flavor; not only Greeks, but also other peoples, consulted its priestesses for help and advice.

Document: An Oracular Consultation

Cyrus had destroyed the empire of **Astyages**, and the power of Persia was steadily increasing. This gave Croesus food for thought, and he wondered if he might be able to check Persian expansion before it had gone too far. [Next comes the account of the oracles he consulted, as described above in "Keep in Mind as

You Read."] His object was to test the knowledge of the oracles, so that if they should prove to be in possession of the truth he might send a second time and ask if he should undertake a campaign against Persia.

The Lydians whom Croesus sent to make the test were given the following orders: on the hundredth day, reckoning from the day on which they left **Sardis**, they were to consult the oracles, and inquire what Croesus ... was doing at that moment. The answer of each oracle was to be taken down in writing and brought back to Sardis. No one has recorded the answer of any of the oracles except that of Delphi; here ... the Priestess gave them ... the following reply:

> ... *The smell has come to my sense of a hard-shelled tortoise*
> *Boiling and bubbling with lamb's flesh in a bronze pot.*
> *The cauldron underneath is of bronze, and of bronze the lid.*

The Lydians took down the **Priestess' answer** and returned with it to Sardis.

When the other messengers came back with the answers they had received, Croesus opened all the rolls and read what they contained. None had the least effect on him except the one which contained the answer from Delphi ... [H]e accepted it with profound reverence, declaring that the oracle at Delphi was the only genuine one in the world, because it had succeeded in finding out what he had been doing. And indeed it had; for after sending off the messengers, Croesus had thought of something which no one would be likely to guess, and with his own hands, keeping carefully to the prearranged date, had cut up a tortoise and a lamb and boiled them together in a bronze cauldron with a bronze lid ...

Croesus now attempted to win the favor of the Delphian Apollo by a magnificent sacrifice. Of every kind of appropriate animal he slaughtered three thousand; he burnt in a huge pile a number of precious objects—couches overlaid with gold or silver, golden cups, tunics, and other richly colored garments—in the hope of binding the god more closely to his interest. And he issued a command that every Lydian was also to offer a sacrifice according to his means. After this ceremony, he melted down an enormous quantity of gold into one hundred and seventeen ingots [each weighing over 100 pounds. Additionally, he ordered an image of a solid gold lion to be fabricated; weight: 570 pounds]. ...

This was by no means all that Croesus sent to Delphi; there were also two huge mixing-bowls, one of gold which was placed on the right-hand side of the entrance to the temple, the other of silver, on the left ... In addition, Croesus sent four silver casks ... and two sprinklers for lustral water, one of gold, the other of silver ... There were many other gifts of no great importance, including round silver basins, but I must not forget to mention a figure of a woman, in gold, four and a half feet high, said by the Delphians to represent the woman who baked Croesus' bread. Lastly, he sent his own wife's necklaces and girdles. These, then, were the offerings which Croesus sent to Delphi ...

The Lydians who were to bring the presents to the temples were instructed by Croesus to ask the oracles if he should

---

Astyages: King of the Median Empire, who ruled for 35 years before being dethroned by Cyrus in 550 BCE. He was the grandfather of Cyrus, and had tried to put Cyrus to death when the latter was an infant because of an oracular prophecy. No wonder that many years later, Cyrus wanted to oust him from his kingship!

Priestess' answer: Answers to questions put to the Delphic oracle were delivered via the priestesses who tended the shrine.

Sardis: Capital city of Lydia, famous for the quality of its handcrafted products and also noted for its gold and silver coins, the first city in the ancient world to produce such coinage.

stater: A commonly used gold coin.

TWO NON-ORACULAR DELPHIC CLAIMS TO FAME

An uncertain number of maxims were carved into the columns and other portions of Apollo's temple at Delphi. Three of these sayings—often attributed to the Seven Sages—have achieved lasting fame: "Know yourself"; "Nothing in excess"; "Be a guarantor for debts (like a co-signer for a loan, in modern times), and ruin is at hand."

Also, Delphi was famous for the quadrennial Pythian Games held within its precincts, an athletic competition second only to the Olympics in fame and prestige. The stadium where the footraces were held is of particular interest. It was carved into the side of a steep mountain in an area barely long enough to accommodate the *stade* race (about 220 yards). At the far end, where the finish line was located, there was very little space between that line and a solid wall of mountain rock, so sprinters must have had to put on the brakes very quickly at the end of the race to avoid slamming directly into the wall!

---

undertake the campaign against Persia . . . On their arrival, therefore, they offered the gifts with the proper ceremony and put their question in the following words: "Croesus . . . has given you gifts such as your power of divination deserves, and now asks if he should march against Persia . . ." To this question, [the oracle] . . . foretold that if Croesus attacked the Persians, he would destroy a great empire . . .

Croesus was overjoyed when he learned the answer . . . and was fully confident of destroying the power of Cyrus. To express his satisfaction, he sent a further present to Delphi of two gold **staters** for every man . . . The Delphians in return granted in perpetuity to Croesus and the people of Lydia the right of citizenship for any who wished, together with exemption from dues, front seats at state functions, and priority in consulting the oracle. [Tr. Aubrey de Selincourt. *Herodotus: The Histories.* (1.47–54.). Penguin Books, 1954. Page numbers: 57, 58, 59, 60.]

AFTERMATH

As Herodotus explains, "Croesus was overjoyed when he learned the answer which the oracles" gave, and so he make plans to attack the Persians, disregarding or forgetting the fact that Apollo's oracular responses were often ambiguous; by attacking the Persians, Croesus *did* destroy a great empire: his own! For Cyrus and his army ultimately besieged and occupied Sardis; Croesus was taken prisoner. According to the biographer Plutarch, Cyrus was about to have Croesus executed, when Croesus three times cried out the name "Solon," the famous Athenian legislator/philosopher/businessman. Solon had visited Croesus some time before and had tried to teach him that no one can be considered truly happy until death, because only then can an assessment be made of the quality of that person's life. Croesus had thought that that was ridiculous, and that money and possessions, temporal things, equate to happiness. But in the end, he had lost all of his fabulous wealth and was about to lose his life; too late, he saw the value of Solon's words. But Cyrus was so impressed with this idea, and with other things that Croesus told him, that he decided to spare the life of the Lydian king.

ASK YOURSELF

1. If the Oracle of Apollo at Delphi was the most prestigious Greek oracle, why do you suppose Croesus bothered also to send messengers to six other oracles?

2. Does Herodotus give us any indication of whether he believes in pronouncements from the Delphic Oracle, either on this occasion or any time?

3. Describe the contents of the "magnificent sacrifice" that Croesus ordered to be prepared in honor of Apollo. What does this tell us about the wealth of Croesus and his kingdom?

4. Why do you think Herodotus refers to "round silver basins," the golden statue of Croesus's bread baker, and the necklaces and girdles of Croesus's wife as "gifts of no importance"?

TOPICS TO CONSIDER

- What do you suppose accounts for the enduring longevity, credibility, and popularity of the Oracle of Apollo at Delphi? After all, its often ambiguous responses could lead questioners astray, or even to ruin, as in the case of Croesus.

- When Croesus sent the messengers to the seven different oracles, with the test about his activities on the hundredth day, Herodotus tells us that the Oracle at Delphi was the only one to come up with the correct response. How could the priestesses, or the god, or whoever, possibly have known what Croesus had been doing on that day (boiling the turtle/lamb soup in a bronze cauldron)?

- Herodotus informs us that after the messengers returned from Delphi with the news that the oracle had correctly described Croesus's hundredth-day activities, Croesus immediately began busying himself with assembling "a magnificent sacrifice" in honor of Apollo. What do you suppose was his purpose in preparing such a treasure trove of expensive gifts? Could it have been a bribe for another favorable response? Or something else? Can you think of any modern examples or instances where a person might say a prayer to God or some other divine or supernatural being, along with an offer to perform some service, in exchange for the prayer being answered favorably?

Further Information

Broad, William J. *The Oracle: Ancient Delphi and the Science Behind Its Lost Secrets.* New York, 2006.

Burkert, Walter. *Greek Religion* (tr. into English by John Raffan.) Cambridge, MA, 1985.

Fontenrose, Joseph Eddy. *The Delphic Oracle: Its Responses and Operations, with a Catalogue of Responses.* Berkeley, CA, 1978.

Website

Delphi. www.delphi-site.com/mobile.html

Bibliography for Document

Blanco, Walter (tr.). *Herodotus: The Histories.* New York, 1992.

de Selincourt, Aubrey (tr.). *Herodotus: The Histories.* Baltimore, 1954.

Godley, A. D. (tr.). *Herodotus.* Volume I. [LCL.] Cambridge and London, 1920.

Matz, David. *Ancient World Lists and Numbers: Numerical Phrases and Rosters in the Greco-Roman World.* Jefferson, NC, 1995.

36. Julius Caesar Becomes a God

INTRODUCTION

The Roman poet Publius Ovidius Naso ("Ovid"; 43 BCE–17 CE) was the author of a wide variety of works, especially love poems. The document is excerpted from his long epic poem about Greek and Roman mythology: *Metamorphoses*.

KEEP IN MIND AS YOU READ

1. Ovid's *Metamorphoses* consists of a collection of many mythological stories, retold in poetic form. Their common theme: some kind of transformation. Most of the entries in the collection are focused on Greek mythology, but the final few selections are purely Roman. The document relates Ovid's description of the deification of Julius Caesar. This is the final scene portrayed in his *Metamorphoses*.
2. In the opening lines of his *Metamorphoses*, Ovid describes the work as a poem which encompasses all of human history.
3. The ancient Romans could and did adopt adults into their families, especially as sons. Julius Caesar did this with his grand-nephew, whose original name was simply Gaius Octavius. When Caesar's will was read after his assassination, it was revealed that he had adopted young Octavius (he was about 18 years of age at the time) as his son. As a result, Octavius acquired his adoptive father's full name—Gaius Julius Caesar—along with his own family name, Octavius, appended in a slightly different form, Octavianus. So his full name became Gaius Julius Caesar Octavianus. The Roman Senate granted him the honorary title "Augustus" in 27 BCE, and it is by this name that he is probably most commonly known today.

Document: From Mortal to God

Caesar is a god in his own land. The first in wars and peace, he rose by wars, which closed in triumphs, and by civic deeds to glory quickly won, and even more his offspring's love exalted him as a new, a heavenly, sign and brightly flaming star. Of all the achievements of great Julius Caesar not one is more ennobling

glorious son: Julius Caesar had no biological sons. The "glorious son" referenced here is his son by adoption, Gaius Julius Caesar Octavianus, better known as Octavian and later as Augustus.

Nestor's years: Nestor was the proverbially old chieftain who accompanied the Greeks to Troy during the Trojan War.

offspring born: Augustus and his wife Livia did not have any surviving sons, so Augustus was succeeded by his stepson Tiberius, Livia's son by a previous marriage. The phrase "offspring born" refers to Tiberius.

peace established: Augustus was widely credited with founding the *Pax Romana*, "Roman peace," a long period of relative tranquility after the bloody and destructive civil wars of the 40s and 30s BCE.

wise laws: As emperor, Augustus introduced many legal, political, military, and social reforms into Roman life. A full description of these enactments can be found in the *Life of Deified Augustus*, written by the Roman biographer Suetonius (ca. 70–140 CE), especially in Chapters 29 through 56.

to his fame than being father of his **glorious son**. Was it more glorious for him to subdue the Britons . . . or lead his fleet victorious[ly in Egypt] . . . to have some triumphs and deserve far more, than to be the father of so great a man, with whom as ruler of the human race, O gods, you bless us past all reckoning?

And [to prevent that son from being considered a mere mortal], Julius Caesar must change and be a god. [Next, the goddess Venus appears; she fears that Caesar, a descendant of her son Aeneas, the long-ago founder of the Roman race, might fall victim to an assassination plot, and so she appeals to all the gods to prevent such a tragedy. The gods are sympathetic but helpless, because even they are not strong enough to alter the dictates of fate. The king of the gods, Jupiter, reassures her that Caesar's adopted son Augustus will avenge the inevitable assassination and usher in a Golden Age in Rome. Jupiter speaks]: "With **peace established** over all the lands, he then will turn his mind to civil rule and as a prudent legislator will enact **wise laws**. And he will regulate the manners of his people by his own example. Looking forward to the days of future time and of posterity, he will command the **offspring born** of his devoted wife, to assume the imperial name and the burden of his cares. Nor till his age shall equal **Nestor's years** will he ascend to heavenly dwellings and his kindred stars. Meanwhile transform the soul [i.e., of Julius Caesar], which shall be reft from this doomed body, to a starry light, that always god-like Julius may look down in future from his heavenly residence upon our Forum and our Capitol."

Jupiter had hardly pronounced these words, when kindly Venus, although seen by none, stood in the middle of the Senate-house, and caught from the dying limbs and trunk of her own Caesar his departing soul. She did not give it time so that it could dissolve in air, but bore it quickly up, toward all the stars of heaven; and on the way, she saw it gleam and blaze and set it free. Above the moon it mounted into heaven, leaving behind a long and fiery trail, and as a star it glittered in the sky. There, wondering at the younger Caesar's [i.e., Augustus's] deeds, Julius confessed that they were superior to all of his, and he rejoiced because his son was greater even than himself. [Tr. Brookes Otis. *Ovid: Metamorphoses 15*. http://www.theoi.com/Text/OvidMetamorphoses15.html]

AFTERMATH

"If the pronouncements of prophets contain any truth, I will live on in fame, throughout all the future generations." These are the final words of Ovid's *Metamorphoses*, and they reflect the notion shared by many Greek and Roman authors that their written works would last forever. In Ovid's case, at least, that prophecy still rings true.

ASK YOURSELF

1. What does Ovid mean by the phrase "he [Julius Caesar] rose by wars"?
2. What reason or justification does Ovid give for the deification of Julius Caesar?
3. The general theme of Ovid's *Metamorphoses* involves the concept of change, or transformation. How does the deification of Caesar fit into this theme? Into what was he transformed?

TOPICS TO CONSIDER

- Lucius Annaeus Seneca (sometimes called the "Younger Seneca," 4 BCE– 65 CE) is generally thought to be the author of a parody of the deification process of emperors. Its title: *Apocolocyntosis*, a play on the formal word for deification—apotheosis—and roughly translated as "Pumpkinification." Read Seneca's *Apocolocyntosis* (it is very short!). What elements of satire and parody do you notice in it? Which Roman emperor's apotheosis is Seneca mocking? Are there any similarities between Seneca's satire and Ovid's account of Caesar's apotheosis? (A translation of the *Apocolocyntosis* may be found at http://ancienthistory .about.com/library/bl/bl_text_seneca_apocol.htm.)

- In our culture we seldom, if ever, hear of families adopting full-grown adults as their sons or daughters. Why do you suppose the ancient Romans did this? What would be the advantages?

- Several of the first-century CE Roman emperors were deified, including Augustus, Claudius, Vespasian, and Titus. Many subsequent emperors also received this honor. Still others demanded to be worshipped as gods while they lived but were never formally granted deification after their deaths. Research this issue. What seem to be the prime requirements for deification? What are the procedures involved in declaring an emperor a god? Can you think of any modern societies or nations in which the leader is regarded as a god, or almost a god?

- In the document excerpt, Ovid clearly writes a very favorable, even flattering, account of Augustus and his deeds. Yet early in the first century CE, Augustus decreed that Ovid be exiled from Rome for life. The poet was sent to live in the region of the Black Sea, a wild, uncultured place and an extremely hostile environment for a man of Ovid's sophistication and elegance. Although he begged on a number of occasions to be allowed to return to Rome, Augustus never relented. Find out why Augustus apparently decided that Ovid should receive such a terrifying punishment. (The true reason is uncertain, but it is quite easy to draw conclusions.) Are there similar, modern examples of authors being forced to leave their homes and go into exile or hiding because of something they had written?

- Read over the sections of Suetonius's biography of Augustus referenced above. Do you agree with Ovid's assessment that he was a "prudent legislator" who "enact[ed] wise laws"?

Further Information

Boyle, A. J. and J. P. Sullivan (eds.). *Roman Poets of the Early Empire*. London, 1991.

Frankel, Herman. *Ovid: A Poet between Two Worlds*. Berkeley, CA, 1945.

Galinsky, G. K. *Ovid's Metamorphoses: An Introduction to the Basic Aspects*. Berkeley and Los Angeles, 1975.

Otis, Brooks. *Ovid as an Epic Poet*. Cambridge, 1996.

Website

Extensive bibliography for Ovid: http://uts.cc.utexas.edu/~silver/Ovid/ovid-biblio.html

Bibliography for Document

Humphries, Rolfe (tr.). *Ovid: Metamorphoses*. Bloomington, IN, 1955.

http://www.theoi.com/Text/OvidMetamorphoses15.html

37. Job Description for a Vestal Virgin

INTRODUCTION

In its earliest days, Rome was ruled by a series of seven kings. The second of these was Numa Pompilius (traditional dates of his reign: 714–671 BCE). The document is excerpted from Plutarch's biography of Numa.

KEEP IN MIND AS YOU READ

1. At least some of the early Roman kings were considered semilegendary, but Numa seems to be fairly well attested. He is credited with a number of religious reforms and innovations, including the establishment of various cult of priests and priestesses, religious rites, and the construction of temples.
2. One of the best known of the priestly cults that Numa reputedly founded was actually a cult of priestesses: the Vestal Virgins. Their job was to tend the temple of Vesta, the Roman goddess of home and hearth. There were six Vestals, each of whom was expected to serve a term of 30 years.

Document: A Vestal's Duties

To Numa is . . . ascribed the institution of that order of high priests who are called Pontifices, and he himself is said to have been the first of them . . .
[Plutarch next embarks upon an interesting discussion of the etymology of the word Pontifices (sg. Pontifex). The word might be derived from the Latin word *potens* ("powerful"), given that these priests were serving powerful gods. Another explanation, which Plutarch considered spurious, is that it came from a combination of the Latin words *pons* ("bridge") and *facere* ("to build"), a "bridge-builder." The pontifices numbered among their duties the performing of religious sacrifices at bridges over the Tiber River, and beyond that, they were also responsible for the maintenance of bridges.]

The chief of the Pontifices, the Pontifex Maximus, had the duty of expounding and interpreting the divine will, or rather of directing sacred rites,

fasces: The *fasces* carried by security officers called *lictors*. The *fasces* were rods bound together by leather straps, a symbol of Roman authority and power. Usually, only high-ranking government officials enjoyed protection from lictors, so the fact that they also accompanied Vestal Virgins in public is another example of the esteem and respect accorded to the Vestals.

right to make a will: The right to make a will was generally reserved for the *paterfamilias*, the father of the family.

Servius: Rome's sixth king (full name: Servius Tullius), who reigned ca. 579–535 BCE.

not only being in charge of public ceremonies, but also watching over private sacrifices and preventing any departure from established custom, as well as teaching whatever was requisite for the worship or propitiation of the gods. He was also overseer of the holy virgins called Vestals; for to Numa is ascribed the consecration of the Vestal Virgins, and in general the worship and care of the perpetual fire entrusted to their charge. It was either because he thought the nature of fire pure and uncorrupted, and therefore entrusted it to chaste and undefiled persons, or because he thought of it as unfruitful and barren, and therefore associated it with virginity . . .

In the beginning, then, they say that Gegania and Verenia were consecrated to this office by Numa, who subsequently added to them Canuleia and Tarpeia; that at a later time two were added by **Servius**, making the number [six] which has continued to the present time. It was ordained by the king that the sacred virgins should vow themselves to chastity for thirty years; during the first decade they are to learn their duties, during the second to perform the duties they have learned, and during the third to teach others these duties. Then, the thirty years being now passed, any one [of the priestesses] who wishes has the liberty to marry and adopt a different mode of life, after laying down her sacred office. We are told, however, that few have welcomed the indulgence, and that those who did so were not happy, but were a prey to repentance and dejection for the rest of their lives, thereby inspiring the rest with superstitious fears, so that until old age and death they remained steadfast in their virginity.

But Numa bestowed great privileges upon them, such as the **right to make a will** during the lifetime of their fathers, and to transact and manage their other affairs . . . When they appear in public, the **fasces** are carried before them, and if they accidentally meet a criminal on his way to execution, his life is spared; but the virgin must make oath that the meeting was involuntary and fortuitous, and not of design. He who passes under the litter on which they are borne is put to death. For their minor offenses, the virgins are punished with stripes, the Pontifex Maximus [chief priest, as mentioned above] sometimes scourging the culprit on her bare flesh, in a dark place, with a curtain interposed. But she that has broken her vow of chastity is buried alive . . . [Tr. Bernadotte Perrin. *Plutarch's Lives. Life of Numa* (9, 10). Volume I. LCL, 1914. Page numbers: 337, 339, 341, 343.]

AFTERMATH

Numa's long reign was characterized by an extended period of peace; Plutarch writes that "there is no record either of war, or faction, or political revolution while Numa was king." There was a temple in Rome dedicated to the two-faced Roman god Janus. This temple had double doors, and when these doors were open, it signified that the Romans were at war; when closed, that peace was upon the land. (The open doors indicated that the god

SAVED BY THE VESTALS

Plutarch writes that, should a Vestal Virgin have a chance encounter with a condemned criminal on his way to execution, the criminal's life would automatically be spared. Apparently, the Vestals' power to induce pardons went beyond the realm of mere chance. In his *Life of Julius Caesar*, the biographer Suetonius notes that when Caesar was a young man, he married a lady named Cornelia. This Cornelia hailed from a family who was at odds with the Roman dictator Sulla; Sulla pressured Caesar to divorce his new wife, but Caesar refused to comply. Accordingly, Caesar's name was placed on a hit list, with the result that he had to flee for his life. However, the Vestal Virgins, as well as some of Caesar's political allies, intervened on his behalf and prevailed upon Sulla to remove his name from the list. Sulla reluctantly did so.

had left his temple and the city, with the Roman army, to assist it in upcoming battles; the closed doors symbolized the opposite, that no wars were being fought.) Plutarch reports that from the beginnings of Rome, down to his own lifetime (a period of some 800 years), the temple doors had been shut only three times: once in 235 BCE, shortly after the end of the First Punic War; again after Augustus had defeated the forces of Mark Antony at the Battle of Actium in 30 BCE; and for a third time during the reign of Numa, when the doors were closed not for a brief period of time, but for the entirety of his reign.

ASK YOURSELF

1. What were the chief duties of the pontifices?
2. What privileges did the Vestal Virgins enjoy? What were they supposed to learn during each 3 of the 10-year increments of their terms as Vestals?
3. What punishment was prescribed for a Vestal Virgin who broke her vow of chastity?

TOPICS TO CONSIDER

- Plutarch generally wrote biographies in pairs—a famous Roman matched with a famous Greek. (Hence, the title *Parallel Lives* is sometimes given to his biographies.) His prime criteria for selecting the two individuals to be paired in this way were the similarities that each displayed. The Greek leader with whom Plutarch linked Numa was the Spartan king Lycurgus. Research the life of Lycurgus, and determine the commonalities between

WANTED: APPLICANTS FOR THE POSITION OF VESTAL VIRGIN

Would-be Vestal Virgins were required to fulfill some fairly unique and stringent requirements, as the essayist Aulus Gellius explains: "[I]t is unlawful for a girl to be chosen who is less than six, or more than ten years old; she must also have both father and mother living. She must be free too from any impediment in her speech, must not have impaired hearing, or be marked by any other bodily defect. She must not herself be freed from paternal control . . . [N]either one nor both of her parents may have been slaves or engaged in mean occupations . . . [T]he daughter of a man without residence in Italy must not be chosen." Aulus Gellius. *Attic Nights* 1.12; tr. Rolfe.]

him and Numa that likely led to Plutarch's decision to pair the two of them.

- ☙ Which of the two derivations of the word pontifex (*potens*, "powerful," or *pons/facere*, "bridge-builder") seems more logical? Why do you suppose Plutarch judged the second explanation to be ridiculously erroneous?
- ☙ Plutarch does not specify the kinds of duties the Vestal priestesses were required to perform. Find out what these duties were. Why did it take the priestesses 10 years to learn these duties?
- ☙ Plutarch writes that few Vestal Virgins married after their 30-year term of service was completed, even though it would have been permissible for them to do so. Why do you suppose most of them did not marry?

Further Information

Scheid, John. *An Introduction to Roman Religion*, translated by Janet Lloyd. Bloomington, IN, 2003.

Staples, Ariadne. *From Good Goddess to Vestal Virgins: Sex and Category in Roman Religion*. London, 1998.

Worsfold, T. Cato. *History of the Vestal Virgins of Rome*. Plymouth, UK, 1934.

Websites

Six Vestal Virgins. http://ancienthistory.about.com/cs/rome/a/aa1114001.htm

Vestal Virgins. http://www.unrv.com/culture/vestal-virgins.php

Bibliography for Document

Perrin, Bernadotte (tr.). *Plutarch's Lives*. Volume I. [LCL.] London and Cambridge, 1914.

Rolfe, John C. (tr.). *The Attic Nights of Aulus Gellius*. Volume I. [LCL.] Cambridge and London, 1927.

SAFETY

38. A Case of Assault and Battery

INTRODUCTION

The public career of ancient Athens' most famous lawyer and orator, Demosthenes (384–322 BCE), spanned over 40 years. Some 58 extant orations are credited to his name, although contemporary scholars consider several of these to have been produced by other speakers of the time. The speech *Against Conon*, however, is deemed to be genuine Demosthenes.

KEEP IN MIND AS YOU READ

1. Demosthenes's speeches and court cases can be conveniently divided into three categories: private speeches, involving matters such as inheritances, wills, debt payments, perjury, and assaults; semipublic speeches, argued on behalf of citizens directly involved in public affairs or public policy issues; and public speeches, in which orations are delivered to gatherings of citizens, on topics such as national security, military matters, and treaties. *Against Conon* clearly belongs in the first category, private speeches.
2. Two years before, while stationed at a military fort (Panactum) north of Athens, the young plaintiff, Ariston, had been viciously assaulted by the sons of a man named Conon; Demosthenes describes the attack in graphic detail. Then, when all of them had subsequently returned to Athens—with bad blood still apparently lingering—Ariston was assaulted again, by the same group of muggers, this time aided by several friends and even Conon himself.
3. Note that Demosthenes speaks in the voice of his client, Ariston.

Document: Demosthenes for the Prosecution

With gross outrage have I met ... at the hands of the defendant, Conon, and have suffered such bodily injury that for a very long time neither my relatives nor any of the attending physicians thought that I should survive. Contrary to expectation, however, I did recover and regain my strength, and then I brought

general: *Strategos* in Greek, from whence came our English words "strategy" and "strategic." The word had a more specific meaning in the Athenian democracy of the fifth century BCE. There, 10 military leaders were elected to one-year terms, 10 annually. So these 10 *strategoi* became very prominent in the affairs of the state, politically as well as militarily.

mess: The Greek word is *sussitoi*, literally "together/eat," or the people with whom one partakes of a meal; "messmates."

summary seizure; highwayman; indictments: Summary seizure: The technical term is *apagoge*, referring to the capture of a criminal in the act of doing the crime and bringing him before a magistrate. **Highwayman:** The Greek word is *lopodutes*, literally "someone who slips into someone else's clothes," a "clothes stealer." The word then broadened in meaning to refer to any kind of a thief or robber. **Indictments:** The technical term is *graphe*, from the word meaning "to write," and thence, a "written" statement.

taxiarchs: According to A. T. Murray, the taxiarchs were "commanders of the infantry detachments."

tent: The Greek word used by Demosthenes is *skene*, which was also a technical term from the world of ancient theater; it referred to the painted backdrop of a stage setting. Our word "scene" is a direct descendant of *skene*.

against him this action for the assault. All my friends and relatives, whose advice I asked, declared that for what he had done the defendant was liable to **summary seizure** as a **highwayman** or to public **indictments** for criminal outrage. But they urged and advised me not to take upon myself matters which I should not be able to carry, or to appear to be bringing suit for the maltreatment I had received in a manner too ambitious for one so young. I took this course, therefore, and, in deference to their advice, have instituted a private suit. [Demosthenes next implores the jury to listen with open minds to his description of Ariston's sufferings, and to his appeal for justice to be served. He then explains that Ariston had journeyed to Panactum, and that Conon's sons, who spent most of their afternoon and evening in their customary overconsumption of alcohol, had camped nearby.]

Well, at whatever time the others might be having their dinner, these men [i.e., Conon's sons] were already drunk and abusive, at first toward our . . . slaves, but in the end toward ourselves. For, alleging that the slaves annoyed them with smoke while getting dinner, or [inappropriately taunted them], or whatever else they pleased, they used to beat them . . . [T]here was nothing in the way of brutality and outrage in which they did not indulge. When we saw this, we were annoyed and at first [complained to] them, but they mocked at us, and would not [stop], and so our whole **mess** in a body—not I alone apart from the rest—went to the **general** and told him what was going on. He rebuked them with stern words, not only for their brutal treatment of us, but for their whole behavior in camp. Yet so far from desisting, or being ashamed of their acts, they burst in upon us that very evening, as soon as it grew dark, and, beginning with abusive language, they proceeded to beat me, and they made such a clamor and tumult about the **tent**, that both the general and the **taxiarchs** came and some of the other soldiers, by whose coming we were prevented from suffering, or ourselves doing, some damage that could not be repaired, being victims as we were of their drunken violence. When matters had gone thus far, it was natural that after our return home there should exist between us feelings of anger and hatred. However, on my own part I swear by the gods I never saw fit to bring an action against them, or to pay any attention to what had happened. I simply made this resolve: in future, to be on my guard, and to take care to have nothing to do with people of that sort.

[Tr. A. T. Murray. *Demosthenes: Private Orations.* (*Against Conon* 1; 4–6). Volume VI. LCL, 1939. Page numbers: 127, 129, 131.]

HOW MUCH WAS TOO MUCH?

The Greeks and Romans both enjoyed parties called *symposia*, literally, a "drinking together." These festive gatherings, usually held at private homes, involved discussions on popular or philosophical topics, as well as entertainments, music, and, of course, the consumption of wine, always mixed with water. (It was considered uncouth to consume unmixed wine.) Sometimes, the *symposia* could get out of hand, especially if the master of ceremonies—the symposiarch—failed to regulate the flow of wine, or if the party were "crashed" by unwelcome guests who were already inebriated. The latter event happened at a famous symposium hosted at the home of an Athenian named Agathon; the details are provided by Plato in his dialogue entitled *Symposium*. Well after the party had gotten underway, the flamboyant young man-about-town Alcibiades showed up, already drunk, and disrupted the proceedings by refusing to cooperate with the host's request that he contribute something relevant to the topic of discussion.

A fragment from a lost play by the comic playwright Eubulus (ca. fourth century BCE) gives us a hint about the standards governing the quantity of wine consumption at a symposium, or anywhere else, for that matter. The god of wine (fittingly enough) Dionysus is the speaker: "For sensible men, I prepare only three kraters [a krater was a large bowl in which the wine was mixed, and from which it was served]: one for health, which they drink first, the second for love and pleasure, and the third for sleep. After the third one is drained, wise men go home. The fourth krater is not mine anymore—it belongs to bad behavior; the fifth is for shouting; the sixth is for rudeness and insults; the seventh is for fights; the eighth is for breaking the furniture; the ninth is for depression; the tenth is for madness and unconsciousness."

[Symposium. http://en.wikipedia.org/wiki/Symposium]

It would appear that Conon and his sons, and their friends, customarily kept on drinking at least as far as the fourth round of kraters.

AFTERMATH

Demosthenes goes on to describe the second attack (two years later, after having returned to Athens) that Ariston suffered at the hands of Ctesias, son of Conon. Ariston was out for a walk in the agora with his friend Phanostratus, when the two of them were set upon by Ctesias and five named men, including Conon himself, as well as "a number of others." Ariston was nearly killed in the melee; to add insult to injury, one of the attackers "began to crow, mimicking fighting cocks that have won a battle, and his fellow [attackers egged him on to] flap his elbows against his sides like wings." Many witnesses were called, and many depositions read, to corroborate Ariston's case. Demosthenes reminded the jury that

CRACKING DOWN ON THE DRUNKS

A legislator by the name of Pittacus (ca. 650–570 BCE), from the city-state Mytilene (the chief city of the island of Lesbos in the Aegean Sea between Greece and Asia Minor), is best remembered for his law that doubled the punishment for any convicted defendant who committed his crimes while drunk. Aristotle writes that Pittacus believed intoxicated men were more prone to committing violent crimes, and that their antisocial behavior while drunk could not be condoned or excused with the argument that they did not know what they were doing while under the influence.

Pittacus was also noteworthy for his inclusion on the list of the famous Seven Sages of Greece.

Conon and his associates had never done any kind of useful service for Athens, but that they did have well-documented reputations for hard drinking, public brawling, and generally lawless behavior, whereas Ariston, by contrast, had always been a model citizen.

ASK YOURSELF

1. We have no indication within the document about whether Demosthenes won the case. But based upon the arguments he made, how likely do you think it is that he did prevail? Why or why not?

2. Imagine that you were the defense lawyer hired by Conon to defend him and his sons in this case. What arguments could you use in their defense? Our sources indicate that Ctesias (Conon's son) claimed that Ariston started the fight and then exaggerated the extent of his injuries. And in any event, he argued, it was not a real fight, but rather some innocent horseplay that got a little out of hand, sort of a "boys will be boys" scenario. Do you think this defense would be plausible? How could Demosthenes counter it?

3. According to Demosthenes, the general in charge of the fort, when informed of the brutality of Conon's sons, "rebuked them with stern words." Was this a sufficient response to the problem? If not, what more should the general have done? In an unquoted portion of the document, Demosthenes relates Ariston's opinion that Conon should have dealt with his sons' lawlessness. Would this have been an effective approach? Why or why not?

TOPICS TO CONSIDER

- The historian Xenophon (ca. 430–355 BCE) states in his *Memorabilia* that the following types of criminals are liable to the death penalty: thieves, highwaymen, kidnappers, and temple robbers [1.2.62]. Under that definition, Conon and his family would qualify for execution. What would be the arguments for and against the supreme penalty for these individuals?

- A. T. Murray, the translator of this passage, writes in an explanatory footnote: "[Since w]e are told by Aristotle . . . that young men of military age, in the second year of their training, patrolled the country and spent their spare time in forts [such as at Panactum], it may be that no formal military expedition is meant. In that case, the loose discipline [resulting in the kinds of destructive and anti-social behavior exhibited by Conon's sons] is more understandable." Is this a plausible explanation for their behavior? Would the jury likely be swayed? Are you?

Further Information

Bonner, B. J. *Lawyers and Litigants in Ancient Athens*. Chicago, 1927.

Carey, C. and R. A. Reid. *Demosthenes: Selected Private Speeches*. Cambridge, 1985. (Note: The speeches are in Greek; however, the English-language introductions and commentaries are informative and useful.)

Doherty, F. C. *Three Private Speeches of Demosthenes*. Oxford, 1927.

Kennedy, George. *The Art of Persuasion in Greece*. Princeton, 1963.

MacDowell, Douglas M. *The Law in Classical Athens*. London, 1978.

Website

Who Was Demosthenes? http://www.toastmasters.state.ct.us/demosthenes/resources/
whowasdemosthenes.htm

Bibliography for Document

Barker, Ernest (tr.). *The Politics of Aristotle*. Oxford, 1958.

Marchant, E. C. (tr.). *Xenophon: Memorabilia and Oeconomicus*. Volume IV. [LCL.]
Cambridge and London, 1923.

Murray, A. T. (tr.). *Demosthenes: Private Orations*. Volume VI. [LCL.] Cambridge and
London, 1939.

39. WOMEN? TAKING OVER THE ACROPOLIS?

INTRODUCTION

Women? Taking over the Acropolis? It would have been unthinkable, the epitome of lawless behavior in ancient Athens . . . had it ever happened. But no scenario, no topic, was too far-fetched for the fertile imagination of the comic playwright Aristophanes.

KEEP IN MIND AS YOU READ

1. Aristophanes's play *Lysistrata* was produced in 411 BCE. Just a few years before (415 to 413), the Athenians had undertaken one of the most ill-considered and disastrous actions of the long-enduring Peloponnesian War: an invasion of the faraway island of Sicily. This scheme had been promoted by some of the most reckless demagogues in the city, but despite the vacuity of their arguments, they were wildly successful in persuading a large majority of their fellow citizens to assent to it. One of the few to oppose the plan was the famous philosopher Socrates, whose reading of various omens indicated devastation for Athens. The invasion of Sicily resulted in the near complete destruction of the Athenian navy and ushered in the beginning of the end of the Athenian cause in the Peloponnesian War.

2. Part of Aristophanes's genius was his ability to create wildly improbable—or impossible—comic scenes and situations. He did this time and time again, but probably nowhere more outrageously than in *Lysistrata*. The very idea that women—mere *women*—could seize and occupy the Acropolis (the citadel of Athens and location of some of the most important religious shrines and public buildings in the city) would have been laughable, completely impossible in real-life Athens. But such a scenario was completely possible in the mind of Aristophanes. The leader of the assault was the title character, Lysistrata, whose name appropriately means "army dissolver."

3. Neither the Greeks nor the Romans had modern-style professional police forces to keep order and enforce the laws. The Athenians, however, maintained a quasi-police force made up of Scythian archers (see sidebar), under the general control of the *probouloi*, a "Committee of Ten for the Safety of the State." One of these 10 *probouloi*, the Magistrate, appears in the document.

4. Three women finally emerge from behind the protective gates of the Acropolis: Lysistrata and two of her co-conspirators, Calonice and Myrrhine. A fourth woman, Stratyllis, leader of a group of old women, also appears.

Document: Ill-Behaved Women

Adonis: A handsome young man beloved by the goddess Aphrodite (and therefore, presumably, also by mortal women). He was killed by wild boars.

Artemis: How appropriately ironic that Lysistrata should appeal to the bow-and-arrow-equipped huntress goddess Artemis, in her threat against the Scythian archer-policeman!

Assembly: The main legislative body in the Athenian democracy. All male citizens were eligible to participate in its debates, deliberations, and votes.

Cholozyges: According to Benjamin Rogers, Demostratus's nickname was *Bouzyges*, "Ox-Yoker," perhaps slightly pejorative, like the modern term "dirt farmer" or "sod buster." Aristophanes created a new nickname for the estimable Demostratus, *Cholozyges*, "Anger-Yoker." (Aristophanes was a master at fashioning neologisms, and this is yet another example.) The document translator, Alan Sommerstein, renders the word as "from Angeriae," his own neologism, which plays off the anger theme.

Demostratus was a leading demagogue of the time; in his biography of Nicias (chapter 12), Plutarch remarks that Demostratus was aggressively demonstrative in his support of the proposed Sicilian Expedition. Nicias, on the other hand, was one of the few prominent

(The situation: The women have successfully taken over the Acropolis, having just turned back a gaggle of ridiculously feeble old men who had tried to evict them. "As if in answer to their call, an elderly magistrate [a *proboulos*, as mentioned in "Keep in Mind as You Read"] of severe appearance enters, attended by four Scythian policemen. The women . . . await developments. The Magistrate has not, in fact, come in answer to the men's appeal, and he at first takes no notice of their bedraggled appearance [they had just been doused with pitchers of water by the women]. Of the women, he takes no notice at all.).

MAGISTRATE: I hear it's the same old thing again—the unbridled nature of the female sex coming out. All their banging of drums in honor of that Sabazius [an eastern god] . . . and singing to **Adonis** on the roofs of the houses, and all that nonsense. I remember once in the **Assembly**—Demostratus, may he come to no good end, was saying we ought to send the expedition to Sicily, and this woman, who was dancing on the roof, she cried, "O woe for Adonis!," and then he went on and said we should include some heavy infantry from **Zacynthus**, and the woman on the roof—she'd had a bit to drink, I fancy—she shouted, "Mourn for Adonis, all ye people!" but the damnable scoundrel from [**Cholozyges**] just blustered on and on. Anyway . . . that's the sort of outrage that women get up to.

LEADER OF THE OLD MEN: Wait till you hear what this lot have done. We have been brutally assaulted, and what is more, we have been given an unsolicited bath out of these pots . . . and all our clothes are wringing wet. Anybody would think we were incontinent!

MAGISTRATE: Disgraceful. Disgraceful. But by Poseidon the **Shipbuilder**, I'm not surprised. Look at the way we pander to the women's vices—we positively teach them to be wicked. That's why we get this kind of conspiracy. Think of when we go to the shops, for example. We might go to the goldsmith's and say, "Goldsmith, the necklace you made for my wife—she was dancing last night and the clasp came unstuck. [Please reset it for her.]" Or perhaps we go into a shoemaker's . . . and we say, "Shoemaker, the toe-strap on my wife's sandal is hurting her little toe—it's rather tender, you know. [Please refit it for her.]" And now look what's happened. I, a member of the Committee of Ten [see "Keep in Mind as You Read"] having found a source of supply for timber to **make oars, and now requiring money to buy it**, come to the Acropolis and find the women have shut the doors in my face! [*Now speaking to the four Scythian policemen, who have apparently done nothing up to this point to apprehend and arrest the women.*] No good standing around! Fetch the crowbars, somebody, and we'll soon put a stop to this nonsense. [*To two of the policemen.*]: What are you gawking at, you fool? And you? Dreaming about [the bar scene], eh? [*Crowbars are brought in.*] Let's get these bars under the doors and lever them up. I'll help. [*They begin to move the crowbars into position, when Lysistrata, Calonice, and Myrrhine open the gates and come out.*]

LYSISTRATA: No need to use force. I'm coming out of my own free will. What's the use of crowbars? It's intelligence and common sense that we need, not violence.

MAGISTRATE: You disgusting creature! **Officer**! Take her and tie her hands behind her back.

LYSISTRATA: By **Artemis**, if he so much as touches me, I'll teach him to **know his place**! [*The policeman hesitates.*]

politicians who opposed it. Aristophanes, a relentless critic of the Peloponnesian War, not surprisingly expresses a wish (via the Magistrate) that Demostratus might "come to no good end" and refers to him as a "damnable scoundrel."

know his place: Aristophanes uses the word *demosios* to refer to the policeman, literally "public [servant]," but the word seems to have a slightly pejorative connotation, something like "disrespected" or "low-ranking" public servant.

make oars, and now requiring money to buy it: The Magistrate reveals his true purpose in coming to the Acropolis, as mentioned just above. The Peloponnesian War had begun some 20 years earlier, and so by this time, war materiel was in short supply. The Magistrate, having (apparently) unexpectedly come upon "a source of supply for timber," is anxious to close the deal, but he needs money in order to do this.

no plunder will be taken. In the many battle scenes described in Homer's epic poem the *Iliad*, it is a mark of high honor and great distinction for a warrior to strip the armor off an enemy soldier whom he has slain, and there is a concomitant obligation on the part of the fallen soldier's comrades to protect that armor. A literal translation of Lysistrata's words indicate that she has ordered her female troops not to try to strip the vanquished Scythian policemen of their weaponry.

Officer: The Greek word used here, *toxotes*, and translated as "officer," literally means "archer."

Pandrosus: Pandrosus was a minor goddess who served as a priestess of Athena. A shrine on the Acropolis was dedicated to her.

relay: Referring to the seemingly constant stream of women pouring forth from the Acropolis. The Greek word is *exodos*, literally "out onto the road," and the source of our word "exodus."

Shipbuilder: The Magistrate has come to the Acropolis to obtain money for building ships, so shipbuilding is on his mind. (The Parthenon, the famous temple dedicated to Athena on the Acropolis, was used as a kind of repository of money, almost like a bank.)

Zacynthus: A small island off the west coast of Greece, and a staunch ally of Athens during the Peloponnesian War. But it does not seem to have had much to offer in the way of military hardware or manpower, so it seems odd that Demostratus would suggest recruiting "some heavy infantry" from that place. Possibly Aristophanes is making a wry comment that the Athenians have sunk so low after the Sicilian disaster that they must appeal to the likes of the Zacynthians for military assistance.

MAGISTRATE: Frightened, eh? Go on, the two of you, up-end her and tie her up!

CALONICE [interposing herself between second policeman and Lysistrata]: If you so much as lay a finger on her, by **Pandrosus**, I'll hit you so hard, you'll [spill out your guts] all over the place.

MAGISTRATE: Obscene language! Officer! [*To third policeman*]. Tie this one up first, and stop her mouth.

MYRRHINE [interposing herself between third policeman and Calonice]: By the Giver of Light [another name for Artemis], if you touch her, you'll soon by crying out for a cupping glass!

MAGISTRATE: What's all this? Officer! [*to fourth policeman*] Get hold of her. I'm going to stop this **relay** sometime.

STRATYLLIS [intervening in her turn]: By the Bull Goddess [yet another name for Artemis], if you go near her, I'll make you scream! [*Giving an exemplary tug to fourth policeman's hair.*]

MAGISTRATE: Heaven help me, I've no more archers! Well, we mustn't let ourselves be worsted by women. Come on, officers, we'll charge them, all together.

LYSISTRATA: If you do, . . . you'll find out that we've got four whole companies of fighting women in there, fully armed.

MAGISTRATE [calling her bluff]: Twist their arms behind them, officers. [*The policemen approach the four women with intent to do this.*]

LYSISTRATA [to the women inside]: Come out, the reserve! . . . Come to our help! [*Four bands of women emerge from the Acropolis.*] Drag them along! Hit them! Shout rude words in their faces! [*The policemen are quickly brought to the ground, and punched and kicked as they lie there.*] All right—withdraw—**no plunder will be taken.** [*The women retire into the Acropolis.*]

MAGISTRATE [his hand to his head]: My bowmen have been utterly defeated!

[Tr. Alan H. Sommerstein. *Aristophanes: The Acharnians; The Clouds; Lysistrata.* (*Lysistrata* ll. 390 ff.) Penguin Books, 1973. Page numbers: 196, 197, 198, 199.]

SCYTHIAN POLICEMEN? REALLY?

The Athenian police force, such as it was, consisted primarily of archers from the untamed land of Scythia, located in modern Romania. The Scythians seemed an odd culture group from which to recruit law enforcement officers. Consider the description of them by the fifth-century BCE historian Herodotus:

> As regards war, the Scythian custom is for every man to drink the blood of the first man he kills. The heads of all enemies killed in battle are taken to the king . . . Many Scythians sew a number of scalps together and make cloaks out of them . . . [Many other gruesome stories of Scythian atrocities are related next] . . . Once a year the governor of each district mixes a bowl of wine, from which every Scythian who has killed his man in battle has the right to drink. Those who have no dead enemy to their credit are not allowed to touch the wine, but have to sit by themselves in disgrace—the worst, indeed, which they can suffer. Any man, on the contrary, who has killed a great many enemies, has two cups and drinks from both of them at once. [Herodotus. *The Histories* 4.65; tr. de Selincourt.]

AFTERMATH

The rebellious women who took over the Acropolis eventually surrendered, but only after exacting from the men a pledge to end the Peloponnesian War, which was the women's objective in the first place. In reality, the war did go on, finally coming to an inglorious conclusion for Athens, in 405, when the Spartans occupied the city and burned much of it.

ASK YOURSELF

1. According to the Magistrate, what is the main reason that the women of Athens are engaging in such lawless behavior? Is his theory defensible?
2. The Magistrate references the god Poseidon with the epithet "Shipbuilder," but this is an unusual name for Poseidon. With what epithet(s) is he more commonly associated?
3. What is the Magistrate's attitude toward women in general? What does he think about the actions of Lysistrata and her followers?

TOPICS TO CONSIDER

- Based on what Herodotus wrote about Scythian culture and some of their barbarous practices, why do you suppose the Athenians would want Scythians as police officers? Herodotus describes the Scythians as fierce warriors. Why, then, do you think they were so inept in their role as police officers? (Aristophanes portrays them as completely unable to take the women into custody.)
- A follow-up to the previous question: Can you think of any similar examples in modern times in which inappropriately recruited or trained security officers were used to keep order or to enforce laws?
- Why do you suppose Aristophanes did not assign any speaking parts to the Scythian policemen?

  ➶ If Aristophanes would use a word like *demosios* to describe one of the police officers—a word that implies a lack of respect—what does that tell us about the Athenian attitude in general toward their Scythian police force?

  ➶ Can you think of any contemporary situations, either in the United States or abroad, in which riots broke out, and the rioters intimidated and overcame law enforcement personnel in the same manner as did Lysistrata and her intrepid band of "four whole companies of fighting women"?

Further Information

Dover, Kenneth J. *Aristophanic Comedy*. London, 1972.

Ehrenberg, Victor. *The People of Aristophanes*. Oxford, 1951.

Whitman, C. H. *Aristophanes and the Comic Hero*. Cambridge, 1964.

Websites

Lysistrata by Aristophanes. Plot summary. http://www.cummingsstudyguides.net/Lysistrata.htm

Lysistrata: An Introduction to the Play by Aristophanes. http://theatredatabase.com/ancient/aristophanes_005.html

Bibliography for Document

Rogers, Benjamin Bickley (tr.). *Aristophanes. The Lysistrata; The Thesmophoriazusae; The Ecclesiazusae. The Plutus*. Volume III. [LCL.] Cambridge and London, 1924.

de Selincourt, Aubrey (tr.). *Herodotus: The Histories*. Baltimore, 1954.

Sommerstein, Alan H. (tr.). *Aristophanes: Lysistrata and Other Plays*. New York, 1973.

40. A Tribune Speaks, a Riot Ensues

INTRODUCTION

When we think of dangers arising from street fights, muggings, and assaults, our initial image of the perpetrators is probably one of desperate or violent criminals. And most ancient Romans probably thought along the same lines. So it must have come as a great shock when the riot that erupted in 133 BCE, and resulted in the loss of some 300 lives, was fomented not by the criminal element but by some of the most highly respected members of the Roman Senate.

KEEP IN MIND AS YOU READ

1. The office of tribune was established in the fifth century BCE as an annual magistracy. Tribunes—10 each year—were charged with protecting the interests of the plebeians (Romans who were not of noble birth, and generally not the wealthiest citizens), especially in the legislative assemblies. Tribunes had the unusual power of virtually shutting down the Roman government by interposing their veto of any proposed legislative action that they deemed harmful to plebeian interests; one tribunician veto was sufficient to accomplish this. In actual practice, the tribunes seldom exercised this extraordinary power, although Gracchus himself had been the victim of such a move during his tribunate when a fellow tribune, Marcus Octavius, vetoed the land reform measure that Gracchus had proposed.

2. Tiberius Gracchus successfully ran for the office of tribune in the fall of 134 BCE, with his tenure for one year, beginning in 133 BCE. The trouble described below was sparked when Gracchus announced that he intended to run for reelection. By custom, Roman officeholders were not permitted to do this; "one (year) and done" was the rule. Hard-line conservatives like Nasica were outraged, and perhaps a little frightened, by Gracchus's attempt to breach tradition.

3. Gracchus's signature political issue was land reform. Rome, and Italy generally, was suffering from the twin problems of homelessness and hunger, and Gracchus was determined to try to effect a solution. Many of the homeless people, especially in the rural areas, had lost their ancestral land holdings due to the devious and often illegal machinations of rich land speculators in Rome. Gracchus announced during his campaign for the tribunate that, if elected, he would introduce legislation

designed to bring about a more equitable division of farm land. Naturally, the wealthy occupiers of the lands opposed this effort, with the result that Gracchus's year as a tribune was marked by intense controversy. Ultimately, however, he succeeded in passing his land reform measure. His opponents probably felt that they could endure one year of Gracchus, secure in the knowledge that he could not run for re-election. So his proclamation that he would indeed run for another one-year term as tribune increased the already considerable animosity toward him, and probably led directly to his assassination.

Document: The Downfall of Tiberius Gracchus

asking for a crown: The Romans hated the idea of being ruled by a king, and any credible politician who was believed—rightly or wrongly—to be aiming at royal power for himself would encounter fierce and intense opposition.

consul: Publius Mucius Scaevola is meant. He was a political ally and adviser of Gracchus, so it is hardly surprising that he refused Nasica's demand that he "act . . . to put down the tyrant."

girded up their togas: The equivalent of our colloquialism "rolling up one's sleeves." The loosely hanging toga had to be rolled up in order to free the wearer's arms for using the spear shafts effectively.

Nasica: Full name: Publius Cornelius Scipio Nasica Serapio, and a cousin of Tiberius Gracchus. But he was no friend of Gracchus; he staunchly opposed his cousin politically and would not tolerate his efforts to run for reelection to the tribunate.

the officers use to keep back the crowd: The Greek reads *aneirgousi ton ochlon*, "they keep back the crowd," but without a noun to indicate the identity of "they." Apparently, "they" were some sort of security detail, perhaps analogous to lictors (see sidebar, below).

Tiberius passed on this news [of a possible assassination attempt] to his supporters who were standing round him, and they at once **girded up their togas**. Then they broke up the staves which **the officers use to keep back the crowd**, distributed these, and prepared to defend themselves against the attackers. Those who were standing farther away were at a loss to know what was happening and asked what it meant. Thereupon, Tiberius raised his hand to his head intending, since the people could not hear his voice, to signify that his life was in danger. But when his enemies saw this gesture, they rushed to the Senate and reported that Tiberius was **asking for a crown**, and that they had the proof of this in the signal he had just given. This created an uproar in the Senate, and **Nasica** demanded that the **consul** must now act to protect the state and put down the tyrant. The consul answered in conciliatory fashion that he would not be the first to use violence, and would put no citizen to death without a regular trial. On the other hand, he declared that, if Tiberius should incite or oblige the people to pass any illegal resolution, he would not consider it to be binding. At this, Nasica sprang to his feet and shouted, "Now that the consul has betrayed the state, let every man who wishes to uphold the laws follow me!" Then he drew the skirt of his toga over his head [in preparation for the stave-wielding violence he apparently anticipated] and strode out towards the Capitol. The Senators who followed him wrapped their togas over their left arms [leaving their right arms free for staves] and thrust aside anyone who stood in their path. Nobody dared to oppose them out of respect for **their rank**, but those whom they met took to their heels and trampled down one another as they fled.

The senators' followers were armed with clubs and staves, which they had brought from their houses. The senators themselves snatched up the legs and fragments of the benches which the crowd had broken in their hurry to escape, and made straight for Tiberius, lashing out at those who were drawn up in front of him. His protectors were quickly scattered or clubbed down, and as Tiberius turned to run, someone caught hold of his clothing. He threw off his toga and fled in his tunic, but then stumbled over some of the prostrate bodies in front of him. As he struggled to his feet, one of his fellow tribunes, Publius Satyreius . . .

> **their rank:** The Roman Senate was comprised of the most experienced and distinguished citizens, so they automatically commanded respect.

dealt the first blow, striking him on the head with the leg of a bench. Lucius Rufus claimed to have given him the second, and prided himself upon this as if it were some noble exploit. More than three hundred men were killed by blows from sticks and stones, but none by the sword . . .

This is said to have been the first outbreak of civil strife in Rome which ended in bloodshed and death of citizens, since the expulsion of the kings [which occurred around 509 BCE, with the overthrow of Tarquinius Superbus]. All the other disputes, although they were neither trivial in themselves nor concerned with trivial objects, were resolved by some form of compromise . . . But the conspiracy which was formed against [Gracchus] seems to have had its origin in the hatred and malevolence of the rich rather than in the excuses which they put forward for their action. [Tr. Ian Scott-Kilvert. *Plutarch: The Makers of Rome, Nine Lives.* (*Tiberius Gracchus* 19, 20.) Penguin Classics, 1975. Page numbers: 171, 172.]

AFTERMATH

The assassination of Tiberius Gracchus ushered in a new era in Roman history, in which many of the traditional institutions and customs of the Republic began to be ignored. The violation of tribunician *sacrosanctitas*, in particular, set a dangerous precedent, and this extreme disrespect to tribunes was destined to be repeated in the case of Gaius Gracchus and other tribunes. Some modern historians see 133 BCE as a kind of watershed year in Roman history, when the decline of the Roman Republic first started to gather momentum.

THE ROMAN VERSION OF THE SECRET SERVICE

In order to protect the leading officeholders of the state, the Romans created a cadre of official bodyguards called *lictors*. Whenever the chief magistrates—particularly consuls—appeared in public, the *lictors* preceded them and cleared a path for them. The *lictors* carried a bundle of rods bound together with leather straps and with axe-heads protruding from each end—the *fasces* (hence our word "fascist")—which symbolized the power of the magistrate to mete out punishments to lawbreakers: the rods for flogging and the axe-heads for execution. They could also use the *fasces* in a practical way, as a weapon, should the magistrate be threatened with attack. Each consul was assigned 12 *lictors*; lesser ranking officials had fewer *lictors*. Unfortunately for Tiberius Gracchus, tribunes did not qualify for this Roman version of Secret Service protection. Perhaps Gracchus would have survived the attack on his life had *lictors* been provided for him.

LIKE BROTHER, LIKE BROTHER

Tiberius Gracchus's brother Gaius, nine years his junior, held the office of tribune in 123 and again in 122. Gaius, like Tiberius, was a tribune on a mission: to correct what he saw as injustices and especially to be an advocate for the less fortunate citizens. Like Tiberius, Gaius ran for reelection to the tribunate, but unlike his brother, he succeeded. However, his effort to obtain a *third* term as tribune failed, and, like his brother, he was killed in a civil disturbance that followed.

ASK YOURSELF

1. Why do you suppose Plutarch emphasizes that of the 300 casualties of the riot, all were killed "by blows from sticks and stones, but none by the sword"?

2. Plutarch writes that when Gracchus raised his hand to his head, his enemies interpreted that gesture to signify that he "was asking for a crown." Do you think they really believed that that was what he was requesting, or did they simply use that as an excuse to chase him down and kill him?

3. What is your sense of the general political climate in Rome in 133? What could Roman political leaders have done to make the situation less hostile and confrontational?

TOPICS TO CONSIDER

- Tribunes were reputed to enjoy the special status of *sacrosanctitas*, the belief that they were to be free from physical threats or actual harm; it was a kind of "hands-off" policy to ensure the safety of tribunes when they appeared in public, and one that all Romans had respected for many years. Why, then, do you suppose that Roman citizens in this instance were not only willing to violate the *sacrosanctitas* of Tiberius Gracchus, but to do so in the most gruesome manner, by murdering him? And the ringleader of the attack seems to have been—if Plutarch is to be believed—Gracchus's own cousin, Nasica. What could account for such a display of violence on the part of one family member toward another?

- Some modern historians believe that the two named murderers of Gracchus, Publius Satyreius and Lucius Rufus, were never prosecuted for their crime. And there is no ancient evidence that would indicate whether a prosecution ever did occur. So what might be the speculative arguments in favor of, or against, the theory that they were never prosecuted?

- There were always two consuls in office each year, but Plutarch references only one of them, and does not even specify his name. Plutarch is usually a little more detail oriented than this, so why do you suppose he omits relatively important identity information in this instance?

- Plutarch is generally a very objective writer and seldom tries to instruct his readership how to interpret historical events. In his biography of Tiberius Gracchus, do you agree that he maintains this objectivity, or not? What indications, if any, are there that would support your answer?

Further Information

Boren, Henry C. *The Gracchi*. New York, 1968.

Earl, Donald C. *Tiberius Gracchus: A Study in Politics*. Bruxelles-Berchem, 1963.

Scullard, H. H. *From the Gracchi to Nero: A History of Rome from 133 B.C. to A.D. 68*. London, 1959.

Website

Tiberius Gracchus. http://medeaslair.net/tgracchus.html

Bibliography for Document

Scott-Kilvert, Ian. *Plutarch: Makers of Rome*. New York, 1965.

41. Everybody Talks about the Weather, but No One Does Anything about It

INTRODUCTION

The source of information for this document is to be found among the letters of Pliny the Younger.

KEEP IN MIND AS YOU READ

1. The addressee of this letter is one Minicius Macrinus, to whom Pliny had written in several other letters. He hailed from Brescia, in northern Italy, in the same general location as Pliny's hometown of Como.
2. Pliny begins his letter with the same topic that often occupies the first lines of modern letters: the weather!

Document: Storms, and Then Floods

Can the weather be as bad and stormy where you are? Here we have nothing but gales and repeated floods. The **Tiber** has overflowed its bed and deeply **flooded its lower banks**, so that although it is being drained by the canal cut by the Emperor [Trajan, who ruled 98–117 CE], with his usual foresight, it is filling the valleys and inundating the fields, and wherever there is level ground, there is nothing to be seen but water. Then the streams which it normally receives and carries down to the sea are forced back as it spreads to meet them, and so it floods with their water the fields it does not reach itself. The **Anio**, most delightful of rivers—so much so that the houses on its banks seem to beg it not to leave them—has torn up and carried away most of the woods which shade its course. High land nearby has been undermined, so that its channel is blocked in several places with the resultant landslides. And in its efforts to regain its lost course it has wrecked buildings and forced out its way over the debris.

People who were hit by the storm on higher ground have seen the valuable furniture and fittings of wealthy homes, or else all the farm stock, yoked oxen, plows and plowmen, or cattle left free to graze, and among them trunks of trees

Anio: The Anio River, a major tributary of the Tiber, arises in central Italy and runs its course for about 67 miles before its confluence with the Tiber. Two large aqueducts drew water from the Anio and helped to supply Rome with the hundreds of thousands of gallons that daily poured into the city. Hence, it is not surprising that Pliny would refer to this river as *delicatissimus*, "most delightful."

flooded its lower banks: See the sidebar, below.

Tiber: The fabled Tiber River wended its way through the downtown area of Rome.

widespread confusion: The Latin is *varie lateque*, with the former connoting a wide variety of debris floating on the floodwaters and the latter suggesting that these waters were widely dispersed.

or beams and roofs of houses, all floating by in **widespread confusion**. Nor have the places where the river did not rise escaped disaster, for instead of floods they have had incessant rain, gales and cloudbursts which have destroyed the walls enclosing valuable properties, rocked public buildings, and brought them crashing to the ground. Many people have been maimed, crushed, and buried in such accidents, so that grievous loss of life is added to material damage.

My fears that you have been through something like this are proportionate to the danger—if I am wrong, please relieve my anxiety as soon as possible, and let me know in any case. Whether disaster is actual or expected, the effect is much the same, except that suffering has its limits but apprehension has none; suffering is confined to the known event, but apprehension extends to every possibility. [Tr. Betty Radice. *Pliny: Letters and Panegyricus*. (8.17). Volume II. LCL, 1969. Page numbers: 49, 51.]

AFTERMATH

Although Tiber River flooding remained a serious public safety issue even after the floods described by Pliny and Tacitus, it was not until the nineteenth century that large stone flood walls were built along the river's banks, to keep the water confined to its channel. The ancient Roman engineers and architects most likely had the expertise to design and construct such walls, but they did not do so. The reasons for this were several: floodwaters generally receded quickly; Rome's fabled Seven Hills had sufficient elevation and space to afford a safe haven to people in harm's way during flooding; the sophisticated system of aqueducts continually brought fresh water into the city, so the danger of drinking water contaminated by flooding was minimal; the sewer system was also very efficient, so that foul water and water-borne debris could be washed away quickly; and their belief in floods as religious

FATHER TIBER OUT OF CONTROL!

Flooding of the Tiber River was a continuing problem in ancient Rome; still extant are 42 literary descriptions of 33 different floods between 414 BCE and 398 CE. One of the most destructive of these occurred about 70 CE; it is described in vivid detail by the historian Tacitus, in his *Histories* [1.86; tr. Moore.]

[There was] a sudden overflow of the Tiber, which, swollen to a great height, broke down the wooden bridge [the Sublician Bridge, the oldest bridge in Rome] and then was thrown back by the ruins of the bridge which dammed the stream, and overflowed not only the low-lying level parts of the city, but also parts which are normally free from such disasters. Many were swept away in the public streets, a larger number cut off in shops and in their beds. The common people were reduced to famine by lack of employment and failure of supplies. Apartment houses had their foundations undermined by the standing water and then collapsed when the flood withdrew.

omens gave at least some Romans a sense that these inundations, catastrophic though they might be, were somehow ordained by the gods and therefore not susceptible to human control.

ASK YOURSELF

1. What were some of the dangers that resulted in Rome when the Tiber River flooded?
2. What people were directly affected by the flood? What kinds of property damages occurred?
3. What does Pliny mean by the last sentence in his letter ("whether disaster is actual or expected the effect is much the same . . .")?

TOPICS TO CONSIDER

- ❧ The Romans excelled in the art of civil engineering. Given this fact, why do you suppose the Tiber River flooded so often, and so destructively, over the course of so many years, without Roman engineers and architects devising a system of flood control that could have prevented, or at least minimized, the destruction caused by the flooding?
- ❧ Does the flooding described by both Pliny and Tacitus sound similar to any of the natural disasters that have afflicted the modern world in recent years?
- ❧ Does Pliny's account in any way suggest the existence in ancient Rome of an agency similar to the Red Cross, the National Guard, or emergency response teams to deal with a natural disaster such as the one he describes? If those agencies did not exist, how do you suppose the Romans would cope with calamities like raging floods?

Further Information

Adam, Jean-Pierre. *Roman Building: Materials and Techniques.* Bloomington, IN, 1994.
Aldrete, Gregory S. *Floods of the Tiber in Ancient Rome.* Baltimore, 2007.
Connolly, P. and H. Dodge. *The Ancient City.* Oxford, 1998.
Platner, Samuel B. and T. Ashby. *A Topographical Dictionary of Ancient Rome.* London, 1929.
Richardson, L. *A New Topographical Dictionary of Ancient Rome.* Baltimore, 1992.

Bibliography for Document

Aldrete, Gregory S. *Floods of the Tiber in Ancient Rome.* Baltimore, 2007.
Burstein, Stanley, a review of Aldrete's book (*supra*), in the History Cooperative database: http://www.historycooperative.org/journals/ht/41.1/br_1.html
Moore, Clifford H. (tr.). *Tacitus: The Histories, Books I-III.* Volume II. [LCL.] Cambridge and London, 1925.
Radice, Betty (tr.). *Pliny: Letters and Panegyricus.* Volume II. [LCL.] Cambridge and London, 1969.
Westcott, John H. (ed.). *Selected Letters of Pliny.* Norman, OK, new edition, 1965.

SPORTS AND GAMES

42. The Goddess Was on His Side

INTRODUCTION

Homer's *Iliad*, organized into 24 chapters called "Books," covers the last few months of the 10-year Trojan War. Its pages are filled with stirring tales of gods and goddesses, victory and defeat, treachery and deceit, high passions and fierce rivalries. In Book 16, Homer describes a turning point in the war: the killing of the Greek soldier Patroclus by the best of the Trojans, Hector. The death of Patroclus set off a chain of events that dominates the last part of the *Iliad*, but the focus in this chapter is on Book 23, where the preeminent Greek warrior Achilles sponsors a series of eight athletic contests to honor the memory of Patroclus, who was his close friend.

The fourth event in the games, recounted in the document to follow, was a footrace. The contestants: Odysseus; Antilochus, who was earlier involved in a chariot-racing controversy; and Ajax, son of Oileus (there were two Ajaxes, differentiated by their patronymics; the other Ajax was the son of Telamon). The prizes: for the winner, a silver mixing bowl, "the finest mixing bowl in all the world." A massive ox awaited the man who finished second, while the third- (and last) place runner would receive half a bar of gold.

KEEP IN MIND AS YOU READ

1. As usual in funeral games, prizes of great value were offered to the contestants. Achilles provided these prizes from among his own possessions, mostly the booty he had amassed during the long years of the war. The relative value of the prizes sometimes seems a little puzzling. Most moderns, for example, would probably consider a solid gold bar to be worth more than a silver mixing bowl. Perhaps the craftsmanship of the bowl, "wrought to perfection" as Homer puts it, conferred on it a greater value than a lump of gold.
2. Footraces, both in the funeral games and in the later Olympic games, were not run on an oval track as today, but rather in a straight line, with a turning post at the far end. The athletes ran toward the post, rounded it, and then ran back to the starting line—which thus also functioned as the finish line.
3. The Greeks generally viewed the gods and goddesses as taking direct roles in human activities. So it is not surprising that Odysseus would pray to Athena for help during the heat of the race, and that she would hear his prayer and provide assistance.

Document: Homer's Account of the Foot Race in the Funeral Games for Patroclus

Argives: The word applies specifically to the natives of Argos, an important city in southern Greece, but Homer uses it generically to refer to all the Greeks.

blazing-eyed Athena: The goddess Athena is depicted in both the *Iliad* and in the *Odyssey* as Odysseus's special helper and protector. Many of her nicknames pertain to her eyes; "gray-eyed" and "flashing-eyed" are commonly employed, in addition to "blazing-eyed," as here.

cheering him on: A majority of the spectators was clearly rooting for Odysseus to win the race.

green old age: The Greeks had an interesting word for an older person who was still fit and active: *omogeron*, literally an "unripe old person," like fruit that had not yet ripened but was still green.

Nestor: Nestor was the wise old man of the Greek forces that were assembled to fight at Troy. Too aged to participate in battle, he was nonetheless very generous (some might say too generous!) with advice to his younger cohorts. Prior to the start of the chariot race in the funeral games, he subjected his son Antilochus to a long monologue about how to win it. One can almost picture the young man's eyes glazing over.

quick at tactics: Homer always describes Odysseus with phrases referring to his mental agility. Unlike many of the other epic heroes, Odysseus was known for his ability to think quickly and to devise schemes to extricate himself from almost any predicament.

[Achilles has announced the three prizes, and calls for three volunteers to compete in the footrace.]

"Now men come forward, fight to win this prize!"
And the racing Oilean [i.e., son of Oeleus] Ajax sprang up at once,
Odysseus, **quick at tactics** too, then **Nestor's** son,
Antilochus, fastest of all the young men in the ranks.
Achilles pointed out the post. They toed the line—
and broke flat out from the start and Ajax shot ahead
with quick Odysseus coming right behind him, close
as the weaver's rod to a well-sashed woman's breast
when she deftly pulls it toward her, shooting the spool
across the warp, still closer, pressing her breast—
so close Odysseus sprinted, hot on Ajax' heels,
feet hitting his tracks before the dust could settle
and quick Odysseus panting, breathing down his neck,
always forcing the pace and all the **Argives** shouting,
cheering him on as he strained for triumph, sprinting on
and fast in the homestretch, spurting toward the goal
Odysseus prayed in his heart to **blazing-eyed Athena**,
"Hear me, Goddess, help me—hurry, urge me on!"
So Odysseus prayed and Athena heard his prayer,
put spring in his limbs, his feet, his fighting hands
and just as the whole field came lunging in for the trophy
Ajax slipped at a dead run—Athena tripped him up—
right where the dung lay slick from bellowing cattle
the swift runner Achilles slew in Patroclus' honor.
Dung stuffed his mouth, his nostrils dripped muck
as shining long-enduring Odysseus flashed past him
to come in first by far and carry off the cup
while Ajax took the ox. The racer in all his glory
just stood there, clutching one of the beast's horns,
spitting out the dung and sputtering to his comrades,
"Foul, by heaven! The goddess fouled my finish!
Always beside Odysseus—just like the man's mother,
rushing to put his rivals in the dust!"
They all roared with laughter at his expense.
Antilochus came in last and carried off his prize
with a broad smile and a joke to warm his comrades:
"I'll tell you something you've always known, my friends—
down to this very day the gods prefer old-timers.
Look at Ajax now, with only a few years on me.
But Odysseus—why, *he's* out of the dark ages,
one of the old relics—
but in **green old age**, they say. No mean feat

AGE AND TREACHERY ALWAYS OVERCOME YOUTH AND SKILL

Odysseus had a well-deserved reputation for sneakiness, especially as a competitive athlete, and he often defeated opponents much younger than he. The *Odyssey* also offers several interesting instances of Odysseus the aging athlete overcoming unsuspecting, youthful challengers. Perhaps the best example of these kinds of encounters occurs in Book 8, where Odysseus has been shipwrecked on the island of the Phaeacians. Several of the young Phaeacians, who had a chance meeting with Odysseus but of course had no idea of his identity, decided to be neighborly and invite him to join in their athletic contests—although the reader does get the impression that there was a certain smirking cockiness in their invitation.

After enduring some taunting from his Phaeacian hosts, Odysseus angrily jumped to his feet, not bothering to change into athletic apparel, nor even to stretch or warm up. He grabbed a discus that was lying nearby on the ground, one that was even heavier than those the young Phaeacian athletes had heaved. He whirled around and let it fly; Homer says that the spectators "went flat on the ground," so astonished and surprised were they at Odysseus's strength and throwing skill. The discus flew through the air and landed far beyond the farthest throw that any of the young men had achieved.

The adrenaline gushed. Odysseus next turned to those (formerly!) smirking Phaeacians and furiously challenged them to any other kind of contest. A footrace? No volunteers arose. Wrestling? Silence. Boxing? Not today. Archery? Some other time. Javelin throwing? Forget it.

Finally, Alcinous, the king of the Phaeacians, stepped forward and called a halt to the games and the challenges, suggesting instead that they all turn their attention to a banquet and dancing, more "Phaeacian-like" pursuits.

to beat him out in a race, for all but our Achilles."
Bantering so, but he flattered swift Achilles
and the matchless runner paid him back in kind:
"Antilochus, how can I let your praise go unrewarded?
Here's more gold—a half-bar more in the bargain."
He placed it in his hands, and he was glad to have it.
[Tr. Robert Fagles. *Homer: The Iliad*. (Book 23.) Penguin Books, 1990. Page numbers: 582, 583, 584.]

AFTERMATH

The three contestants in the footrace all had interesting post-race adventures. The most famous of these is the story of Odysseus's 10-year homeward journey after the Trojan War, as recounted in Homer's *Odyssey*.

Ajax drowned on his voyage home after the war. This Ajax was always viewed as a brash and irreverent sort; after successfully weathering a storm at sea and guiding his ship and crew to safety, he loudly boasted that he had bested both the deities and the ocean waves. The god Poseidon, infuriated by this unwarranted insolence, shattered with his fearsome trident the point of land from which Ajax uttered his boast, sinking both it and Ajax into the depths of the onrushing waters.

Antilochus, young, handsome, and a close friend of both Patroclus and Achilles—it was Antilochus who had the unhappy duty of informing Achilles about Patroclus's death—was subsequently killed while defending his father Nestor against an attack by the Ethiopian king

Memnon. The three friends—Antilochus, Patroclus, and Achilles—were buried in the same tomb and were reunited in the afterlife. When Odysseus made his descent into the Underworld (in Book 11 of the *Odyssey*), he saw all three of them together.

ASK YOURSELF

1. Achilles was a fast runner; Homer often refers to him as "swift-footed Achilles." He probably could have won the footrace easily if he had competed. In fact, Antilochus admits, at the end of the document, that Achilles could outrun even Odysseus. Why do you suppose, then, that he sat it out?

2. Why did Ajax complain so bitterly about losing the race to Odysseus? What do you think about his contention that a goddess was the cause of his defeat?

3. The response of the spectators—laughter—to Ajax' unfortunate fall seems a little inappropriate. Why do you suppose they laughed at him? Was it merely because he looked foolish, having fallen in cattle droppings, or did their laughter also display a lack of respect for him?

4. If Odysseus had fallen instead of Ajax, is it likely that the spectators would have greeted him with laughter?

5. Quite a change has taken place in Antilochus. A little earlier in Book 23, he angrily complained when it appeared that he might be deprived of the second-place prize in the chariot race. But he seems to be perfectly content with having finished last in the footrace. Why the change in attitude?

TOPICS TO CONSIDER

- In Homer's description of the eight events in the funeral games for Patroclus, it seems as if the chariot race is the most important one. It is described first, and in the greatest detail. Think about why the Greeks of Homer's time apparently considered chariot racing so prestigious.

- The attitude displayed by the Homeric athletes toward winning and losing seems to be very different from the way in which Olympic athletes (centuries later) viewed the matter. As noted, disputes did arise in the funeral games for Patroclus, but more often, the competitors seemed to behave like Antilochus after the footrace: even though he finished last, he was still good-humored about it and willing to give due credit to the winner. No defeated Olympic athlete would have displayed such magnanimity. Two of the events in the funeral games did not even have a winner: the wrestling match, which ended in a tie, and the archery contest, which was cancelled because everyone knew that Agamemnon was unbeatable. Consider some possible reasons why the participants in the funeral games seemed to have such a polite outlook on the question of winning and losing.

- The Roman poet Virgil (70–19 BCE) authored the *Aeneid*, an epic poem about the Roman hero Aeneas and the founding of the Roman race. In Book 5, Virgil describes a series of athletic events staged in honor of Anchises, Aeneas's deceased father. Consider the similarities and differences between the funeral games for Patroclus and the funeral games for Anchises.

Further Information

Bowra, Sir Maurice. *Tradition and Design in the Iliad*. London, 1930.

Edwards, Mark W. *Homer: Poet of the Iliad*. Baltimore and London, 1987.

Nagy, Gregory. *The Best of the Achaeans: Concepts of the Hero in Archaic Greek Poetry*. Baltimore and London, 1979.

Schein, Seth. *The Mortal Hero: An Introduction to Homer's Iliad*. Berkeley, Los Angeles, and London, 1984.

Wace, Alan J. B. and Frank Stubbings. *A Companion to Homer*. London, 1962.

Website

Homer's Iliad and Odyssey. http://library.thinkquest.org/19300

Bibliography for document

Fagles, Robert (tr.). *Homer: The Iliad*. New York, 1990.

43. The (Ancient) World's Greatest Athlete

INTRODUCTION

The sixth-century BCE wrestler Milo of Croton (a southern Italian town noted for the many champion athletes born there) was without a doubt the most successful competitor in ancient Olympic history. It might not be too far a stretch to consider him the most dominant Olympic athlete ever. As Pausanias informs us below, he won the championship in six consecutive Olympiads. No Olympic athlete, ancient or modern, has ever accomplished a comparable feat. And he nearly won a seventh; he was undone by a certain Timasitheus (also from Croton, interestingly), who apparently employed a strategy of running around the wrestling ring, and forcing Milo—who must by that time have been 40 years of age or older—to chase him. Eventually, youth and stamina overcame age and experience.

Pausanias also notes that Milo won seven wrestling championships at the Pythian Games. Other sources add that Milo won 10 times at the Isthmian Games and 9 more at the Nemean Games, giving him an astounding total of 32 championships at the four most prestigious and competitive athletic venues.

In addition to his athletic excellence, he was something of a showman, delighting in tests of strength and skill. Many of these displays are described in the passage quoted from the pages of Pausanias. And like many oversized athletes throughout history, Milo had an enormous appetite, reportedly downing 20 pounds of meat and bread and three pitchers of wine at a single sitting. He is said to have once carried a four-year-old bull around the stadium, and then to have butchered it and consumed it in its entirety. Another time, at a festival in honor of Zeus, he lifted onto his shoulders a four-year-old steer, paraded with it among the festivalgoers, and then supposedly butchered and ate it.

KEEP IN MIND AS YOU READ

1. Statues of victorious athletes were set up in the area around the temple of Zeus, the god to whom the Olympic games were dedicated. Victorious athletes were also praised in verse written by epinicean poets. These poets—who could perhaps be characterized as the western world's first sports writers—specialized in writing odes that honored successful athletes. The best known epinicean poet was Pindar (518–438 BCE). About 45 of his elegantly written poems survive to the present day.

2. Winning the Olympic championship in wrestling was exceptionally difficult. The number of wrestlers who could enter the lists for wrestling is not known, but apparently, the entrants had to wrestle a series of elimination matches prior to the start of the games, so that the number of finalists was reduced to 16. These surviving 16 were paired up by lot; no effort was made to seed them or to match them according to weight. The wrestling event then proceeded in the manner of a single-elimination tournament featuring the (presumably) finest 16 wrestlers in the Greek world. Hence, in order to win the overall championship, a wrestler had to defeat four extremely skilled opponents, in four grueling matches, and most likely, all in the same day. (No wonder the aging Milo had difficulty keeping up with his young rival Timasitheus!)

Document: Pausanias's Account of Milo of Croton [6.14.5–8]

Milo won six victories for wrestling at Olympia, one of them among the boys; at [the Pythian Games] he won six among the men and one among the boys. He came to Olympia to wrestle for the seventh time, but did not succeed in mastering Timasitheus, a fellow-citizen who was also a young man, and who refused . . . to come to close quarters with him. It is further stated that Milo carried his own statue into the **Altis**. His feats with the pomegranate and the [discus] are also remembered by tradition. He would grasp a pomegranate so firmly

Detail from a sarcophagus shows young Greeks engaged in a wrestling contest, Greek, marble relief, sixth century BCE. (Gianni Dagli Orti/Corbis)

> **Altis:** the sacred grove that surrounded the temple of Zeus in Olympia, where the statues of victorious athletes were placed. A statue of Milo was erected in the Altis, and interestingly, Milo's statue was crafted by his fellow Crotoniate, a sculptor named Dameas.

that nobody could wrest it from him by force, and yet he did not damage it by pressure. He would stand upon a greased [discus], and make fools of those who charged him and tried to push him [off of it]. He used to perform also the following exhibition feats: He would tie a cord around his forehead as though it were a ribbon or a crown. Holding his breath and filling with blood the veins on his head, he would break the cord by the strength of these veins. It is said that he would let down by his side his right arm from the shoulder to the elbow, and stretch out straight the arm below the elbow, turning the thumb upwards, while the other fingers lay in a row. In this position, then, the little finger was lowest, but nobody could bend it back by pressure. [Tr. W. H. S. Jones. *Pausanias: Description of Greece.* (6.14.5–8.) Volume III. LCL, 1933. Page numbers: 83, 85.]

AFTERMATH

Many notable wrestlers competed in the sport after Milo. Examples: Epharmostus of Opus (fifth century BCE), who won championships at the Olympic, Isthmian, and Nemean games, as well as a number of other places, including Arcadia, Argos, Athens, Marathon, and Pellana; Praxidamas of Aegina (fifth century), who triumphed five times in the Isthmian games and three times in the Nemean, and whose son, Alcimidas, won the boys' wrestling crown at Nemea; Thaeaus of Argos (fifth century), winner of three Isthmian championships, one each at the Pythian and Nemean games, as well as at Argos, Sicyon, and Athens; Caprus of Elis (fourth century), a uniquely versatile competitor who was the first man in Olympic history to claim championships in both wrestling and the pankration at the same festival. But none of these athletes, accomplished as they were, matched Milo's excellence. No one else ever did, either.

CROTON: HOME OF FINE-QUALITY ATHLETES

The southern Italian city of Croton was famous for the many superb athletes it produced. Milo was undoubtedly the best known and most successful of these, but there were others. Astylus, early fifth century BCE, was a champion sprinter. He won both the *stade* and the *diaulos* races in the same Olympiad three consecutive times, in 488, 484, and 480. Such a unique double victory, accomplished three times, was unmatched in the ancient Olympics.

Phayllus, also early fifth century, won three victories in the Pythian Games: two in the pentathlon, and one in the stade (200-yard) race. An epigram concerning Phayllus records that he long-jumped 55 feet (probably a triple jump) and threw the discus 95 feet.

And in one Olympiad, the top seven finishers in the *stade* sprint race were all from Croton, thus occasioning a famous saying: "The last of the Crotoniates was the first among all other Greeks."

GREEK NAMES

The ancient Greeks did not have a "first name, middle name, last name" in the same way as do Americans and members of other modern societies. They generally had a given name, roughly equivalent to a modern first name, followed by their place of origin. Hence, "Milo of Croton." An alternative form: identifying a person by referencing his father's name, a patronymic naming system. Milo's father's name was Diotimus, and Pausanias sometimes refers to Milo by his patronymic: "Milo, son of Diotimus." Compare modern patronymics, such as names that end with the -son suffix: Johnson (i.e., "son of John"), Jackson, Peterson, Stevenson, etc.

ASK YOURSELF

1. Milo apparently enjoyed competing in informal contests of strength and skill, in addition to those described in the document. What do you suppose motivated him to want to do this?
2. In the introduction to the document, it was stated that Milo was the greatest ancient Olympic athlete, and possibly the greatest of all time. Does this seem plausible? Is there a way to prove this contention, or is it more likely that it is an issue for which a consensus will never be achieved?

TOPICS TO CONSIDER

ক Ancient athletes like Milo enjoyed the adulation of an adoring public, much like modern athletes and other celebrities. The ancient athletes were

A FAMOUS ATHLETIC FAMILY

Possibly the most noteworthy athletic family in the history of the ancient games came from the island of Rhodes, in the eastern Mediterranean. Pausanias informs us that the "elder statesman" of this distinguished group, Diagoras, won a boxing crown in the Olympics of 464 BCE. His sons Acusilaus, Damagetus, and Dorieus were all champion athletes. There is a story that Acusilaus and Damagetus, having triumphed at the same Olympiad, hoisted their father onto their shoulders and carried him through the crowd, who tossed flowers at him and congratulated him on his sons' athletic excellence. Dorieus, the youngest son, won the pankration in three successive Olympiads (432, 428, and 424), as well as eight crowns in the Isthmian games and seven in the Nemean. Two of Diagoras's grandsons also claimed Olympic glory: Eucles, who triumphed in boxing in the Olympics of 396, and Peisirodus, in boys' boxing, in 388.

Pindar wrote an epinicean ode (*Olympian 7*) in honor of Diagoras, that "mighty, fair-fighting man" (tr. Swanson), in which he indicates that Diagoras won twice at Olympia, four times at the Isthmian games, and an unspecified number of times at Nemea, as well as one or more victories at games in Athens, Argos, Thebes, Arcadia, Boeotia, Aegina, and Pellana.

Plutarch and Cicero both relate the following incident from Diagoras's old age: On the day when he had seen his two sons crowned at Olympia, a Spartan supposedly approached him and said, "Die, Diagoras, for you could never ascend to heaven." The point seemed to be that the old man had reached the apex of happiness, and nothing—not even heaven itself—could surpass the joy a father would feel at the Olympic success of his offspring.

Today, we might use the words "athletic dynasty" to describe this family!

immortalized by statues in the Altis (sort of like a Hall of Fame.of Olympic champions), and praised in verse by well-paid professional poets. Furthermore, they brought fame and glory to their families and home-towns by virtue of their athletic accomplishments. Consider why human beings, both ancient and modern, idolize(d) their athletic heroes, some-times to great extremes.

      The ancient Olympics were first staged in 776 BCE. They continued to be held every four years for more than a millennium. The modern version of the games has been continuously run since 1896 (with the exceptions of the war years of 1916, 1940, and 1944). So one could argue that Olympic competitions constitute one of the most enduring, most popular, and most widely watched events in the history of the western world. Consider why this is so, why it is that the Olympics have inspired and cre-ated such a long-standing interest among both competitors and fans.

Further Information

Gardiner, E. N. *Athletics of the Ancient World.* Oxford, 1930.

Harris, H. A. *Greek Athletes and Athletics.* Bloomington, IN, 1964.

Harris, H. A. *Sport in Greece and Rome.* Ithaca, NY, 1972.

Kyle, Donald. *Athletics in Ancient Athens.* Leiden, The Netherlands, 1987.

Matz, David S. *Greek and Roman Sport. A Dictionary of Athletes and Events.* Jefferson, NC, 1991.

Robinson, Rachel S. *Sources for the History of Greek Athletics.* Cincinnati, 1955.

Website

Milo of Kroton. http://www.perseus.tufts.edu/Olympics/milo.html

Bibliography for Document

Jones, W. H. S. (tr.). *Pausanias: Description of Greece.* Volume III. [LCL.] Cambridge and London, 1933.

Swanson, Roy Arthur. (tr.) *Pindar's Odes.* Indianapolis and New York, 1974.

44. "Put Me In, Coach": A Famous Athletic Trainer

INTRODUCTION

Hiring a personal trainer is not a modern phenomenon; ancient Greek athletes often had their own personal coaches, who advised them on everything from dietary regimens, to training methods, to lifestyle options. We even have a detailed training manual, authored by a certain Philostratus; the date is uncertain, but it may have been written in the third century CE. In addition to training advice, Philostratus also offers opinions on other relevant topics, such as an athlete's family background: "Now since it is best to begin with a man's birth, the coach should proceed first to investigate the parentage of the boy athlete, that is, to see if the parents were married when young, both of good stock, and free from diseases . . . Young parents . . . bestow strength upon the athlete, pure blood, powerful frame and untainted humors as well as normal size, and I would still further claim that they bestow also a wholesome beauty" [Philostratus. *On Gymnastics* 28; tr. Robinson.].

We know the names of several coaches, and perhaps the most successful of these was the fifth-century BCE wrestling trainer Melesias. Pindar's eighth *Olympian Ode* honors Alcimedon of Aegina, the winner of the boys' wrestling, in 460; Melesias coached Alcimedon, and according to Pindar, Alcimedon's victory was the 30th earned by wrestlers who learned their craft under Melesias's tutelage.

KEEP IN MIND AS YOU READ

1. Greek athletes sometimes became coaches after their retirement from active competition, in much the same manner as retired athletes in modern times. This was clearly the case with Melesias; Pindar notes that "he won in his / own right at Nemea, / and, later in the men's pancration / bouts." From this, it seems clear that Melesias excelled both in wrestling and in the pancration, but he apparently specialized in coaching wrestlers. Keep in mind also how Pindar emphasizes to young athletes dreaming of Olympic glory that it would be to their advantage to secure the services of an experienced coach who had been there, done that: "Untested men [that is, those who had never competed and won] speak unreliably. / But Melesias speaks with authority / about these feats to neophytes . . . "

2. Pindar often incorporated mythic allusions into his poetry, as, for example, the last two lines of the document: "Hades holds no qualms/for one who wins." The

meaning seems to be that a victorious athlete is already immortal, by virtue both of his success and Pindar's poem in his honor, so he need not worry about what might happen to him in the afterlife.

Document: "Coach" Melesias: Pindar, Olympian 8

he sent four badly beaten boys/back home in shameful silence, to defer/the choristers of catcalls: An excellent example of Pindar's skill in seamlessly combining two somewhat different topics in the same sentence. The comment about "four badly beaten boys" is a reference to the procedure followed in wrestling (and also most likely in boxing and the pancration): prior to the official start of the games, wrestlers would be required to engage in a series of elimination matches—the exact number is anybody's guess—to narrow the field of finalists to 16. These 16 would then compete for the championship, in a single-elimination format. So in order to win a wrestling crown, an athlete would have to defeat four opponents, almost certainly on the same day, no small task considering that these 16 could fairly be said to be the best wrestlers in the Greek world.

Even to make it to the "final 16" would have required considerable skill. And yet so intense was the emphasis on winning that simply making it to that select group of 16 would mean nothing for any wrestler who failed—and there would be 15 failures!—to capture the championship. To lose was worse than disgraceful; hence

And, if I've rushed to glorify Melesias'
wrestler-boys in poetry,
may envy hurl no jagged stone at me:
for I recall he won in his
own right at Nemea,
and, later in the men's **pancration**
bouts. Teaching comes the easiest to one
who knows; and it is pointless not to learn.
Untested men speak unreliably.
But Melesias speaks with authority
about these feats to neophytes whose highest
dreams are of the prize performances at consecrated games.
Alcimedon has brought Melesias
his thirtieth victory:
divinely lucky, with no lack of manliness,
**he sent four badly beaten boys
back home in shameful silence, to defer
the choristers of catcalls**,
and gave his father's father strength enough
to wrestle with old age:
Hades holds no qualms
for one who wins.
[Tr. Roy Arthur Swanson. *Pindar's Odes.* (*Olympian 8.*) Indianapolis and New York, 1974. Page numbers: 35, 36.]

AFTERMATH

All three of the wrestlers trained by Milesias and honored by Pindar hailed from families with long-standing athletic traditions. While nothing is known of the progeny of Alcimedon, Timasarchus, or Alcimidas, it would not be surprising if their sons and/or grandsons carried on their families' athletic prowess.

After winning a championship at a major athletic festival like the Olympic or Nemean Games, a victorious athlete could expect to receive a sumptuous welcome upon his return to his hometown. Expensive gifts, free meals at the town hall, or cash prizes might all be showered upon the conquering hero. It is highly likely that all three of Milesias's wrestlers enjoyed these kinds of perquisites when they came home.

ASK YOURSELF

1. Compare Pindar's style of poetry to that of Homer. Both authors describe athletic competitions in their respective documents, but there are quite a few differences in the way each poet goes about doing so. What differences do you notice? What do you suppose accounts for those differences?
2. Does Pindar give us any hints about why Melesias was so successful as a coach? Does he anywhere suggest that Melesias's experience as an athlete helped to prepare him to become a first-rate coach?
3. What modern examples can you think of in which two or more members of the same family were successful athletes? And modern examples of former athletes who later became successful coaches?

Pindar's totally unsympathetic comment about the four wrestlers defeated by Alcimedon having to return home "in shameful silence," to endure the jeers and the catcalls of their fellow townspeople.

pancration (pronounced "pan-krat-ee-on," not "pan-kra-shun.") A word meaning "all/strength," the pancration was a brutal event, a combination of boxing and wrestling, in which just about every kind of blow, hold, or kick was permitted, somewhat like modern cage fighting. The only prohibitions: no biting; no gouging.

TOPICS TO CONSIDER

- In modern sports, the skill of a coach is often measured by the number of victories his/her teams have accumulated, and perhaps also by the number of individual awards won by the players on those teams. It seems as if the same kinds of standards were applied to ancient Greek coaches like Melesias. Consider why coaches are evaluated by these criteria. Is there a more accurate way to assess their effectiveness?
- Pindar writes that Melesias was "divinely lucky" to have been so successful as a wrestling coach. It seems like a strange phrase, since Pindar elsewhere often praises the work ethic and self-discipline of both athletes and their trainers. Why do you suppose, then, that he would use the word "lucky" to describe Melesias?

A BOGUS COACH

Women were not permitted to attend the Olympic games as spectators, but the mother of the champion boxer Peisirodus (q.v.), Pherenice (the daughter of the famous boxer Diagoras, and therefore also a member of that famous family of athletes) was so eager to watch her son compete that she disguised herself as his coach; she did so by completely enveloping herself in a cloak, in the manner of the other coaches. The deception worked until her son's moment of victory, when Pherenice, in her exuberant leaping and cheering, inadvertently allowed the cloak to drop from her body, immediately revealing her feminine qualities. The Olympic authorities were uncertain about what action to take; some felt that Pherenice should be put to death for such a sacrilege, but cooler heads fortunately prevailed, in deference to the considerable athletic prestige of her family. So Pherenice apparently received no punishment, but the authorities did enact a new regulation, that henceforth, all trainers and coaches must be "clad" in the same way as the athletes: *au naturel*.

MILESIAS'S OTHER SUCCESS STORIES

Pindar briefly mentions Milesias in two of his other victory odes. Milesias served as the trainer for Timasarchus of Aegina, who won a boys' wrestling championship at Nemea, ca. 473 BCE (Pindar's fourth *Nemean Ode*), and Alcimidas of Aegina, also victorious in boys' wrestling, ca. 461 BCE at Nemea (the sixth *Nemean Ode*). In the case of the latter, his was the 25th victory won by a member of his athletically inclined family.

Further Information

Bowra, C. M. *The Odes of Pindar*. Baltimore, 1969.

Hornblower, Simon. *Thucydides and Pindar: Historical Narrative and the World of Epinikian Poetry*. Oxford, 2004.

Nisetich, Frank J. *Pindar's Victory Songs*. Baltimore, 1980.

Race, William H. *Pindar*. Cambridge, MA, 1997.

Website

Works by Pindar. http://classics.mit.edu/Browse/browse-Pindar.html

Bibliography for Document

Swanson, Roy Arthur (tr.). *Pindar's Odes*. Indianapolis and New York, 1974.

45. The Resume of Ancient Rome's Superstar Charioteer

INTRODUCTION

Roman chariot racing was a high-risk, high-reward profession. Princely fortunes awaited those lucky few who enjoyed long careers on the racetrack. The satirist Juvenal, writing perhaps with equal measures of envy and exaggeration, claims that the charioteer Lacerta could amass wealth amounting to 100 times the net worth of a successful lawyer. In the same vein, the epigrammatist Martial writes that a driver named Scorpus could rake in 15 heavy bags of gold in only an hour of successful racing.

But the most proficient of them all was undoubtedly the second-century CE charioteer Appuleius Diocles. Racing for all four factions over the course of his lengthy 24-year career, he tallied an astounding 1,462 wins and set several (most likely) unbreakable statistical records. The minutely detailed inscription that appears below preserves the numbers. This inscription has occasionally been interpreted as a memorial to a recently deceased Diocles, but its tone and content point more strongly to understanding it as a summary of his career after his retirement from the track.

KEEP IN MIND AS YOU READ

1. Roman charioteers did not necessarily hail from downtown Rome, or even from Italy. Diocles, for example, came from Lusitania, a section of western Spain in Roman times, Portugal on the map of modern Europe.
2. The Romans counted their years according to the names of the two consuls who held office during that particular year. This system worked because the consulship was an annual magistracy, with a high turnover rate: two new consuls each year.
3. Most Roman chariot races featured *quadrigae*, chariots pulled by four horses, yoked four across. It was apparently noteworthy—and unusual—when different arrangements were employed, such as three-horse, six-horse, or even seven-horse teams.
4. Some races were run cooperatively, team races, with members of the same faction assisting each other strategically. However, the details or rules of such races are unknown.

Document: The Diocles Inscription (Corpus Inscriptionum Latinarum [Collection of Latin Inscriptions] 6.10048)

Appuleius Diocles, a driver of the Red **faction** from Lusitania in Spain, aged 42 years, seven months, 23 days. He first drove for the White faction, during the consulship of Acilius Aviola amd Corellius Pansa [122 CE]. He first won in the same faction, during the consulship of Manlius Acilius Glabrio and Caius

---

HOW MUCH MONEY IS 35,000,000 SESTERCES?

The inscription informs us that Diocles won in excess of 35,000,000 sesterces over the course of his 24 years of competitive charioteering. But how much money is that exactly? Or even approximately? Comparing ancient currencies to modern is always problematic, but perhaps a way can be found to provide us with at least a general idea of the buying power of his winnings.

The relationships of the salaries earned by certain Roman workers is known from the Edict of the Emperor Diocletian (ca. 300 CE), a document that specified maximums on wages and prices, a kind of Roman wage/price freeze. Although the edict postdated Diocles by about 150 years, it nonetheless contains the most complete surviving information about Roman wage structures, and provides enough detail to make at least some general comparisons with Diocles's earnings.

Among the professions mentioned in the edict, lawyers could receive the highest legal wage, 4,000 sesterces for pleading a case. Teachers of Greek, Latin, literature, and geometry might make a maximum of 800 sesterces per student, per month. An artist was limited to 600 sesterces per day, while a mosaic maker could earn a daily wage of 240 sesterces. Bakers, blacksmiths, wagon wrights, stone masons, cabinet makers, and carpenters could each bring home 200 sesterces for a day's work. Daily wages for camel or mule drivers, water bearers, and sewer cleaners were capped at 100 sesterces, while shepherds, at the lowest level of the wage scale, were eligible for a meager daily maximum of 80. Remember, too, that these figures were the *maximums*; there was no guarantee that any worker would be paid the highest legally permissible wage.

On the other hand, Diocles's earnings of 35,000,000 sesterces (rounded off), distributed over 24 years, would have yielded an average annual income of about 1,460,000. Even if Diocles competed every day of a 365-day year (which he surely did not), it would still have meant an average *daily* salary for him of 4,000 sesterces, far higher than that offered by any of the occupational categories previously mentioned. Lawyers could earn 4,000, but that was not a daily wage; it was to be paid for pleading a case, which would undoubtedly require many days, or weeks, of preparation and courtroom jousting.

An additional indication of the enormity of a sum of 35,000,000 sesterces is that admission to the Equestrian Order—Rome's upper middle class, sometimes called the "knights"—required a net worth of at least 400,000 sesterces. A typical Roman equestrian almost certainly earned a comfortable, if not lavish, income; yet Diocles could make several times an equestrian's amount in a year, or less, of successful charioteering.

Was Diocles permitted to keep all 35,000,000, or was he required to surrender at least some of it to his faction, or to the imperial treasury, or to some other person or organization (although probably not to an agent; the practice of professional athletes hiring legal or financial representatives awaited a more mercenary era)? The answer to this question is unknown. But even if he had to put half of his winnings into someone else's upturned palm, the remainder—17,500,000 sesterces—would still have made him a multimillionaire by today's standards.

It appears that the practice of paying handsome salaries to top-ranked athletes is hardly a new phenomenon.

Bellicius Torquatus [124 CE]. He first drove for the Green faction during the consulship of Torquatus Aspens and Annius Libo [128 CE]. He first won for the Red faction during the consulship of Laenus Pontianus and Antonius Rufinus.

Summary [of his career]: He drove chariots for 24 years, having been sent from the gate 4,257 times [i.e., he competed in 4,257 races]. He won 1,462: from the procession [the first race of the day] 110 wins. Singles races [where he competed on his own, instead of cooperatively with other faction teammates]: 1,064 wins. Of these, he won the major prize 92 times: 30,000 **sesterces** 32 times, including three times with a six-horse team [four horses was the standard number]; 40,000 sesterces 28 times. He won 50,000 sesterces 29 times; of these, one was with a seven-horse team. He won 60,000 sesterces three times. He won 347 doubles races and 51 triples races. In the three-horse chariots, he won the 15,000 sesterces prize four times. He placed [i.e., finished first, second, or third] 2,900 times.

He finished second 861 times, third 576 times. He failed to place 1,351 times. He won ten times for the Blue faction, 91 times for the White faction, including two wins worth 30,000 sesterces each. He won 35,863,120 sesterces [over the course of his entire career]. Furthermore, he won three races in two-horse chariots. He won once for the Whites, and twice for the Greens, in three-horse chariots. He won by taking the lead at the start 815 times. He won by coming from behind 67 times. He won after deliberately falling behind 36 times. He won using various other strategies 42 times. He won on the stretch

---

THE FACTIONS: RED, WHITE, GREEN, AND BLUE

Factions were official organizations of racing companies whose responsibility it was to provide horses, chariots, drivers, and equipment. Originally, there were only two factions, the White (*factio alba*, or *albata*) and the Red (*factio russata*). Early in the first century CE, two more were formed, the Green (*factio prasina*), and the Blue (*factio veneta*). Spectators usually became fans of a particular faction; their attitude toward individual drivers depended upon the drivers' faction affiliation. The Green and Blue factions seemed to be the most popular, which raises the interesting, although unanswerable, question of why a charioteer of Diocles's undoubted skill and reputation spent most of his career with the Reds.

Chariot racing was apparently an institution that inspired the loyalty and partisanship of royalty and commoner alike. The emperor Caligula (reigned 37–41 CE) was reportedly so addicted to the fortunes of the Greens that occasionally, he even ate and slept in their stables. Nero (reigned 54–68 CE), too, was a fan of the Green faction. Other first-century CE emperors, like Vitellius and Domitian, favored the Blues.

Sometimes, the enthusiasm for the races and the factions became overdone, to say the least. At the first-century BCE funeral of Felix, a Red faction driver, one of his fans committed suicide by throwing himself onto Felix's funeral pyre. But perhaps the most telling description of rabid and demonstrative spectator behavior comes to us from the pen of the satirist Juvenal: "All Rome today is in the Circus [Maximus; the monstrous, 250,000-capacity racetrack in Rome]. A roar strikes my ear, which tells me that the Green has won; for had it lost, Rome would be as sad and dismayed as when the Consuls were vanquished in the dust of Cannae." [Juvenal. *Satire* 11; tr. Ramsay.]

The Battle of Cannae (216 BCE), during the Second Punic War against Hannibal and the Carthaginians, was viewed by many Romans as their worst military setback ever; upwards of 50,000 Roman soldiers were killed in a single day of fighting. Yet so high did racing passions run for some fans that a defeat of the Green faction represented, for them, a greater tragedy than even the Cannae disaster!

run 502 times, including 216 wins over the Green faction, 205 against the Blue faction, and 81 against the White faction. He gained the 100th wins for nine horses, and the 200th win for one horse. [Tr. The author.]

AFTERMATH

Chariot racing continued to be popular for several centuries after Diocles's retirement in 146 CE. With the decline and eventual fall of Rome, the focal point of chariot racing shifted to the eastern empire and specifically to Constantinople, where a hippodrome was built and racing, replete with factions, was introduced. Partisanship ran high, and in January of 512 CE, a spectator riot erupted, in which some 30,000 people were killed. The glory days of chariot racing were over forever after this tragic event.

ASK YOURSELF

1. It seems clear that Diocles (and other top-shelf charioteers) could earn far more money than most of the fans in the stands who came to see them race. The situation is much the same today, with professional athletes—especially baseball, football, and basketball players—being paid much higher salaries than most of the spectators. Why do you suppose that societies, ancient and modern, have somehow made a collective decision that athletes deserve more money than nearly anyone else? Is this fair or unfair?

2. The inscription indicates that Diocles raced for all four factions at one time or another during his career. However, we do not know the reasons why a charioteer would switch factions, or under what circumstances he was permitted to switch, or whether it was even his decision to do so. Perhaps faction management made these kinds of personnel decisions. What do you think about this? What might be some of the reasons for a charioteer to change factions? Why do you suppose Diocles stayed with the Reds for most of his career, even though the Greens and Blues were more prestigious and more successful?

3. What would be the advantages, and disadvantages, of the various racing strategies enumerated in the inscription? In particular, why might a charioteer *deliberately* fall behind at the beginning of a race and then try to come back to win, as Diocles did 36 times?

TOPICS TO CONSIDER

- The Circus Maximus was the largest racetrack in the entire Roman world. Estimates of its seating capacity are generally in the 250,000 range, making it more than twice as capacious as the largest stadium or arena in the United States. And contemporary evidence—the quotation from Juvenal, for example—indicate that the building accommodated capacity crowds on many of the racing days. Consider the reasons for the immense popularity of spectator sports, both ancient and modern.

- Although chariot racing was undoubtedly very popular, with an intensely devoted fan base, a majority of these race fans seemed to have a sort of contemptuous attitude toward individual charioteers. One would never see a "respectable" Roman socializing with a charioteer, or a gladiator. The situation today is obviously quite different; most modern sports fans would love to "hang out" with their heroes. Consider why or how these different attitudes might have arisen.

≈ Consider the statistical detail in the inscription, and the fact that Diocles was by no means the only Roman charioteer for whom we have such a complete account of his career numbers. Consider, too, the near-obsession with the numbers game exhibited by modern professional sports organizations, and whether there are similarities between ancient and modern attitudes about the importance of statistical records.

Further Information

Balsdon, J. P. V. D. *Life and Leisure in Ancient Rome*. New York, 1969.
Harris, H. A. *Sport in Greece and Rome*. Ithaca, NY, 1972.

Websites

The Circus: Roman Chariot Racing. http://www.vroma.org/~bmcmanus/circus.html
Chariot Races. http://www.pbs.org/empires/romans/empire/chariot.html
A movie to check out: *Ben-Hur*, the 1959, version, starring Charlton Heston in the title role. The chariot race, about two-thirds of the way through the film, is a classic scene in the history of American cinematography. Particularly impressive is the attention to accurate historical detail. For example: Roman chariot races were always run counterclockwise, around a very long and narrow dividing wall (the *spina*) in the middle of the racetrack. Laps (usually seven) were indicated by the lowering of images of dolphins. Both of these details were portrayed in the film.

Most races featured a *pompa*, a ceremonial, one-lap parade around the track of all the chariots prior to the start of the race. *Quadrigae*, chariots pulled by four horses, yoked four abreast, were standard. Horses were specially bred for racing, and were unusually high-strung, powerful animals. A great deal of strength and skill was required of the charioteers to control them. Drivers sometimes used whips to encourage or restrain the horses, although it was a special distinction to win a race *sine flagello*, without using a whip. All these aspects of Roman racing were effectively portrayed, although only the villain of the story, the Roman tribune Messala, wielded a whip during the race.

After the *pompa*, as the chariots and horses were lining up and readying themselves for the start of the contest, a Roman magistrate appears on the scene to make some prefatory remarks. Among other things, he introduces to the crowd the individual charioteers who will be competing that day. Interestingly, all eight of them come from widely varying cities, countries, or regions. This, too, is in keeping with the realities of Roman chariot racing: as noted before, charioteers came from virtually every corner of the Roman world.

Even the smallest details were not overlooked by the film's writers. For example, as the hero, Judah Ben-Hur, is making his final preparations prior to the start of the race, he is shown inserting a small knife into his belt. Roman charioteers often equipped themselves in this fashion, because of their habit of looping the slack of the reins around their waists, to give themselves extra control and leverage. The downside of such a practice, however, would become apparent should the driver ever be thrown out of his chariot; if he failed to extract his knife quickly and sever the reins, he could be dragged along the ground behind the horses, with serious injury or even death a distinct possibility.

BIOGRAPHICAL SKETCHES OF IMPORTANT INDIVIDUALS MENTIONED IN TEXT

Aristophanes (ca. 445–380 BCE). Aristophanes, called "that most clever man" by Aulus Gellius (see below), was one of the premier comic playwrights of the late fifth and early fourth centuries. His plays were invariably original, witty, satirical, sprinkled with neologisms; his invented word *spermagoraiolekitholachanopolides* ("lettuceseedpankcakevendorsofthemarketsquare"), 31 letters in Greek, slightly more in the English translation, must hold some sort of word-length record. That record-setting word appeared in his anti-Peloponnesian war play *Lysistrata*. He also wrote plays satirizing education, the Athenian court system, tragic plays, and the teachings of the philosopher Socrates.

Aristotle (384–322 BCE). Aristotle was one of the most prolific authors in the history of Greek and Roman literature. A true polymath, he was interested in everything from logic to poetry, from astronomy to zoology, from ethics to politics. He created a system of classifying birds and animals that formed the basis for the Linnean system of binomial nomenclature still in use today. Altogether, some 400 written works have been attributed to Aristotle.

Athenaeus (fl. ca. 200 CE). Athenaeus's *Deipnosophistae* (*Witty Dinner Conversationalists*) is a vast compendium of all kinds of information that one might reasonably expect to be discussed over the dinner table by knowledgeable and clever dinner guests. Examples of their highly varied dinnertime discussion topics: the merits of lentils and lentil soup; the use of silver utensils at a dinner party; Aristotle's assertions about the natural world; riddles and enigmas; the themes and scenes embossed onto drinking cups; famous courtesans; the various kinds of wreaths; a mass wedding organized by Alexander the Great.

Aulus Gellius (ca. 123–165 CE). Aulus Gellius, jurist, rhetorician, and man of letters, is famous for his *Attic Nights*, a 20-book collection of information and anecdotes on a wide variety of topics. In part, he collected and recorded these selections for the entertainment and education of his children. The title, *Attic Nights*, is derived from the period of time that he spent in Athens, where he began writing his book "during winter, with its long nights."

Celsus (first century CE; full Roman name: Aulus Cornelius Celsus). Celsus was a learned scholar who wrote an encyclopedic compendium covering agriculture, medicine, military affairs, oratory, and philosophy. However, only the portion on medicine survives intact, so Celsus today is remembered primarily as a source on Roman medical practices. In this work, he covers diseases, drugs, surgery, and anatomy, as well as the history of medicine and suggestions for maintaining good health.

Cicero (106–43 BCE; full Roman name: Marcus Tullius Cicero). Cicero wore many hats during his life: orator, lawyer, statesman, politician, diplomat, philosopher, epistler, poet. He was, and is, regarded as the best lawyer the Romans ever produced, in a culture that brought forth numerous highly skilled and effective legal professionals. Likewise, he was, and is, regarded as the best Latin prose writer the Romans ever produced, in a culture that spawned many excellent such writers. He is probably best known for his courtroom and political speeches, especially the four orations he delivered in November and December of 63, in which he exposed and denounced the aspirations of the would-be revolutionary Catiline. A nineteenth-century artist's conception of the delivery of one of the Catilinarian speeches appears on the cover of this volume.

Demosthenes (384–322 BCE). Generally regarded as the greatest of the (many) outstanding ancient Greek orators, Demosthenes is credited with some 58 extant orations, although a few of these may have been written by other orators of the time. He received an early, and personal, introduction to the world of Athenian law: when he turned 18 years of age (his father had died when he was 7) and attempted to claim his inheritance, he found that his three guardians had mismanaged and plundered the estate. So he took them to court and won his case, although the estate had been so completely drained that what remained was only a fraction of the original worth.

Herodotus (490–425 BCE). Herodotus claims the distinction of being the first true historian in western literature. The nine books of his *Histories* are filled with a mixture of facts, legends, stories, and myths, sometimes not logically ordered. By modern standards, his work might seem unprofessional, with a gullibility unbecoming of a historian. But he was a true pioneer, one who invented the genre as he wrote, and as such, he deserves the title bestowed upon him by Cicero: the "Father of History."

Hippocrates (ca. 460–370 BCE). The most famous name in ancient medicine, Hippocrates today is most widely associated with the celebrated Hippocratic Oath. Although Hippocrates was almost certainly a historical personage, and a practicing physician, modern historians are divided in their assessments of how much of the so-called Hippocratic Collection of medical works can actually be credited to him. However, it seems very likely that Hippocrates did author a number of medical works, now lost, and that much of the Hippocratic Collection was written by physicians unknown today.

Homer (dates uncertain). Homer is widely regarded as the greatest epic poet of antiquity, perhaps of all time, and yet nothing is known for certain about his life. When and where he was born, where he lived and worked, whether he truly was a blind poet—all these raise questions for which we have no answers. Some historians even suggest that he was not a real person at all, and that the name "Homer" was actually a kind of generic term referring to a whole consortium of writers. But the consensus down through history seems to be that he did exist, and that he is to be credited with two of the most famous epic poems of all time, *Iliad* and *Odyssey*.

Horace (65–8 BCE; full Roman name: Quintus Horatius Flaccus). Horace, considered one of the greatest Roman poets, authored several collections of verse, including *Odes, Satires, Epistles,* and *Epodes,* as well as a poetic hymn, *Carmen Saeculare,* celebrating Rome's founding. Horace was the originator of the still-famous phrase *Carpe diem,* "Seize the day."

Julius Caesar (100–44 BCE; full Roman name: Gaius Julius Caesar). Caesar is much more often remembered as a general and a politician than as a man of letters, but he wrote enduring commentaries about his military experiences in the Gallic Wars (58–50) and the civil war (49–45). Legions of Latin students will recognize the famous opening words of his Gallic commentary: *Gallia est omnis divisa in partes tres*: "All Gaul is divided into three parts."

Juvenal (ca. 60–130 CE; full Roman name: Decimus Junius Juvenalis). The Roman poet Juvenal wrote 16 satirical poems, many of them bitter comments on the perils of life in Rome, the difficulties of making a living, and a social system that seemed to favor the rich and influential. He is the source of several famous phrases, including *mens sana in sano corpora* ("a sound mind in a sound body"), and his acerbic comment that the average person in Rome cared only for *panem et circenses,* "bread and circuses," or in other words, food and entertainment.

Livy (59 BCE–17 CE; full Roman name: Titus Livius). One of the most celebrated Roman historians, Livy set out, around the age of 30, to write a comprehensive history of Rome, from its founding up to his own time. Forty years later, he completed the massive project: *Ab Urbe Condita (From the Founding of the City).* Unfortunately, only about 25 percent of his manuscript is still extant; however, even the surviving portions provide a good deal of information, especially about the earliest days of the monarchy and the Republic, as well as a detailed account of the Second Punic War, including the famous story of Hannibal and the Carthaginians crossing the Alps Mountains with elephants in tow.

Lucian (fl. second century CE, perhaps 120–200). Lucian was a Greek satirist and essayist. A prolific writer, he authored works on rhetoric, literature, and philosophy. His wide variety of satirical dialogues focused on topics such as philosophy, religion, and human pretentiousness. He traveled widely, working as a rhetorician and lecturer, before eventually making a home for himself in Athens, where he perfected his satirical writing style.

Marcus Terentius Varro (116–27 BCE), a scholarly antiquarian called by Quintilian "the most learned of Romans," reputedly wrote over 70 books. Of these, substantial portions remain of only two of them: *On the Latin Language* and *On Farming.*

Martial (ca. 40–104 BCE; full Roman name: Marcus Valerius Martialis). The poet Martial wrote over 1,500 epigrammatic poems, most of them in a satirical or social commentary mode mocking the flaws, foibles, and inconsistencies of Roman society; mooches, gold-diggers, and legacy hunters are the lowlife types often skewered by Martial. Additionally, he authored a collection of poems called *Liber Spectaculorum (Book of Spectacles),* commemorating the dedication of the famous Roman amphitheater the Coliseum, in 80 CE.

Ovid (43 BCE–17 CE; full Roman name: Publius Ovidius Naso). Ovid was a versatile Roman poet whose works range from *Amores* and *Ars Amatoria* (love poems) to *Fasti,* a poem devoted to the Roman calendar and the important historical events and religious observances connected with specific days. *Metamorphoses,* perhaps his most famous work, contains a series of mythological stories, all of which involve some sort of change or transformation. Ovid spent the last nine years of his life in exile from Rome, at a place called Tomi, on the Black Sea (the ancient Roman equivalent of Siberia). He had somehow gravely offended the emperor Augustus, but to this day, the specific nature of his offense is unknown.

Pausanias (fl. second century CE**).** Pausanias traveled widely throughout ancient Greece and viewed many famous architectural monuments, works of art, historical sites, and cities. During his travels, he often spoke to the "locals" in order to gather information and better understand the places he visited. The result of all this activity was one of antiquity's most notable travelogues, *Description of Greece*. The work is divided into 10 books, each describing a specific region of Greece. In Books 5 and 6, Pausanias focuses on Elis, the area in which Olympia was located; in these two books, he cites the names of over 200 Olympic athletes, sometimes with biographical data.

Petronius (fl. first century CE**; full Roman name: Gaius Petronius Arbiter).** Petronius is most famously credited with authoring the *Satyricon*, a ribald tale of the adventures of a certain roguish character named Encolpius. The best-known incident in the extant portion of the work is *Cena Trimalchionis* (*Trimalchio's Dinner*), a description of an elaborate Roman dinner party hosted by the utterly buffoonish, nouveau-riche Trimalchio. At one time, Petronius was in the good graces of the emperor Nero, but they had some sort of serious falling out, and Petronius was forced to commit suicide, probably in the year 65 CE.

Pindar (518–438 BCE**).** Pindar could be dubbed one of history's first sportswriters, since he made his living by writing epinicean poetry: poems in honor of victorious athletes at the great athletic competitions of ancient Greece, including the Olympic Games. Pindar's poetic skill was widely known; if a triumphant athlete wanted a victory ode in his honor, he could hire Pindar to write it, who likely commanded a hefty fee for his services. Pindar had a healthy respect for his abilities; he once claimed that his poetry soared like an eagle in flight, whereas that of his rival epinicean poets resembled the meanderings of low-flying crows.

Plato (427–347 BCE**).** Over the course of some 50 years, the philosopher Plato wrote 25 (mostly book-length) philosophical dialogues; among the most famous of these are his *Republic*, about an ideal society, and his *Apologia*, a transcript of the speech his mentor Socrates delivered in his own defense at his trial in 399. Plato, a skilled teacher like Socrates, often conducted classes and gave lectures in a grove of olive trees near Athens; the name of the grove was Academia, a word that thus became associated with Plato's school and, in later times, with higher learning in general.

Pliny the Elder (23–79 CE**; full Roman name: Gaius Plinius Secundus).** He is called "the Elder" to distinguish him from his nephew Pliny the Younger (see just below). Pliny the Elder was the consummate man of learning and knowledge. His *Natural History*, which—according to him—contains 20,000 facts gleaned from 2,000 writings of 473 authors, covers every conceivable topic pertinent to the natural world: astronomy; topography; hydrology; human physiology and psychology; land animals; sea animals; birds; insects; forest trees; fruit trees; shrubs and flowers; agricultural crops; noncultivated plants; drugs and medicines; metals, gems, and rocks. He was a victim of the volcanic eruption of Mount Vesuvius in 79.

Pliny the Younger (62–114 CE**; full Roman name: Gaius Plinius Caecilius Secundus).** Pliny the Younger enjoyed a distinguished career as an orator, statesman, diplomat, and litterateur. He is primarily remembered today as an epistler; 247 of the letters he wrote to friends still survive, while an additional 121—written to, and received from, the emperor Trajan—are also extant. He wrote two of his most famous letters to the historian Cornelius Tacitus, describing the volcanic eruption of Mount Vesuvius in 79; hence, his birth year (62) is pretty well established, because he states in one of those letters that he was 17 years of age when the eruption occurred.

Plutarch (ca. 46–120 CE). Plutarch is most noted as a biographer—he wrote 50 biographies of famous Greeks and Romans—but he also authored a massive collection of short essays entitled *Moralia* (*Moral Essays*). Plutarch was an erudite, intelligent writer, one of our best and most reliable sources of information about the ancient world. Ironically, both he and the poet Pindar hailed from Boeotia, a district not far from Athens and a place proverbial for the backwardness of its inhabitants; and yet two of the most accomplished and sophisticated writers in the history of Greek literature came from there.

Quintilian (ca. 35–95 CE; full Roman name: Marcus Fabius Quintilianus). Quintilian was a lawyer, teacher, and orator, and the author of a book on oratory called *Institutio Oratoria* (*Institutes of Oratory*). In this book, he meticulously describes the many aspects of the profession, including proofs, kinds of evidence, methods of influencing judges, appropriate use of humor, style and word usage, figures of speech, gestures, and dress. Perhaps most interesting, however, are the early chapters in his book, in which he discusses educational principles and the proper training of an orator.

Seneca the Younger (4 BCE–65 CE; full Roman name: Lucius Annaeus Seneca). Seneca produced a lengthy corpus of written works during his lifetime: 10 dialogues; three moral essays; a book on natural phenomena; nine tragic plays; and an interestingly amusing satire on the deification of the emperor Claudius, the *Apocolocyntosis*, or *Pumpkinification*. In 65, he was accused of complicity in a plot to assassinate the emperor Nero, and was forced to commit suicide.

His father, Seneca the Elder (55 BCE–41 CE), was also a noted author.

Suetonius (ca. 70–140 CE; full Roman name: Gaius Suetonius Tranquillus). Suetonius wrote biographies of Julius Caesar and the first 11 Roman emperors. He also authored biographies of other noted individuals, including grammarians, rhetoricians, and poets.

Tacitus (ca. 55–117 CE; full Roman name: Cornelius Tacitus). The highly respected Roman historian Tacitus authored *Annals*, covering the years 14 to 68 CE, and *Histories*, covering 69 and 70. He also wrote a biography of his father-in-law, *Agricola*, a description of Germany (*Germania*), and a treatise on oratory (*Dialogue on Oratory*). He claimed in the *Annals* that his approach to historical writing was *sine ira et studio*, "without anger and prejudice."

Terence (195–159 BCE; full Roman name: Publius Terentius Afer). A native of Carthage in North Africa, the Roman playwright Terence was born a slave; fortunately, he had an enlightened owner who brought him to Rome, educated him, and eventually freed him. Terence went on to write six comedies, all extant. His cognomen, Afer ("African"), reflects his birthplace.

Tertullian (ca. 160–225 CE; full Roman name: Quintus Septimus Florens Tertullianus). Like Terence (above), Tertullian was a native of North Africa. At some point, he converted to Christianity, and became the earliest Christian patristic writer. Among his many works (some written in Greek, others in Latin), the most notable is perhaps the *Apology*, a defense of Christianity.

Virgil; sometimes spelled Vergil (70–19 BCE; full Roman name: Publius Vergilius Maro). Virgil is generally regarded as the finest ancient Roman poet. He wrote several collections of poetry, including *Georgics* (on farming) and *Eclogues* (pastoral poems), but his best-known work is the epic poem about the founding of the Roman race, *Aeneid*. He worked on the *Aeneid* for the last 10 years of his life, finally completing it shortly before his death. He had intended to spend an additional three years editing and polishing it; unfortunately, his death cut short those plans. Although he had specified in his will that the entire manuscript was to be destroyed if he died before completing his revisions, the emperor Augustus intervened and ordered it to be published as it was.

Vitruvius (fl. ca. early first century CE; full Roman name: Vitruvius Pollio). Vitruvius was a Roman architect and engineer whose manual on architecture, *De Architectura*, is the only text of its kind surviving from antiquity. The manual covers topics such as city planning, construction materials and methods, public and private buildings, house decoration, water quality and testing, aqueduct and pipe construction, and civil and military machines.

Xenophon (430–355 BCE). Xenophon was a Greek historian and essayist, and a student of the philosopher Socrates. His most famous work is probably *Anabasis*, a firsthand account of the battles and adventures of King Cyrus the Younger of Persia and the Ten Thousand, an army composed of Greek mercenaries who assisted Cyrus in warfare against his brother, Artaxerxes. A versatile author, he also produced works on hunting; on the trial of Socrates; on household management; on the Athenian economy; and an account of conversations at a dinner party, as well as treatises on military matters, history, and philosophy.

GLOSSARY

Definitions and explanations of most terms, place names, archaeological remains, etc., appear within the text, especially in footnotes to specific documents or in sidebars. For information about individual ancient authors, please consult the *Author Bio* section; no authors' names will appear in the glossary.

Acropolis: the large elevation in Athens and location of many famous buildings, notably the Parthenon; literal meaning of the word: "top [of the] city."

agora: the downtown area of a Greek city; *agora* is often translated by the misleadingly limited word "marketplace."

Athens: the premier polis of ancient Greece, particularly in the fifth century BCE. Pericles praised his city's eminence in his famous *School of Greece* speech in 430 BCE.

consul: the highest elected official in the Roman government, during the period of the Republic (509–27 BCE). Two were chosen annually.

drachma: the basic unit of exchange in the Greek monetary system, approximately the average daily wage paid to a middle-class worker.

forum: the downtown area of a Roman city.

Gracchus: full Roman name: Tiberius Sempronius Gracchus. Tribune in 133 BCE; championed a fairer distribution of farmland between wealthy landholders and homeless, impoverished citizens.

Olympic Games: a quadrennial athletic festival, first held in 776 BCE, at Olympia, in the southwestern area of the Peloponnesus.

ostracism: a method of expelling from Athens an unscrupulous or power-hungry politician for a period of 10 years.

Parthenon: the magnificent and expensive temple dedicated to the goddess Athena and located on the Acropolis in Athens.

Peloponnesian War: the devastating conflict between Athens and Sparta, and their allies: 431–404 BCE.

Peloponnesus: the large southern peninsula of Greece.

Pericles: ca. 495–429 BCE. An outstanding orator and politician, and driving force behind the Athenian Golden Age of the mid- to late fifth century.

polis: Greek word meaning "city-state." Polises were independent countries—hundreds of them—dotting the Greek peninsula and elsewhere in the Greek world.

Punic Wars: a series of three wars between Rome and Carthage: 264–241 BCE.; 218–201; and 149–146.

Roman Republic: a time period (509–27 BCE) when the chief officials of the Roman government were chosen in elections. The Republic replaced the monarchy (753–509).

sestertium: a basic unit of exchange in the Roman monetary system; pl. *sesterces.*

Socrates: 470–399 BCE; the Athenian philosopher, tried and condemned in 399. His teachings and ideas are preserved exclusively in the writings of others, notably Plato.

Solon: ca. 640–560 BCE; noted Athenian legislator, businessman, poet, philosopher, and world traveler. Given sole authority in 594 to reform the Athenian law code.

Sparta: one of the most influential of the Greek polises and a major rival of Athens, especially in the fifth century BCE.

Thebes: a famous and powerful polis north of Athens, once ruled by the star-crossed King Oedipus.

tribune: an elected official of the Roman government whose primary responsibility was to protect the interests of the plebeians. Ten were chosen annually.

Trojan War: fought ca. 1200–1190 BCE, between the Trojans (and their allies), and the Greek polises. Homer writes that over 1,000 Greek ships sailed to Troy to carry on this war.

BIBLIOGRAPHY

BIBLIOGRAPHICAL NOTES

A sourcebook such as *Voices of Ancient Greece and Rome* could never be compiled without the assistance of countless translations, commentaries, dictionaries, and reference works. To provide each of these resources with the appropriate recognition would be a daunting task; however, several of them can be singled out.

First and foremost are the translations of the works of Greek and Roman authors to be found in the Loeb Classical Library series (LCL). These translations are highly readable, well annotated and indexed, invariably feature useful and interesting introductions to the translations, and offer the additional advantage of providing the Greek or Latin text on the page facing the English translation. All the major ancient authors are represented in the series, and these volumes collectively form a true *sine qua non* for anyone wishing to seriously study and research any aspect of life in antiquity.

Also indispensible are major reference works such as *The Oxford Classical Dictionary (OCD)* and *Harper's Dictionary of Classical Literature and Antiquities*. These and similar resources save the day again and again for the author who cannot quite remember details like Suetonius's birth year, or the length of time required for the construction of the Parthenon, or the number and titles of the surviving plays of Aristophanes, or hundreds of other factoids that are critically important for a sourcebook like *Voices*.

Many of the definitions or explanations of Greek and Latin words and phrases appearing in *Voices* have been provided by the premier lexicons of the two ancient languages: Liddell and Scott's *A Greek-English Lexicon* and Glare's *Oxford Latin Dictionary*. Older, but still serviceable, is Lewis and Short's *A Latin Dictionary*. The LCL editors and translators also offer perceptive comments on some of the trickier or more obscure Greek and Latin words that occur in the original sources.

For quick and concise information about mythological characters or places, it would be difficult to imagine a more useful reference work than J. E. Zimmerman's *Dictionary of Classical Mythology*. All major gods, heroes, and legendary notables are represented within its pages, as well as brief citations of the ancient literature in which they appear.

Special mention ought to be made of Lillian Feder's *Apollo Handbook of Classical Literature*. This very readable reference contains biographical information for all major ancient authors, as well as informative synopses of their works. "Synopsis," indeed, may not be the operative word, because many of the entries pertaining to these works are quite detailed, and this feature is perhaps what constitutes the greatest utility in Feder's book.

Naphtali Lewis and Meyer Reinhold have collected a wide assortment of source material in their two-volume set *Roman Civilization Sourcebook I: The Republic* and *Roman Civilization Sourcebook II: The Empire*. Both volumes are well stocked with pertinent selections from ancient sources, as well as introductions and commentaries.

Few websites are mentioned in the bibliographies, partially because of their impermanence and partially because of their potential for purveying inaccurate information. However, relevant Internet sites, including translations of ancient works, can be quickly accessed via search engines by readers who prefer electronic media to hard copy.

TRANSLATIONS AND EDITIONS OF ANCIENT AUTHORS

Babbitt, Frank Cole (tr.). *Plutarch's Moralia*. Volume III. [LCL.] London and New York, 1931.

Barker, Ernest (tr.). *The Politics of Aristotle*. Oxford, 1958.

Blanco, Walter (tr.). *Herodotus: The Histories*. New York, 1992.

Brownson, Carleton L. (tr.). *Xenophon: Anabasis*. Volume III. [LCL.] London and Cambridge, 1922.

Bury, The Rev. R. G. (tr.). *Plato: Timaeus; Critias; Cleitophon; Menexenus; Epistles*. [LCL.] London and Cambridge, 1929.

Butler, H. E. (tr.). *The Institutio Oratoria of Quintilian*. Volume I. [LCL.] Cambridge and London, 1920.

Clement, Paul A. (tr.) *Plutarch's Moralia*. Volume VIII. [LCL.] London and Cambridge, 1969.

Cornford, Francis MacDonald (tr.). *The Republic of Plato*. New York and London, 1941.

Creekmore, Hubert (tr.). *The Satires of Juvenal*. New York, 1963.

de Selincourt, Aubrey (tr.), revised by A. R. Burn. *Herodotus: The Histories*. Baltimore, 1954.

de Selincourt, Aubrey (tr.). *Livy: The War with Hannibal, Books XXI-XXX*. Baltimore, 1965.

Dover, Kenneth (ed.). *Aristophanes: Clouds*. Oxford, 1968.

Fagles, Robert (tr.). *Homer: The Iliad*. New York, 1990.

Fairclough, H. Rushton (tr.). *Virgil: Eclogues; Georgics; Aeneid*. Volume I. [LCL.] Cambridge and London, 1916.

Fowler, Harold N. *Plato: Cratylus; Parmenides; Greater Hippias; Lesser Hippias*. [LCL.] London and New York, 1926.

Fuller, Edmund (tr.). *Plutarch: Lives of the Noble Greeks*. New York, 1968.

Glover, T. R. (tr.). *Tertullian: Apology; De Spectaculis*. [LCL.] Cambridge and London, 1931.

Godley, A. D. (tr.). *Herodotus*. Volume I. [LCL.] Cambridge and London, 1920.

Granger, Frank (tr.). *Vitruvius on Architecture*. Volume I. [LCL.] Cambridge and London, 1934.

Grant, Michael (tr.). *Selected Political Speeches of Cicero*. New York, 1969.

Gulick, Charles Burton (tr.). *Athenaeus: The Deipnosophists*. Volume I. [LCL.] London and New York, 1927.

Gummere, Richard M. (tr.). *Seneca: Ad Lucilium Epistulae Morales*. Volume II. [LCL.] London and Cambridge, 1920.

Harmon, A. M. (tr.). *Lucian*. Volume V. [LCL.] Cambridge and London, 1936.

Henderson, Jeffrey (tr.). *Aristophanes: Clouds; Wasps; Peace.* [LCL.] Cambridge and London, 1998.

Hubbell, H. M. (tr.). *Cicero: De Inventione; De Optimo Genere Oratorum; Topica.* [LCL.] Cambridge and London, 1949.

Humphries, Rolfe (tr.). *Ovid: Metamorphoses.* Bloomington, IN, 1955.

Jones, W. H. S. (tr.). *Hippocrates.* Volume I. [LCL.] Cambridge and London, 1923.

Jones, W. H. S. (tr.). *Pausanias: Description of Greece.* Volume III. [LCL.] Cambridge and London, 1933.

Jones, W. H. S. (tr.). *Pliny: Natural History.* Volume VIII. [LCL.] London and Cambridge, 1963.

Lamb, W. R. M. (tr.). *Plato: Laches; Protagoras; Meno; Euthydemus.* [LCL.] Cambridge and London, 1924.

Marchant, E. C. (tr.). *Xenophon: Memorabilia and Oeconomicus.* Volume IV. [LCL.] Cambridge and London, 1923.

Miller, Walter (tr.). *Cicero: De Officiis.* [LCL.] London and New York, 1913.

Moore, Clifford H. (tr.). *Tacitus: The Histories, Books I–III.* Volume II. [LCL.] Cambridge and London, 1925.

More, Otis. *Ovid: Metamorphoses.* http://www.theoi.com/Text/OvidMetamorphoses15 .html

Murray, A. T. (tr.). *Demosthenes: Private Orations.* Volume VI. [LCL.] Cambridge and London, 1939.

Palmer, George Herbert (tr.). *The Odyssey: Homer.* New York, 1962.

Perrin, Bernadotte (tr.). *Plutarch's Lives.* Volume I. [LCL.] London and Cambridge, 1914.

Perrin, Bernadotte (tr.). *Plutarch's Lives.* Volume V. [LCL.] London and Cambridge, 1917.

Peterson, Sir William (tr.). *Tacitus: Dialogus; Agricola; Germania.* Cambridge and London, 1914.

Rackham, H. (tr.). *Pliny: Natural History.* Volume III. [LCL.] London and Cambridge, 1940.

Radice, Betty (tr.). *Pliny: Letters and Panegyricus.* Volumes I and II. [LCL.] Cambridge and London, 1969.

Ramsay, G. G. (tr.). *Juvenal and Persius.* [LCL.] Cambridge and London, 1918.

Rieu, E. V. (tr.). *Homer: The Iliad.* Baltimore, 1950.

Rogers, Benjamin Bickley (tr.). *Aristophanes: The Lysistrata; The Thesmophoriazusae; The Ecclesiazusae; The Plutus.* Volume III. [LCL.] Cambridge and London, 1924.

Rolfe, John C. (tr.). *The Attic Nights of Aulus Gellius.* Volume I. [LCL.] Cambridge and London, 1927.

Rolfe, John C. (tr.). *Suetonius.* Volume II. [LCL.] Cambridge and London, 1914.

Sage, Evan T. (tr.). *Livy.* Volume IX. [LCL.] London and Cambridge, 1935.

Scott-Kilvert, Ian (tr.). *Plutarch: Makers of Rome.* New York, 1965.

Scott-Kilvert, Ian (tr.). *Plutarch: The Rise and Fall of Athens; Nine Greek Lives.* New York, 1960.

Sommerstein, Alan H. (tr.). *Aristophanes: The Acharnians; The Clouds; Lysistrata.* New York, 1973.

Spencer, W. G. (tr.). *Celsus: De Medicina.* Volume I. [LCL.] London and Cambridge, 1935.

Sullivan, J. P. (tr.). *Petronius: The Satyricon and the Fragments.* Baltimore, 1965.

Swanson, Roy Arthur (tr.). *Pindar's Odes.* Indianapolis and New York, 1974.

Tredennick, Hugh (tr.). *Plato: The Last Days of Socrates.* Baltimore, 1954.

Watts, N. H. (tr.). *Cicero: The Speeches.* [LCL.] London and New York, 1923.

Westcott, John H. (ed.). *Selected Letters of Pliny.* Norman, OK, new edition, 1965.

Williams, W. Glynn (tr.). *Cicero: The Letters to His Friends*. Volume I. [LCL.] Cambridge and London, 1927.

MODERN SOURCES

Aldrete, Gregory S. *Floods of the Tiber in Ancient Rome*. Baltimore, 2007.

Balsdon, J. P. V. D. *Life and Leisure in Ancient Rome*. New York, 1969.

Cary, M. *A History of Rome, Down to the Reign of Constantine*. London, first edition, 1935.

Gardiner, E. Norman. *Athletics of the Ancient World*. Oxford, first edition, 1930.

Harris, H. A. *Sport in Greece and Rome*. Ithaca, New York, 1972.

Jarrett, James L. *The Educational Theories of the Sophists*. New York, 1969.

Lesky, Albin, translated by James Willis and Cornelis de Heer. *A History of Greek Literature*. New York, English translation, 1966.

Lewis, Naphtali and Meyer Reinhold (eds.). *Roman Civilization: Sourcebook I, The Republic*. New York, 1951.

Lewis, Naphtali and Meyer Reinhold (eds.). *Roman Civilization: Sourcebook II, The Empire*. New York, 1955.

Nevett, Lisa C. *House and Society in the Ancient Greek World*. Cambridge, 1999.

Robinson, Rachel S. *Sources for the History of Greek Athletics*. Ann Arbor, MI, 1927.

Scullard, H. H. *From the Gracchi to Nero. A History of Rome from 133 B.C. to A.D. 68*. London, 1959.

Starr, Chester G. *A History of the Ancient World*. New York, 1965.

REFERENCE WORKS

Berry, George Ricker. *The Classic Greek Dictionary*. Chicago, 1943.

Cary, M. et al. *The Oxford Classical Dictionary*. Oxford, 1949.

Feder, Lillian. *Apollo Handbook of Classical Literature*. New York, 1964.

Glare, P. G. W. (ed.). *Oxford Latin Dictionary*. Oxford, 1982.

Howatson, M. C. (ed.). *The Oxford Companion to Classical Literature*. Oxford and New York, 1989.

Lewis, Charlton T. *An Elementary Latin Dictionary*. Oxford, 1889.

Lewis, Charlton T. and Charles Short. *A Latin Dictionary*. London, 1879.

Liddell, Henry George and Robert Scott, revised by Sir Henry Stuart Jones et al. *A Greek-English Lexicon*. Oxford, 1843. Revised edition published 1996.

Matz, David. *Ancient World Lists and Numbers. Numerical Phrases and Rosters in the Greco-Roman World*. Jefferson, NC, 1995.

Peck, Harry Thurston (ed.). *Harper's Dictionary of Classical Literature and Antiquities*. New York, 1896.

Smith, William (ed.). *A Dictionary of Greek and Roman Geography*. London, 1878.

Zimmerman, J. E. *Dictionary of Classical Mythology*. New York, 1964.

INDEX

ABOUT THE AUTHOR

David Matz is professor of classical languages at St. Bonaventure University, St. Bonaventure, NY. His published works include Greenwood's *Daily Life of the Ancient Romans* and *Daily Life through World History in Primary Documents*, as well as other books on Greek and Roman history and culture.

CPSIA information can be obtained at www.ICGtesting.com
Printed in the USA
LVOW09*1519220416

484627LV00009B/15/P

9 780313 38738